MY LIFE IN THE PITS

ALSO BY RONDA RICH

What Southern Women Know (That Every Woman Should)

MY LIFE
IN THE PITS

LIVING AND LEARNING
ON THE NASCAR
WINSTON CUP CIRCUIT

RONDA RICH

FOREWORD BY RICHARD CHILDRESS

HarperEntertainment
An Imprint of HarperCollinsPublishers

MY LIFE IN THE PITS. Copyright © 2002 by Ronda Rich. All rights reserved. Printed in the United States of America. No part of this book may be used or reproduced in any manner whatsoever without written permission except in the case of brief quotations embodied in critical articles and reviews. For information address HarperCollins Publishers Inc., 10 East 53rd Street, New York, NY 10022.

HarperCollins books may be purchased for educational, business, or sales promotional use. For information please write to Special Markets Department, HarperCollins Publishers Inc., 10 East 53rd Street, New York, NY 10022.

FIRST EDITION

Printed on acid-free paper

Designed by Adrian Leichter

Library of Congress Cataloging-in-Publication Data has been applied for.

ISBN 0-06-000589-0

02   03   04   05   06   RRD   10   9   8   7   6   5   4   3   2   1

To George and Mildred Elliott.

Their lives are gone, but their lessons remain.

CONTENTS

Contents

F O R E W O R D

BY RICHARD CHILDRESS

Dale Earnhardt and I were sitting in my pickup truck at Martinsville Speedway in Virginia watching a downpour of rain wash away a day of practice and qualifying. We were parked near the end of pit road, just watching people and shooting the bull when Dale spied Ronda Rich, sharing an umbrella with Bill Elliott. Dale being Dale, he just couldn't resist having a little fun. When he wasn't in a racecar, he was happiest when he was aggravating someone about something, especially if that someone was Ronda.

He rolled down the window, stuck his head out in the rain, and hollered over to them, "Hey, Elliott! Y'all come here!"

I have to say that neither one of them looked too excited about the invitation, but nonetheless they waded through the puddles and sloshed over to Dale's side of the truck.

Without cracking a smile, he pointed at Bill and said to Ronda in a stern voice, "You need to be *real* careful about the kind of people you hang around with."

She didn't miss a beat. "I am," she replied. "That's why I'm not hanging around with *you*."

I can't count the times I watched those two go toe-to-toe in a battle of wits as Dale tried to get the best of her. Sometimes he did, other times he didn't. But each time, it was quite a sight to behold. She was about a foot shorter, but every bit as determined. I've seen some of the toughest men in the world crumble under that intimidating stare from Dale Earnhardt. But Ronda, nervous or not, matched him stare for stare, word for word. I feel sure it wasn't easy to do, but I know for a fact that it was spunky. To say the least, I was impressed. She was a brave young lady.

I don't think I'll ever forget the first time I saw her in the garage at a Winston Cup race, sometime in 1985. I was on top of the race hauler with my stopwatch, timing Dale's laps during practice. I happened to look down and see this well-dressed young woman in the middle of a sea of dirty mechanics and greasy crew guys. It's an unusual picture that's hard to forget. It wasn't just that she was dressed in nice clothes and high heels, it was also the fact that she was a she. Back in those days, we didn't have many shes in the garage, and none of them dressed like that. The others wore jeans, T-shirts, and sneakers—what you would call sensible clothes for garage work. But that wasn't Ronda's style.

She came into the sport on her own terms in other ways, too. She chose to bridge the gap between a job to be done and friends to be made. Somehow she managed to fit in and find acceptance in a world dominated by men. It couldn't have been easy, but her tenacity opened doors and made her a young pioneer who broke down barriers and helped to pave the way for the dozens of women who enjoy careers in our sport today.

I've always believed that you can tell a winner, pick one right out of a crowd. I don't think it's hard at all to spot the kind of person who has what it takes to rise above adversity, take on the toughest challenges, and persevere with talent and smarts. I am not at all surprised that Ronda took the lessons she learned in Winston Cup racing, focused on the positive aspects, and made a better life for herself. And, now she shares those inspiring lessons of hope, courage, generosity, faith, compassion—of taking risks and chasing dreams—believing that it is her responsibility to return goodness to a world that has been so good to her. Within each story lies a moral, a lesson of life learned by a young girl, naive in the beginning but wise in the end, who spent almost a decade on the Winston Cup circuit. As you will see, she learned her lessons well.

I can say many things about Ronda, but the best thing, as far as I'm concerned, is that she's a good and loyal friend who's there during good times and sad times. "You can count on me," she always tells me. I know that's true. So do all her other friends. She's the kind of person who opens her heart the moment she meets you and invites you in to be her dear friend, no strings attached. Alan Kulwicki, Davey Allison, and Tim Richmond had very different personalities; they were so different from each other that it's hard to imagine that any of them could have had a close friend in common. Yet all three of them shared a strong, true friendship with Ronda, as you will see in the stories that follow. When you know her, that isn't hard to believe. She accepts people for who they are, loves them without judgment, and is always there to encourage and support them. That's the best kind of friend to have.

As you begin this book, you're in for a treat. I promise that. In the pages that follow, Ronda Rich does what she does best: she opens her heart, and in doing so, she presents a touching, entertaining view of a man's world as seen through a woman's eyes. Just wait until you see the tender sides of some of the toughest guys in racing as she writes about the kind of sensitivity and emotions that only a woman would be allowed to see. There's only one person I know who could tell these stories, and that's the young, spirited girl with lots of bravado who grew into the strong, courageous woman with lots of wisdom and compassion. In the education of life, in a place where the teachers were racers rather than scholars, she made a very good student.

MY LIFE IN THE PITS

THE RACING EXPERT

WEARS A SKIRT

One recent Sunday afternoon, I climbed up on a stair machine at a gym and noticed that a NASCAR Winston Cup race was being shown on a television screen in front of the cardio platform. As I began to sweat through the rigors of my workout, I focused my full attention on the race, paying no attention to the baseball game or the golf event that were playing on the other sets.

"You don't like this kind of racing, do you?" asked a doctor who was exercising next to me. He grinned as if it were a stupid question, as if it wasn't possible for a woman like me—a white-collar professional, well-educated, traveled, and especially *feminine*—to like stock car racing. I have heard his tone of voice many times when the subject of NASCAR racing arises. It is one of regal condescension, the kind that seems to call for embarrassment, apology, denial, or defensive explanations. But I no longer explain or defend.

For now I am part of an enormous audience in the world of sports. I am a NASCAR fan.

I turned my attention from the television screen to look him squarely in the eye. "As a matter of fact," I replied coolly, with a confidence I had gained over the years, "NASCAR racing is my favorite sport."

His eyes bulged and his mouth dropped open, but he quickly recovered and assumed a "you're just kidding me" look. "No, it's not," he said, chuckling at either the ridiculousness of the idea or the fact that he had almost been taken in by my reply. Without a smile and without a word, I continued to look straight at him. With a quizzical expression, he tilted his head. "You're not serious, are you?"

"Dead serious. What's wrong with that?"

He began to stammer. "Uh, uh, nothing. I just wouldn't have ever taken you for a stock car fan, that's all. I just thought that was kind of a redneck sport."

I knew the stereotype he had in mind; but before I could continue with a retort intended to increase his discomfort, a businessman on a treadmill behind us spoke up.

"I don't see how you get anything out of this," he interjected. "It's not interesting. All they do is go around in circles."

I smiled, more to myself than to them, remembering when I had once used those same words. That's the battle cry of all those ignorant about one of the world's most fascinating sports. I saw an opportunity to preach to the racing heathens, to convert two fans of other sports, to show them the intrigue and excitement produced by a NASCAR race.

"Oh, but it *is* interesting," I replied enthusiastically. "It's the strategy that makes it interesting."

Both the doctor and the businessman cast their eyes upward to the television screen and watched for a few moments.

"Why don't they all drive on the inside of the track?" the doctor asked. "Why do some of them race in the middle of the track and some up high?"

I laughed, but not because it was a stupid question; it was really a good observation from a racing neophyte. "That's where strategy comes in. Of course, you want to race on the inside of the corners because that's part of the shortest way around the track. If you'll notice, the cars running best are running the apex of the corner. They hug the inside of the track close as they go into the turns, then they bounce up higher to a certain point between the turns on the straightaways and then dive back to the inside for the next turns. If they stayed on the inside all the time, they'd stay on their brakes and lose horsepower and speed. When they bounce up on the straightaway, they can rev up rpms and increase speed. Occasionally, you'll find a track where the outside groove, up high on the track, is the fastest path. But the inside groove in the corner is usually the best because the shortest way is the quickest way."

"Hmmm," the doctor mused. "But why are some cars higher on the track than the ones leading?"

"That's part of the setup strategy," I continued. "You see, it isn't always the car with the best engine or best driver that wins. It's the car that handles best that has the edge, and it takes a lot of strategizing to produce the best car. The driver and crew have to figure out which shocks, springs, gear ratios, tire stagger, and such will help the car 'handle' and take the best way around the track. A good-handling racecar is a fast car. If track conditions change during the race—for instance, because of a brief rainfall, cloud cover, hotter sun, or slicker track created from the rubber of the tires—that will affect the handling, and the strategy has to be improvised."

With amusement, I noted that their interest was piqued, and they began to watch more closely. There were thirty laps to go in the race and the cardio area fell quiet, except for clicking stair climbers, humming treadmills, and buzzing racecars.

"So the car's that leading now is gonna win, right?" someone asked. "There are only thirty laps to go."

"I'd love to see him win," I replied, referring to Dale Earnhardt Jr. "But I'm afraid he won't. The car's that's probably going to win is running fifth right now. Dale Jarrett."

The doctor shot me a skeptical look. "Now, how can you tell that?"

The camera was following the leader as he headed into a turn. "Watch. The back end of his car is a little loose. It's kicking out from under him just a little as he turns into the corners. The handling is off just a tiny bit, but it's enough to make a big difference. He's having to lift off the throttle slightly because if he doesn't, he could lose control. It isn't sticking to the track. It could just spin out and put him into the wall. Every time he does that, he loses a little edge, and the other cars are catching him."

The camera moved to Jarrett and another car running behind him. "Look at how beautifully that car is sticking into the corners. It's picture-perfect. If nothin' happens, that's your winner."

But something did happen. A car spun out and brought out a caution flag with twenty laps to go. The cars had enough fuel to go the distance, so one guy, a race fan, interjected his opinion.

"Oh, they'll all stay out and not pit because they've got enough fuel."

I shook my head. "No, they won't. They'll come in and get tires. If there were only four or five laps left, they wouldn't; but twenty laps is plenty of time to turn this into a shoot-out."

"Why?" the businessman asked.

"New tires—they call them 'sticker' tires because they still have the manufacturer's sticker on them—are the fastest. Before the rubber is worn down, they stick like glue to the track; and with that traction, the car can run faster. The question here is, Do they get two tires or four tires?"

"What's the difference?" the doctor asked.

"Time in the pits. It takes longer to put four tires on than it does two." Dale Jarrett, who came out third from his pit stop, went on to win the race, just as I had predicted thirty laps earlier. He had the best-handling racecar, and his crew chief, Todd Parrott, made the right strategic calls when the unexpected caution flag came out. That's what makes racing interesting—the unpredictability and the strategy involved. It's the combination of the man and the machine that determines the winner. If either is slightly off, they're out of contention. In the early days of stock car racing, the driver was more important than the car, but now a moderate driver in a dominant race-perfect car can beat the best driver.

When the race ended, I smiled triumphantly at the men. They shook their heads in silent amazement. I stepped off the cardio machine, brushed back the damp tendrils that hung around my face, and took a long drink of water from a bottle. I knew I had made a good call, an astute one, but I also was quite aware that in a sport where unpredictability is always predictable, the ticklish fingers of good luck had favorably touched both Dale Jarrett and me.

"That was good," the businessman admitted. "Very good."

The doctor stepped down from the stair stepper, wiped his hands with a towel, and then propped an arm against the machine. "I've got to hand it to you. That was pretty incredible."

I shrugged. "No big deal." I started to leave but stopped and turned to face the two men. I pointed a finger in their direction and said, "But now you've got to admit that there's a lot more to racing than you thought. Right?"

The doctor raised his eyebrows and nodded, his eyes full of puzzled surprise. "There sure is. I had no idea. I just thought they went out there and raced around and around." He wiped his cheek with the sleeve of his T-shirt. He studied me with amusement for a moment and then said, "Hey, you really know your stuff. That's pretty impressive."

I grinned. "Thank you."

"I've just got one more question for you."

"What's that?"

"How in the world did you learn so much about cars and racing?"

That was his best question so far. And the answer is where *this* story begins.

THE GREEN FLAG DROPS

The first time I found myself in the pits of a Winston Cup race was on the dreariest of spring days in 1983, when penny-sized drops of rain were hammering down on the Atlanta Motor Speedway, producing puddles of water on pit road that swooshed around my ankles; soaked my shoes, socks, and feet; and made me miserable, albeit stoic, in the March chill. That was the easy part of the day. The tough part came that night when I peeled off a pair of jeans drenched so thoroughly with water that they weighed almost as much as I did, and so completely covered in red Georgia clay that it took no less than four machine washings to free them from the stubborn, insidious gunk. Thanks to the weekend of rain, the infield was a knee-deep marsh of oozing, deep, orange mud that ensnared car after car and kept massive wreckers busy in a nonstop series of whirling, churning attempts to yank vehicles from their sinking graves. My shoes and jacket did not fare as well as my jeans; the malicious Georgia clay, which harbors multiple minerals and therefore is like black permanent ink when it stains clothes, had ruined them, and they had to be relegated to the trash. Georgia clay, I was to learn, is a lot like the racing fever that infects people and consumes them. Once it is absorbed, it sticks forever and never fades away.

I was then a persistently prissy girl, and I was not happy.

"This newspaper owes me for a pair of shoes and a jacket," I ranted to my sports editor at *The Times* in Gainesville, Georgia, the next morning after I returned from my first major motorsports assignment. I was still in college, working on twin degrees in journalism and broadcasting, and I had managed to talk my way into a job as a sports reporter. Not because I liked sports—when I started out, I knew virtually nothing about any kind of sports—but because my options were either sports or the obituaries.

There are a lot of problems with being an obituary writer. First, there's considerable pressure, particularly in the South and especially in small towns, where the obituaries are the most read, most scrutinized section of a newspaper. There is no room for error. If you get the day, time, or place of the service or burial wrong, a member of the deceased person's family will soon be lying prostrate with grief across your desk, wailing in agony and asking how you could possibly treat the dear departed with such sloppy irreverence. The obituary writer before me had derailed his own promising journalistic career when he had the man who died preaching at his own funeral. Then there is the problem of mobility. Death comes to you, the obituary writer. You only need to wait for the undertaker to show up and hand you the form from which you write. There are no field assignments. You are a desk jockey in the purest form. Finally, there are no bylines. This is the only form of journalism in which the subject completely overrides the reporter in importance. I suppose I'm not very good at being anonymous.

For all these reasons, I quickly determined that I was not destined for a life of lifeless writing. My mother still believes, how-

ever, that as the town's obit writer, I was at the height of my journalistic excellence and that all my accomplishments since then
pale in comparison. But, despite my mama's grave disappointment, I sought refuge in the sports department—bluffing and
maneuvering around my lack of experience and knowledge. Somehow, I survived. And amazingly enough I soon wound up with
the best beats in sports, becoming the single female in the press
boxes of the Atlanta Braves and Falcons and the University of
Georgia Bulldogs, at a time when they were one of the hottest college football teams in the nation. It was exhilarating. Heady.
Intoxicating.

Then my cruel editor decided to send me—I shuddered—to a
stock car race. So on the morning when I sat at my desk complaining about my ruined clothes, it wasn't my wardrobe that truly mattered. What really rankled me was that I had been momentarily
stripped of my prestige and sent on an assignment to cover a lowly
stock car race. I did not want it to become a habit. My editor was
doing what he always did extremely well when I acted like a disgruntled, childish idiot: he was ignoring me. Being ignored just
makes me madder.

"I'm serious!" I raised my voice and made my tone more
emphatic. Finally, he turned away from the page layouts he was
studying and looked at me. The amused twinkle in his eye irritated
me further. "I expect to be completely reimbursed for the cost of my
clothes, not just the dry cleaning." I settled back against my chair,
crossed my arms, and smiled smugly as if I had one-upped him. I
thought I was pretty big stuff. My formal education was nearing its
end. I would soon have not one but two bachelor's degrees and had
managed to earn both of them while working at two to three jobs at
a time. What I didn't know then was that my true, most valuable
education was just beginning.

He chuckled and took a deep drag on one of his ever-present
cigarettes. "Well, good luck in getting it."

"I'm puttin' 'em on my expense report," I warned.

"Give it your best shot."

I turned back to my computer terminal and silently stewed. After several minutes, I swirled my chair around to face him.

"I'm not goin' back to another race," I declared firmly.

His patience was strained. A gurgling, sarcastic snort preceded his words. "My dear, you're gonna learn that sportswriters don't always get to choose what assignments they get. But the good news is that if you stay with it as long as I have, you'll get to be the boss. That's why I cover golf and you cover stock car racing."

He hated racing, too. He had sent me—a rookie reporter so green that I was still attending a snooty women's college that was warping my perception of the real world—to cover a race only because of the enormous amount of letters and phone calls that the newspaper was receiving daily from outraged race fans who wanted to read about their beloved sport. At first, the calls and letters were cordial, respectful, pleading. But when their requests were ignored, they became discourteous, belligerent, and sometimes hostile. Whew. I sure hated to answer the phone when one of the mean ones called! This outpouring of interest, coupled with the fact that a fresh, talented local boy named Bill Elliott was starting to garner some media and fan attention on the prestigious NASCAR circuit had prompted my sports editor to send me to the Atlanta spring race, a two-hour drive from Gainesville.

When I got the assignment, I protested mightily. When that failed, I begged and pleaded. I thought briefly of summoning up tears, but I've never been the type of female to use that ploy. Actually I *was* close to tears at the thought of having to cover a stock car race. I suspected that it was an uncivilized sport to which homage was paid by toothless, beer-bellied men and snuff-dipping women. I had a couple of mountain cousins who fit that description, and *they loved* stock car racing.

"How on earth do you cover racing?" I argued, spreading my arms, palms up. "All they do is go around in circles! Booor-*ring*!"

That's why I smiled when the businessman at the gym made the same comment. It wasn't a smile of condescension or disrespect. It was a smile of amusement at myself, because I remembered how a similar, narrow-minded attitude had almost made me miss a career more exciting and fulfilling than my wildest fantasies. The sport of NASCAR racing and its people would become one of life's sweetest gifts to me. But on that rain-drenched day when I encountered my first stock car event, I was as ignorant as the doctor and the businessman. "So, what am I going to write about?" I pressed my sports editor.

He shrugged. "Write about the Elliott kid. Folks want to know about him."

I hadn't met the hometown favorite that day, but I did see the tall, lanky, red-headed, freckle-faced Bill Elliott for the first time as he hurried through the garage at a long-legged, fast-paced gait. I would soon learn that while Bill Elliott talked more slowly than anyone I had ever known, he moved at the speed of lightning, on-track and off. My sister Louise had been telling me for two years about this guy from Dawsonville, Georgia, who was going to be a famous racer one day. "You need to get in on the ground floor and start writing about him now," she advised. "Don't wait until he's a star and everyone else jumps on the bandwagon."

I did meet Bill's brother Dan, considered by many to be the best-looking, most personable of the three brothers, and his father, George, who would become my mentor and the best teacher that a racing neophyte could have. I wrote the first in what would become a long line of racing stories that day and began an association that would lead me to become the chief chronicler of the Elliotts' early racing careers. I liked my second race better, was intrigued by the third, thoroughly enjoyed the fourth, and by the fifth race I was completely smitten.

In NASCAR racing, the bumper of a car driven by a rookie is painted with a yellow stripe. This reminds the experienced drivers, when they pull up on the car to pass it, that they're dealing with a rookie and should proceed with caution. In those early days, I was certainly a rookie, wearing my own yellow stripes, but I hung in there until I earned the right to be called a veteran. My coverage on the Elliotts would win awards, acclaim for my newspaper, and notoriety for me throughout the Gannett Corporation, and eventually would earn me an invitation to work with *USA Today* in Washington, D.C. The Elliott family, for their part, would teach me a lot about racing and even more about life, love, and loyalty.

Stock car racing, as it turned out, was definitely a better career move than the obituary desk. It was even better than the Braves or Bulldogs. I also picked up lots of useful information during my years in racing, the kind that you can apply in everyday life. For instance, not too long ago, I was in the market for a new car and was shopping at a highbrow dealership. The salesman said, "I know it's not what you're shopping for, but I do have a fabulous preowned two-door." As he talked, he walked toward a stunningly beautiful, shiny red sports car.

"I'm sure you probably don't know much about baseball, but this car was owned by a guy who used to play for the Atlanta Braves for several years before he got traded." The arrogant salesman continued with his story, naming the player almost as an afterthought, since he was certain that I knew nothing of sports.

"Oh, I know him," I commented calmly, evenly.

He raised his eyebrows in slight surprise and nodded. "Oh, so you've heard of him, then?"

"No, I *know* him. I used to be a sportswriter and I covered the Braves. He was always my favorite player to interview."

He looked skeptical but seized the opportunity. "Then maybe you'd be interested in owning this car that was his. C'mon, let's take it for a ride."

He handed me the keys, I slid in behind the steering wheel, and he climbed in on the passenger side. I eased the car out of the parking lot and onto the street. When I accelerated, I felt a slight kick from the automatic transmission. Subtly, I cut my eyes sideward to the salesman, who was looking straight ahead, as if nothing was wrong. His arrogance had already irritated me, but that made me furious because I realized that he thought he was going to sell me a dud because, after all, a "little lady" like me certainly couldn't know anything about the mechanics of a car. Or could she? I accelerated again, forcing the transmission to change gears from second to third. As it switched to high gear, it did so with another subtle kick. Still, he said nothing, coolly acting as if nothing were out of the ordinary.

"There's something wrong with this transmission," I commented grimly. "It has a hard shift to it."

He nodded but continued to look straight ahead. "Yeah," he mumbled. "Something's wrong. I'll have to get service to check it out." Then, afraid he was going to lose a sale—which, by the way, he did—he tried to salvage the opportunity.

"When we get back, you need to drive the sedan version of this car. There's all the difference in the world in the way they drive. Driving the sedan is like gliding on silk."

"Probably because sports cars always have stiffer springs and shocks than sedans. A sports car is designed to enhance performance rather than comfort."

Finally, he turned to look at me, his face a mask of disbelief and shock. I bit the inside of my mouth to keep from smiling and tried to return his incredulous expression with one of complete nonchalance.

"Isn't that right?" I asked, as if it were possible that I was wrong.

"Uh, yeah. Right." He was quiet for a moment before asking, "How is it that you know so much about cars?"

I shrugged. "Oh, just something I picked up somewhere along the way." I neglected to tell him that I had learned it in the garages of the NASCAR Winston Cup Series and that my teachers had been some of the most famous mechanics in motorsports and some of the best automotive engineers that Detroit could offer. Somehow it didn't seem to matter where I had gotten my knowledge, only that I had it.

In addition to Winston Cup races, I also began covering the local short track owned by Bud Lunsford, the South's winningest short track driver with more than a thousand career victories. His daughter, Debbie, became the dearest, best friend I have ever known. So, as the saying goes, I was sitting in high cotton with two of the South's most accomplished racing families—the Elliotts and the Lunsfords—willing to teach me everything I needed to know about what would one day become the nation's number one spectator sport. I quickly became an avid fan and admirer. Within a short time, it would become and remain my sport of choice.

Back at the newspaper, I reversed my position. Instead of arguing against being sent to the races, with great enthusiasm I argued for why I should be covering every major event in the Southeast. "But you have to send me to Darlington!" I would proclaim. "The Southern 500 is one of the biggest of the year and that racetrack is the granddaddy of 'em all. I *can't* miss *Darlington!*"

My poor sports editor, weary of the monster he had created, would shake his head, run his fingers through his hair, and say, "Go. Please just go and get outta my hair!"

I learned quickly that preset ideas and notions can rob a person of great enjoyment and adventure in life and that the nicest gift we can give ourselves is to be open and eager for new experiences. It's like eating tofu. How do you know if you like it or don't, until you try it? I shudder to think how different my life would have been if I had not discovered stock car racing and its people. I would have missed out on strong friendships, memorable moments, and the kind of education that could never have been bought by my parents' hard-earned money. It's true that I would also have escaped many heartaches, sorrows, and tears—for had I not known so many charismatic, memorable characters, I would not have grieved so deeply over the disappearance of their lives. However, although the sorrow has been tremendous, the happiness and soul-warming memories are equal in value to, perhaps even greater than, the sadness. Frankly, I wish there had been less tears and spirit-savaging moments; but I can clearly hear Richard Petty's voice ringing in my ears, saying quite sensibly, "That's just part of the deal." How true. Without the great pain, it would have been impossible to know the tremendous joy.

I didn't make a conscious choice to be adventurous and openminded when the first assignment was forced upon me. I was too young and too stupidly stubborn for that. Sometimes, though, fate saves us from ourselves. It certainly swooped down and rescued me from my own narrow-mindedness. Racing may have been forced upon me, but it set the tone for the rest of my life as I became interested in learning about things that had not previously seemed to interest me.

How completely different and drab my life would have been if not for that unreasonable, obstinate, mean ol' sports editor who insisted that I cover racing.

Oh, how I love that man.

FROM MOONSHINE

TO SUNSHINE

Today, the sport of stock car racing is considered glamorous and chic, with the Winston Cup Series racing in front of sold-out crowds in glitzy cities like Las Vegas and Los Angeles. Every December, NASCAR's championship banquet packs the Grand Ballroom of the Waldorf Astoria on Park Avenue in New York City. But Hollywood, Las Vegas, and New York are a long way, both geographically and culturally, from the birthplace of this enormously popular sport—the backwoods of the Deep South.

The art of stock car racing rose up out of the Depression-smothered mountains of the rural South, born of enterprising men desperate to survive and feed their families. In the rugged terrain of the Carolina and Georgia mountains, crops often failed in the brick-hard dirt, but corn, sturdy and virtually invincible, was always dependable. So much so that it became a problem, growing in such abundance that there was more supply than demand and the farmers quickly and sadly discovered that they could not live on corn alone. The southern Appalachians and the surrounding foothills had been primarily settled by the Scotch-Irish who brought with them three important art forms: storytelling, fiddle playing, and whiskey making. So when times turned tough, these Celtic descendants turned back to the old heritage, called up family recipes, and turned the surplus corn into "lickker."

When Prohibition reigned in the United States, from 1920 to 1933, moonshining was a big business. Ninety percent of the illegal brew was manufactured in the southeastern United States, led by the state of Georgia. But the whiskey makers proved themselves so adept that even the end of Prohibition did not slow their business. Mountain corn liquor, nicknamed "white lightning" because it is as clear as the sparkling river waters from which it is made, was still as popular and as much in demand as it had been during the country's dry spell. Now, the producers were no longer in a business that violated the laws of the land, but they did refuse to pay the exorbitant whiskey tax imposed by the U.S. Treasury. As a result, the corn whiskey continued to be made stealthily and kept away from the nonobliging, uncompromising law enforcers and revenue agents. It was hidden deep in the mountains and brewed under the darkened cloak of night with only the illumination of the moon—thus earning it the mountain moniker of "moonshine."

As in any culture, successful entrepreneurs garner a certain acclaim and fame, and it was no different for these small business owners of the mountains. Even staunch Bible-thumping Protestants, who mostly considered the moonshiners to be disciples of the devil, harbored envy and respect for their money-making ingenuity. In a land and at a time when money reigned supreme, these men were no less than monarchs. I am descended from mountain royalty, a princess produced from a kingdom of paupers. My paternal grandfather and a couple of other relatives were noted moonshiners. My maternal grandfather was one of the mountain preachers who prayed for what were largely considered to be the doomed souls of those covert whiskey makers. Still, in the southern mountains of the 1920s, 1930s, and 1940s, the most celebrated occupations were that of preaching and moonshining, creating a chasm between the men who loved the Lord with all their hearts and those who ran from him with all their might. The primary difference was that one was rich by mountain standards and the other was poor by any standards, even lowly mountain ones. I consider it quite an accomplishment that the blood that courses through my veins was created from a comingling of the righteous and the renegades.

My daddy, the son of a north Georgia moonshiner, grew up to be a respected Baptist minister who gained acclaim for his goodness and his strong, unyielding sense of right and wrong. But even this man of high moral standards was sympathetic to the plight of the farmers turned moonshiners.

"My daddy could grow a bushel of corn and sell it for fifty cents. Or he could take that bushel and turn it into a quart of corn whiskey and sell it for two dollars and a half," he once explained. "Thing was, there wasn't another way to make a livin' back in them days. People were starvin' and losin' their farms because they couldn't pay the taxes on 'em. Now, what would you've done? Sell the bushel for fifty cents or the quart of whiskey for two-fifty?"

While the moonshiners were pulling in what seemed like a king's ransom, the biggest moneymakers were the strong, lionhearted men with nerves of steel who were transporting the illegal brew out of the mountains and into the eager arms of city slickers in places like Atlanta, Knoxville, and Charlotte. These "runners" packed gallons of the smooth punch into cleverly hidden compartments of their Fords, Dodges, and Chevrolets, armed themselves with two or three shotguns, and sneaked off in the darkest part of the night. Without headlamps, they wove their way painstakingly down and around the dangerously snaking mountain roads, most of which were still dirt despite Franklin Roosevelt's best efforts to blacktop them. The sheriffs of the rural counties were fighting valiantly to keep law and order in their neck of the woods, so often they lay in wait for an offending cargo to approach and then hightailed it after the lawbreaker. When that happened, the moonshine runner had two choices: outshoot 'em or outrun 'em. The preferred choice was no bloodshed, so the runner would hit the headlamps, gun the throttle, and head off into the night.

Almost always, with rare exceptions, he would outrun the law car, which was considered to be no more than a temporary nuisance by runners who had the fastest cars and engines that money could buy. The souped-up cars were blindingly quick, thanks to the rapid rpms turned by the supercharged engines. It was, in essence, no more than a piddling game of cat and mouse. The lawmen were frustrated because their standard assembly-line cars were no match for the moonshine runners, who spared no expense in boosting the horsepower of their engines. And, of course, men will be men, so the runners were always bragging among themselves about who had the fastest car. Egos would inflate, tempers would flare, and inevitably money would be wagered.

To settle the dispute and for bragging rights, the challengers would race each other. In the small mountain communities where entertainment other than church meetings was rare, word of an impending challenge would spread and a large crowd would assemble for the event. It wasn't long before the enterprise and ingenuity of the mountain mentality began to emerge and promoters stepped forward to organize these challenges into real races that paid prize money and charged admission. Promoters weren't always honest, and the rules weren't always fair, so it became obvious that there was a need for a governing body to ensure that rules would be standardized and purses would be paid as promised.

My best friend, Debbie, and I often laugh about all the old men we've met who claim to have started NASCAR from these mountain uprisings. Debbie's dad, Bud, himself the recipient of hundreds of trophies from the organized races, will sometimes chuckle and say to one of the pretenders, "I thought old so-and-so started NASCAR. That's what he always says."

But it was indisputably Big Bill France who built the sport into the respectable form of racing it has become, nurtured later by the business acumen and shrewdness of his sons Bill and Jim. As a sanctioning body, NASCAR (National Association for Stock Car Auto Racing) played an important role by organizing a group of racers who were guaranteed to appear in events throughout parts of the South. These racers, some of whom were still running 'shine as their main occupation, soon developed starry reputations and gathered avid followers. And as the basic laws of marketing would predict, the bigger their names became, the more of a draw they were at the gate, pulling in even more money for purses and promoters. The sanctioning body also oversaw the establishment and enforcement of rules and the promotion of the events.

The greatest appeal of this sport is, perhaps, that the racecars are "stock," unlike dragsters or open-wheel cars, which don't look anything like a vehicle that can be purchased by the average citizen. In stock car racing, the Chevrolet Monte Carlo, Ford Taurus, and Dodge Intrepid have the same body style as showroom cars. Of course, these cars are modified for speed and safety, just as the moonshine runners modified their cars. Still, Detroit automakers learned quickly that a winning racecar made for a profitable product. The adage "Win on Sunday, sell on Monday" is as true today as it has ever been, explaining why auto executives shower money on the sport and its teams.

By the mid-1950s, moonshining had for the most part given way to chicken farming. Desperate to fill the consumer demand of a booming postwar population, poultry companies began to supply chicken houses, chickens, and feed to the mountain farmers, who readily turned to poultry production as good, steady sources of income. Many who had lived and worked on the fringes of the law for years were happy to return to a law-abiding, life-sustaining occupation. Of course, there were a few who decided to have the best of both worlds and therefore hid their stills in the chicken houses!

The moonshine makers of the mountains were masterful at what they did. Eventually, they expanded their product lines to include brandy made from abundant fresh fruits like apples and peaches.

Top-notch moonshine is, more often than not, 120-plus proof of smooth, silky liquor. In fact, the first whiskey, called grain alcohol, which is produced from a double and twist run (meaning that the moonshine is run through the still twice) is 150 and 160 proof. Prewar taverns and roadhouses quickly discovered that a little moonshine went a long way in helping them to stretch their pricier inventory. They simply mixed a little of the perfect mountain brew in with the popular brands of whisky, which were a mere 80 or 90 proof. This, of course, helps to explain the high volume of moonshine transported out of the hills and into cities like Atlanta. In its heyday, Dawson County, Georgia, home then to fewer than 3,000 residents, is said to have exported over 50,000 gallons of moonshine *every* week. The county seat, Dawsonville, can lay claim to the nation's first twenty-four-hour gas station, which stayed open to service the runners as they came and went at all hours of the night.

Bill Elliott, who became the town's leading export, used to laugh and say with a wink, "I don't drink it. Never have. But I have used it as fuel!" He wasn't kidding.

Today, a local sign boasts, "Welcome to Dawsonville. Home of 'Awesome Bill' Elliott." The residents are truly proud of this native son turned racing champion, but he was not the first from the tiny mountain hamlet to conquer racing's big leagues. That honor belonged to Lloyd Seay, a young man reputed to be one of the best moonshine runners in the South. The county's sheriff once said, "I only caught him twice and both times I had to shoot his tires out from under him! I shore couldn't outrun him!"

Seay, like many others of his kind, channeled his enormous talent into the newly organized racing events, using the same fast car in which he smuggled illegal whiskey. In 1941, the darkly handsome rogue captured the sport's championship at Lakewood Speedway in Atlanta. It was his third victory in nine days. Flushed with victory, he returned home to Dawsonville to live out what would be his last twenty-four hours. The next morning, the newly crowned racing champion went about business as usual, but an argument with his cousin over a load of sugar to be used in a new batch of moonshine turned bitterly sour. In an instant, moonshine ran thicker than blood when Seay's cousin gunned him down while a stunned group watched in horror. In his last act, Seay fumbled through his own gushing blood, reached into his pocket, and pulled out a fat roll of money. "See that Mama gets this," he gurgled to his best friend. A short time later, Lloyd Seay, a mountain legend and race champion, was dead. He was two months shy of his twenty-first birthday.

Gordon Pirkle, owner of the famous Dawsonville Pool Room, proudly recounts what Bill France Sr. once said when asked by the press just how good Dale Earnhardt was. "He told them reporters that 'Dale Earnhardt is the best driver I've seen since Lloyd Seay.' " Gordon always quickens to add, "Now, he didn't say that Earnhardt was *better* than Lloyd. He said he was the best *since* Lloyd."

I had never heard of Lloyd Seay the first time I visited the Elliott family's modest racing operation, nor had I seen the handsome monument that marks his grave in the center of the town's cemetery. Appropriately, it is decorated with his photograph inside a carved rendition of the car that he drove to victory and racing immortality. In his hometown, Seay's shadow loomed large over the young freckle-faced Dawsonvillian destined to become the first stock car racer to grace the cover of *Sports Illustrated* as well as the first to capture the million-dollar bonus awarded for winning three of the sport's four grandest events (the Daytona 500, Talladega's Winston 500, Charlotte's World 600, and Darlington's Southern 500). "Million Dollar Bill" Elliott and his pit crew of mountaineers would usher in a new era for Winston Cup racing, sending a jolt throughout the sport and the national media that was both stupefying and electrifying.

When I first visited the town on assignment in 1983, I had never heard mention of Lloyd Seay and had never heard the name of Gober Sosebee, who owned a local garage and was another racing legend who had won countless races in the 1950s and 1960s. And I certainly didn't know much about the Elliotts, except that they were a small, simple, somewhat eccentric family with grand dreams that seemed practically impossible. I did not know that a Dawson County resident by the name of Raymond Parks had owned the cars driven by the sport's earliest sensations, such as Seay, Roy Hall, and the Flock brothers, or that when Bill won his first Daytona 500, he became the fifth Dawsonvillian to win a prestigious Daytona title, although the others had won theirs when the race was run on the beach.

I was soon to become an expert, though, because over the next three years I would write countless stories on the Elliotts and remind the world of the greatness of Seay and Sosebee. It was a mountain land of unusual, colorful, and wonderful characters, a place where the long arm of the law belonged to a ruggedly handsome tower of a sheriff, whose own conviction for moonshine running years earlier had resulted in a stint in a federal penitentiary. When a presidential pardon in the early 1970s cleared his record of the felony, the man who once ran from the law became the man who ran the law. In a town where the peacekeepers were once the peace breakers, where the gas station was owned by a hilarious storyteller called Rooster and the best food in town was (and still is) the Bully Burger at the tiny Pool Room, I began the education of a lifetime.

The first thing I learned is that magnificent successes, captivating folks, and record-making trendsetters can be found in the unlikeliest of places.

4

FALLING OUT OF THE SKY
AND INTO RACING

The small plane tilted downward in a plunging nosedive as Bill Elliott flipped a switch and killed the engine. He cut his eyes over to me and grinned mischievously as we began a rapid spiral toward the earth. The plane was suddenly nothing more than dead weight falling from the sky, gaining momentum with each inch. Bravely, I tried to return the smile but all I could think about was the thick forest of Georgia pines and massive oaks that was looming beneath us, growing closer with each fleeting heartbeat. Seconds before we plummeted into the treetops, Bill fired up the engine again and pulled the stunt plane out of its deadly dive.

I swallowed hard, and he threw back his head and laughed. "Scared?" he asked, obviously hoping that the answer was "yes."

I shook my head. "No," I lied. "If you kill me, you have to kill yourself, too, and I'm bettin' on you to think too much of yourself to do that."

Bill Elliott almost killed me more than once, but like a frisky feline armed with nine lives, I stubbornly hung on. I was taking such risks in order to write a fresh, interesting newspaper story or column about these misadventures. I believed I was a very dedicated journalist while my friends and family believed I was just plain stupid. Regardless of the adjective that described me best in those days, I gave Bill another chance to end my life a year later, at Road Atlanta. This time, rather than an airplane, he used a lightning-fast Jack Roush–built Ford Mustang on a course that has twelve wicked turns and a swift back straight. During a test session at the track, I succumbed to the entreaties of many who thought if I was going to write about racecars, I should ride in one. It sounded like a reasonable argument. The crew scrounged up a helmet small enough to fit me, and I climbed in through the right-side window, since racecars do not have doors.

With a look of glee that should have been an ominous clue to his naïve passenger, Bill climbed in the driver's side and very carefully buckled his seat belts. A driver's harness consists of hearty straps that come over the shoulders, across the lap, and up through the straddle. They all come together at a central buckle and are locked together with a special latch. Drivers then pull the adjustment on the shoulder straps very tight until they are sealed like glue to the seat. During the wear and tear of a grueling, bumping race, the shoulder straps can loosen, so conscientious drivers consistently pull them tighter throughout the race, particularly on caution laps and pit stops. For extra safety, the seat is custom-made to the driver's exact measurements and includes a rib protector on the driver's right side that bends slightly around the rib cage and helps to secure him tighter. When properly installed in the seat, the driver is in a cocoon of protection. That's how safe Bill Elliott was in that Michigan-built rocket ship. Here's how safe I was: I had on a helmet custom-made for someone else. Period. I had no seat belts. I didn't even have a *seat*. I also didn't have a net that could prevent me from flying out the window. Stock cars are made with fabricated sheet metal that covers the passenger side and is about elbow-high to the driver. So when I climbed in, my "seat" was a crouching position with my knees drawn toward my chest.

I was skeptically appraising the situation when Bill instructed me, "Hang onto the roll bars" as if we were on a slow-moving subway train and I had only to steel myself against sudden stops and starts. The roll bars are the incredibly strong, padded bars that are part of the roll cage, the hefty inside shell that keeps the roof from crushing down and the sides from being pushed together. Bill flipped the ignition switch and pressed the starting button to fire the engine (racecars don't have normal key ignition starters), looked over at me, and reached up to grab the strap on my helmet and pull it tighter. At the time, I thought that was extremely chivalrous. A few seconds later, I saw nothing remotely connected to chivalry about him.

He cocked his head and grinned. "Ready?"

I smiled and nodded eagerly. "Let's go."

When I agreed to that little exhibition, I assumed that we would travel the 2.5-mile course at a moderate speed of 50 or 60 mph. Bill had already taken a couple of other people for a tour of the track, and that's what he did with them. But that's *not* what he did with me. From the point that he screeched out of the pits, he raced as if he were headed for the checkered flag and a dozen cars were battling him for the lead. It's hard to say when the exact moment of heart-stopping fear began, but I would boldly venture to say that it was as we entered the first turn. By the time we hit the back straight, Bill's notoriously heavy foot had the Mustang churning at a speed close to 180 mph and I was clinging for dear life to the roll bar while the powerful G-forces were trying to suck me out of the window. As I had no seat or seat belt, this would not have been very difficult. A less determined or less desperate person could never have survived. I felt like Gilligan holding on to a skinny palm tree, fighting the fierce tropical winds of a massive hurricane. As I valiantly fought the punishing G-forces, all I could think was, "If we wreck, I'm goin' outta this window and I'll die instantly, and Mr. Compassion over there is gonna walk away without a scratch."

G-forces are a natural phenomenon of speed and although they are normally more brutal to sports cars and open-wheel Indy-style cars because of these cars' low-slung aerodynamics, they can be quite punishing to stock car drivers. And, I might add, to their passengers. The combination of a racer's head and helmet is quite heavy compared with his relatively tiny neck, so it can easily be pulled by the opposing gravitational forces as a car whips into a turn. If the combination of head and helmet weighs ten pounds and the car is pulling two G's, that's a wind pull of twenty pounds on a ten-pound object supported by a spindly neck. Three G's would be thirty pounds, and so forth. While low-riding race cars can commonly pull as many as five G's (anything higher can cause danger in the form of light-headedness and possible blackouts), stock cars are usually more in the range of two and three G's. Nonetheless, it can be quite tiring and uncomfortable. Some tracks—such as Bristol, Tennessee—are so steeply banked and so short in distance that it's almost like one continuous turn. That is quite a grueling punishment for drivers, whose necks are whipped and pulled for hours. And some people argue that racecar drivers aren't athletes! I'd like to see one of those critics fight a 3,400-pound monster with crushing G-forces at the thin-aired mountain altitude of Bristol for four hours.

Perhaps now you'll understand better how close I was to being sucked out of the netless window on that most memorable of rides with Bill Elliott. At the height of the horror—that would be coming down the straightaway at 180 mph with a grip on the roll bar that was rapidly weakening—I glanced over to see Bill looking at me. When he saw the sheer terror on my face, he threw back his head and howled with hilarity. I chose not to waste a morsel of my strength by glaring at him. I saved that for later. A couple of minutes later, he roared into the pits and skidded to a smoking, dragmark-producing stop. He was still laughing.

"Get her out," he told the crew. "I's gonna take her for a second lap, but she'll never make it."

I was a puddle of convulsing nerves as two crew members pulled me—blackened, smut-covered, and disabled—from the car. I was covered with tiny bits of asphalt that had been dislodged by the speeding car and had flown all over me. The crew guys steadied me to keep my knees from buckling under me. I do not exaggerate when I say that I trembled for twelve straight hours. I timed it. Then, I documented it by writing a column about it. That story, along with dozens of others of mine, decorates the walls of the hallowed Dawsonville Pool Room—in fact, my photos and my words cover the bathroom walls, thank you very much. Thanks to Gordon Pirkle, the proprietor, I have my own tiny bit of immortality in a county where immortality isn't awarded lightly and friends aren't made easily.

But as mean as Bill could treat me, I adored him and his entire family. His father, George, the family's wise and shrewd patriarch, became my patient mentor; Mildred, the Elliott matriarch, became my staunchest supporter; Bill and his oldest brother, Ernie, became wonderful, close friends of mine; and Dan, the middle brother—then newly divorced—became my boyfriend. The daughters-in-law, Martha and Sheila, were equally wonderful and kind. In short, the Elliotts, all of them, took me under their wing, welcomed me into their private, secluded fold, and opened their hearts to me. Southerners, particularly those from the mountain regions, are incredibly loyal and never forget their friends. I had written glowingly of the Elliotts before the rest of the world caught on; as a result, when they became the hottest story in motorsports, they provided me with scoop after scoop and the kind of unlimited access that no other journalist had. I became the authority on the Elliotts, the reporter other reporters called when they needed to verify facts. In all honesty, it was my connection with the Elliotts, not talent or ability, that got me to *USA Today*.

I went to church with the Elliotts, flew to races with them on their private planes, and, time after time, dined at their table of friendship and hospitality. The Elliotts are the luckiest thing that ever happened to me, one of those great rewards that life hands you, although you haven't done one darn thing to deserve it. I will always be grateful and indebted to that lovely family.

Still, the Elliotts' greatest gift to me was not a better life or a more successful career. It was, instead, a compelling lesson that conventional wisdom and practicality does not teach, that common sense frequently fails to comprehend, and that reality often ignores. They showed me that in life, it doesn't matter where you come from. All that really matters is where you go. Your potential and dreams are not limited by the world's view of you. They can be expanded and realized by your view of the world. I realized that if you think in terms of possibilities long enough, they eventually turn into probabilities.

The Elliotts and what seemed like a far-fetched dream for stardom rose up from a small town nestled in the foothills of North Georgia, far from the mecca of stock car racing in North Carolina. Dawson County, of course, can lay claim to a substantial role in the birth of NASCAR and stock car racing, but over the three decades before the emergence of the racing Elliotts in the 1980s, the center of talent had shifted to the Carolinas, home to the most powerful team owners, engine builders, drivers, and crew members. Even the Alabama-based Allisons and Neil Bonnett and the Tennessee-based Darrell Waltrip were racing for teams based in North Carolina. The philosophy was simple. If you wanted to race NASCAR, you went to the base of real power and talent. From the beginning, the Elliotts resisted this notion, and their radical concept would raise them to the grandest heights achieved by any team in the 1980s. What many believed would work against them actually worked for them.

The doors of any racing operation revolve constantly—talent and labor steadily come and go, especially at the end of each season. As Richard Petty once noted, "Each time a guy leaves your race team, he takes a little bit of your knowledge and technology with him to his new team." This was one reason that Petty's operation, located in Level Cross, North Carolina, had an edge on its competition for many years. Petty's team was just far enough from the hub of activity in Charlotte to keep crew members from continually uprooting and relocating.

As it turned out, what worked well for Petty worked remarkably well for the Elliotts. If Petty was separated from the sport's hub, the Elliotts were downright segregated. So, location, combined with the innate loyalty of men born and raised in the same community who were neighbors more than coworkers, unparalleled mechanical genius, and indisputable talent, destined the Elliotts for exactly what they became—history makers.

The naysayers, however, didn't give much in the way of good odds for success to what they saw as a straggling bunch of country bumpkins. The other owners and drivers, much to their chagrin later on, underestimated the craftiness, talent, brilliance, incredible work ethic, and uncommonly strong common sense bred into these men of the mountains. In 1985, the Elliott race team, which had been purchased by the Michigan industrialist Harry Melling, would thumb their noses at the bewildered competition. They chalked up eleven wins, including the Daytona 500, and eleven pole positions; won the inaugural Winston Million; and set world speed records that earned Bill Elliott the title "Fastest Man Alive." It was a far cry from the days of "oiling the square," a game that the brothers had played with their friends in which they poured motor oil around the tiny town square and then raced their cars to the oil, where they slipped, slid, and spun out—the countywide pastime for teenage boys.

"You mean the law let you do that and get away with it?" I asked suspiciously.

Bill chuckled. "We only had one—a sheriff. So we sent one car in front of us as a decoy. He raced through town and the sheriff took off after him. Then the rest of us oiled the square and had some fun."

To illustrate the public's general perception of the slow-talking, fast-driving country boys from rural Georgia, I have to look no further than my own family. In September 1984, I accepted an invitation from Dan Elliott to join him and his family in Darlington, South Carolina, for the Southern 500. Ernie, his wife Sheila, Dan, and I were going to fly by chartered plane from Gainesville to Florence, South Carolina (the landing strip behind their shops and their fleet of airplanes were still a couple of years away). Although Dan and I had been dating for a few months, my brother, Randall, who took me to the airport for the departure, had not yet met him. We arrived before the Elliotts and were waiting in our car when we heard a choking, sputtering mechanical cough. We both turned to look as an ancient pickup that looked like the one driven by the Beverly Hillbillies came spitting and jerking past us. In the back of the truck, hanging onto the weathered clapboard cattle railings, were two unkempt, scruffy-looking mountaineers wearing dingy yellow undershirts and gray chino-like work pants. They both wore dusty black billed caps that were splattered with mud. One had a fairly large belly that spilled out from his T-shirt and left the flesh exposed for about an inch between it and his pants. The other was equally dapper. The truck jarred to a stop and the less than agile duo each grabbed a black plastic trash bag, which apparently was their luggage since one of the bags had a hole in it and was spilling out clothes, as they jumped down from the five-foot-high truck bed. This sight was funny and became even funnier when they headed straight to a handsome twin-engine, six-passenger plane and began to board.

I was chuckling and shaking my head in amazement when I looked over at my brother. He wasn't laughing. His face was completely ashen and his dark eyes were saucer-large when he turned to me. His expression was absolute horror when he finally managed to find his voice and ask, "Is that the Elliotts?"

My chuckle turned into screaming laughter and I howled so hard that I was gasping for breath. I couldn't stop laughing. Still, he did not see the absurdity of it and he pressed forth in a hopeful, anxious tone, "It ain't, is it?"

I was still laughing so hard that I couldn't speak. I could only shake my head "no" as tears rolled down my face. The look of relief that spread across his face induced me to laugh harder. A few minutes later, Dan and the rest of the family arrived in separate new Ford vehicles, and both brothers—tall, trim, and stately—were dressed impeccably in handsome casual clothes. After introducing them to my very relieved brother, I joined them on the tarmac. We boarded the plane and while the pilot was rolling up the red carpet and pulling up the steps to close the door, I started laughing again. Questioningly, Dan looked at me as he reached over and picked up a piece of fruit from the catering tray.

"You're not going to believe what just happened. It's hilarious," I said, shaking my head in amusement. Then, pausing frequently to laugh and catch my breath, I told him the story.

For some reason, Dan didn't find it funny at all.

RICHARD PETTY

AND THE CASE OF THE

MISSING PURSE

Talladega, Alabama, is a tiny town where the best of yesterday resides blissfully, creating an odd illusion for those of us accustomed to a more tumultuous modern world. Unfairly, almost sinfully, it tempts visitors to yearn wistfully for the good old days when folks visited on their neighbors' front porch on lazy Sunday afternoons and homemade apple pies cooled on windowsills while children played happily in swings made from old tires.

But in this special town some sixty miles east of Birmingham, in which the residents meander unhurriedly through everyday life and shop at the Piggly Wiggly, where old men congregate in lawn chairs on the asphalt parking lot every day to chew tobacco, whittle, and talk, life quickens to death-defying speeds twice a year when the Winston Cup Series roars into Talladega.

It was here, in the middle of nowhere, that the France family chose to build a superspeedway in the late 1960s. The inaugural race of 1969 at Alabama International Motor Speedway, later renamed Talladega Super Speedway, won a unique place in the annals of racing history because of the fury that arose from the drivers when they discovered that the fast speeds delivered by the incredible 33-degree banking—the turns are equal in height to a four-story building—were blistering their tires and endangering their lives.

Led by the charismatic Richard Petty, who could effortlessly rally troops to follow him into a storm of hellfire and brimstone, the NASCAR stars boycotted the race, packed their trailers and cars, and headed home with scarcely a look back over their shoulders. Big Bill France refused to be bullied. He gathered enough small-time drivers to field the race and awarded fifteen minutes of fame to Richard Brickhouse, who won his only Grand National event (it was renamed the Winston Cup Series in December 1985). Big Bill also competed in the race himself in an attempt to prove how safe the track was. Petty, Cale Yarborough, David Pearson, Bobby Allison, and the other greats returned for the next race after Goodyear had developed a sturdy tire that would withstand 2.66 miles of heart-pulsing speed.

Talladega is, to me, the best racetrack in the world, and my favorite track to visit. After more than thirty years, it is still surrounded by a rural, tree-smothered landscape, although the convenience of Interstate 20 is within walking distance of the front gate. The folks are down-home and eager to please, with a smile, a friendly word, and a hand of kindness. In addition to southern hospitality, the 2,500-acre facility offers spectacular shows, both on the track and in the infield, where blue-collar workers gather for three days of nonstop partying. By Sunday morning, those in the infield are red-eyed from no sleep, red-necked from the sun, and white-faced from too many beers, too many cigarettes, and too little food. Talladega is a place of color and interest, where various cultures converge to share a weekend of passion and fun.

A couple of years ago, I chronicled the Sunday event with a tiny camera, recording the crowds that gathered, the traffic that jammed, the garage folks who worked, the pits that buzzed, and the racecars that hummed for three hours and 188 laps of splendid speed. I took the last shot as we waited in traffic to leave the infield. Two guys, who had definitely enjoyed the day with a beer or two, were passed out in their old Ford pickup, their race hats—embroidered with the names of their favorite drivers—pulled down at an angle over their brows. The windows were rolled down, so I jumped out of our car, ran over, and snapped a close-range photo while my friends doubled over in laughter. It was the perfect photographic recollection of a day at Talladega.

Talladega is also my favorite because it is the site of many of my most vivid memories. I watched with enormous pride as Bill Elliott set three world speed records, twice breaking his own records. I saw Davey Allison run his first Winston Cup race at this track, filling in for Neil Bonnett in a Junior Johnson–owned Chevrolet. A year later, I saw him win his first Cup race in front of his hometown crowd.

This was also the place where Davey would crash his helicopter seven years later while attempting to land so that he could watch his buddy, Bonnett, test. For Davey, born in Hollywood, Florida, and raised in Hueytown, Alabama, a stone's throw from his home track, Talladega represented both the beginning and the end. On the other hand, I saw Davey's dad, Bobby, defy death when his red-and-white Buick lifted off the ground and spun toward the grandstands and into the fence in the most horrific crash I have ever witnessed. It was even more frightening than the crash in which Petty rolled end over end seven times down the front straightaway at Daytona, because Allison's car headed straight toward the spectators. It did injure a few, but fortunately no one died, thanks to a pair of two-inch cables strung behind the fence, which held and caught the car at the last minute.

I once sat in a car with Tim Richmond outside the Talladega media center and heard his endless angry-man rants about the viciousness of the press, which he believed was trying to destroy him. "Look at them," he snarled, motioning toward a large window through which several reporters could be seen. "They're just a bunch of vultures, sitting in there trying to figure out what rotten things they can do next."

I laughed at his silliness, and this struck the wrong chord with him. "You're not taking their side, are you?" His eyes narrowed suspiciously.

"I used to *be* one of them."

"Don't remind me or I'll stop liking you." He wasn't kidding.

Talladega was also the first place where I saw a race on a super-speedway (2 miles or longer). This was, in fact, only the third race I had attended. I had gone as a guest of Dan Elliott and his family. Dale Earnhardt won the race, followed by a train of nine cars that crossed the finish line bumper to bumper, with Dan's brother Bill rounding out the Top 10.

"I'm sorry that we couldn't have given you a better show," George Elliott apologized, meaning that he was sorry that Bill had not won or, at least, finished second.

"Are you kiddin'? It was great!" I replied enthusiastically, already falling helplessly in love with the shiver produced by a flying checkered flag. "I just saw ten cars cross the finish line in less than two seconds. That's amazing."

That day had been eventful from its predawn start. At 5:30 A.M., I had rounded the Dawsonville town square in my little sports car and glanced into my rearview mirror to see the headlights of a sheriff's car blaze to life. The driver was not surreptitious or stealthy but bold and brazen. He tailed me for a few miles, until I turned into the long winding driveway of Dan's ranch-style brick house. The sheriff's car waited at the foot of the driveway until I parked, got out of the car, and was greeted by Dan. The sheriff's car then backed up, turned around, eased onto the road, and drove away.

"That law car followed me here from the town square," I explained, mystified. "I wasn't speeding or anything."

Dan chuckled at the city girl's naïveté. "He didn't recognize the car and knew you weren't from here. He wanted to make certain that you belonged in these parts."

From the beginning of the day, Dan promised a special surprise for me after the race. I was excited, busily trying to imagine what great treat lay in store. I was certain that it had to be something incredibly romantic and thoughtful. Bill sidled up to me before the race started and asked curiously, "Do you have any idea what your surprise is?"

My smile sparkled with excitement as I shook my head. "No. Do you know?"

He nodded and knitted his eyebrows into a slight frown as doubtfulness filled his blue eyes. "Boy, are you going to be surprised," he drawled in a tone that implied "I don't think it's going to give you the kind of joy you're expecting."

Like many other starry-eyed girls, I was a hopeless devotee of romance novels, so I fantasized about that perfect romantic moment. I could barely wait for the race to end, dreamily floating through the hours leading up to my surprise. After the race, as the crew loaded the racecar into the hauler, Dan took my hand and led me around to the passenger side of the cab of the truck. He opened the door, grinned proudly, and exclaimed, "This is it!"

I was bewildered. "This is what?" I asked.

"Your surprise!" His grin broadened, stretching from ear to ear. "We're gonna drive the truck home with the racecar in it!"

My heart sank. "*This* is my surprise?" I said this in a tone of numbed disbelief, but Dan reacted as if I had spoken with giddy excitement.

"And that's not all," he replied, beaming happily as his chest swelled with pride. "We're also gonna stop for pizza!"

That was a moment of revelation: I discovered that racers don't view the world as others do, particularly when it comes to romance. I also learned that when people offer a gift of which they are extremely proud, it is because they believe that it's the best present in all the world. For that reason, we should always let the gesture count more than the gift itself. Though skeptically unenthusiastic, I climbed into the truck for the trip home from Talladega and began to make the best of the situation by chatting endlessly over the CB radio with the truckers who wanted to talk about "ol' number 9." It wasn't the surprise that I would have chosen, but it was unique and it came from a sincere, well-meaning heart. While I have long forgotten many of the floral bouquets I have received over the years, that is one gift and memory I will never forget.

A year later, I rode the same race hauler home from Talladega, but not with Dan, for we had long since parted ways—divided by the fame that engulfed him but thoughtlessly excluded me. Now, it was Richard Petty's fault that I had to ride in the truck, for he had stolen my purse and left town. Well, he didn't exactly steal it. He is, after all, an icon of motorsports as well as an incredibly honest and kind man, and there simply is no better ambassador for the sport. Men like Elliott, Earnhardt, and Jeff Gordon have drawn a great deal of attention to the sport and garnered huge followings of fans; but Richard brought tremendous public relations skills to stock car racing and represented the sport with class and brilliance. It is his car—the familiar 43 painted in "Petty Blue" and orange—in the Smithsonian Institution in Washington, D.C., that symbolizes the modern era of stock car racing.

"I never needed a publicity person," he recently commented after hearing me recount one of my most challenging moments as a publicist on the circuit. He shrugged and continued. "I just went out there and took care of my own thing. I was my own public relations person."

And no one could have done it better. With his trademark cowboy hat, wraparound dark sunglasses, and 100,000-watt smile, he created an unforgettable image, one that couldn't be rivaled by the world's best. He is word-perfect as a quote maker and the epitome of graciousness to the demanding media and his adoring fans. Add all this to the fact that his 200 wins makes him the winningest driver of all time (David Pearson is next, with 105 wins). Petty has won the Daytona 500 a record seven times (the closest contender is Cale Yarborough with four wins) and captured seven championships, a record tied by the late Dale Earnhardt. Even when I knew nothing about racing of any kind, I knew the name Richard Petty and that Petty was king.

But still, he took my purse and left Talladega with it.

My purse was actually contraband buried in the back of his van under other bags and boxes, so he and his wife, Lynda, left without knowing they were taking all my money, my car keys, and—worst of all—my favorite lipstick. I was a sportswriter covering the race, and I had stopped by for a tailgate lunch with the Pettys and my good friends Ed and Randy Parks. This was back in the days before luxury motor coaches, when drivers used custom-made vans. Richard's was navy blue with a painted image of him in a cowboy hat and dark glasses emblazoned on both sides. While I was making a sandwich, I said, "I'm going to put my purse in the back seat of the van." I did, and then I promptly forgot about it.

The race that day was the most exciting I have ever seen. Bill Elliott, who won the pole at a world-record-setting speed of 209.393 mph, an incredible four mph faster than the second-place qualifier, Cale Yarborough, was racing to win a big bonus from Winston. A victory that day, coupled with his earlier win at the Daytona 500, would guarantee him $100,000, a huge amount in those days, and put him in line to win a million dollars if he won at either Charlotte for the World 600 or Darlington's Southern 500. But early trouble with an oil line forced him into the pits for repair and put him two laps down. For the first time in Talladega history, there was no caution flag, but Bill, with his rocket ship, miraculously managed to chase down the field to get back his two laps and win the race by several seconds. Bill's wife, Martha, had taken me to the scoring stand with her to teach me how to score a car. I was completely absorbed in the race and Martha's teaching and oblivious of anything else. As soon as the checkered flag fell, I suddenly remembered my purse and ran to the parking compound, only to discover that the Pettys' van was nowhere to be found. I raced to the garage and found Kyle, Richard's son, who had finished a distant second in the race.

"Kyle!" I screamed frantically. "Where is your dad?"

"He's already gone."

I grabbed his shoulders, shook him, and cried soulfully, "Nooooo!!!! He can't be gone. He can't be!"

Kyle looked around the garage, trying to spot his dad. "I'm sure he is because he fell out early and he wouldn't stick around. He'd leave. Whattaya need?"

"My purse is in their van," I groaned. Kyle rolled his eyes and shook his head.

"Well, your purse is now on its way to Randleman, North Carolina." Good ol' Kyle. You could always count on him to point out the obvious.

With no purse, I had no car keys and no way to get home. I also had colorless, unpainted lips, which was just as bad or worse. After celebrating their victory, the Elliotts offered me a ride home in their plane, since I lived only about thirty minutes from their shop.

"No," I told Bill's brother, Ernie. "That's very nice of you, but that's much too good for me after doing such an idiotic thing. But I would appreciate it if I could hitch a ride home on the truck."

So, again, I rode home in the front cab of the eighteen-wheeler, hauling the winning racecar and listening to congratulations pour in from truck drivers over CB radio. The Pettys sent my purse the next day by UPS.

My newspaper editor at the time, Mike Connell, was so amused by my mishap that he wrote a column about "the sportswriter and her missing purse." What made the story newsworthy was not the role that the legendary Richard Petty played as the bandit but rather that at the time there were not many sportswriters who carried purses. The story got picked up by the newswire, and my stupidity became a source of national amusement.

The most important lesson of that predicament is one every woman will understand—never leave your lipstick in someone else's care. From that moment forward, I always tucked my lip gloss inside my credential holder, because a girl and her lipstick should never be separated.

FAST JETS AND

JUNKYARD CARS

Bill Elliott reached over to answer the ringing telephone with one hand and with the other motioned me into the office of the race shop.

"Mellin' Racin'," he drawled. Then he listened for a moment before replying, "Naw, Bill ain't here. This is Dan."

I clapped my hand over my mouth to stifle my laughter while Bill covered the mouthpiece of the phone to cover his. The three brothers not only looked remarkably alike but sounded similar, so the subterfuge was easy. He talked a few more minutes, hung up, and swiveled his chair around to face me with a delighted twinkle in his Elliott-blue eyes. Those twinkles had become fewer and farther between, owing to the growing demands and stresses of being NASCAR's hottest star.

"I'm not believing you," I said, still laughing with merriment at the sight of seeing my friend enjoy a brief reprieve from the prison of his fame.

"Man, I gotta do somethin'," he explained, shaking his head. "If I talked to everybody who wants to talk to me, I'd never have time to work on the racecar. Don't have much time as it is."

If the history of stock car racing is correctly recorded, it will be written that 1985 was the year when NASCAR first entered the modern era of media adoration—and the lives of Bill Elliott and his family changed forever. These two strands of time are woven together and neither would have happened without the other.

In 1984, unencumbered and uninhibited by a racing world that virtually ignored them, the Elliott brothers had diligently gone about their business in Dawsonville. Each had specific expertise that complemented the other's, and they were working in tandem to create what would become motorsports spinning, race-winning history.

Ernie, the oldest, who oversaw race strategy as crew chief, is a mechanical genius. He proved it with the powerful, sturdy charged engines that he built, engines created from brilliant ingenuity, engines that set world speed records that in all likelihood will never be broken. Dan built the strong transmissions and gears that could sustain the power created by Ernie's masterpieces. Bill, a driver with remarkable skill, proved to be uncommonly talented in setting the car up to racetrack-hugging perfection.

There is a new generation of drivers who have no idea which springs, shocks, or sway bars will work best on which car at which track under which weather conditions. They never lay a hand on the car—wouldn't or couldn't even consider it. But not Bill. He was as gifted under the car as he was in the driver's seat.

Some drivers have difficulty communicating what is wrong with their car in practice or in a race so that the crew will know how to adjust it. Tim Richmond, for instance, knew nothing about the mechanics of a car or how to articulate what was wrong with it. Tim's career took off when Rick Hendrick teamed him with a veteran crew chief, Harry Hyde, who translated Tim's unique verbiage into usable instructions. When Tim complained, "It's got a jiggle in the seat," Harry knew that the car was loose and that the back end was slipping out from under the car as Tim tried to maneuver the turns.

Bill, however, could articulate perfectly what was wrong and then climb under the car and fix it himself.

Many times I would stop by the car at the racetrack and ask the crew, "Where's Bill?" Someone would gesture toward the underneath of the car, where only a pair of sneakered feet connected to long legs clothed in dark blue work pants could be seen. Bill knew that his destiny should not be entrusted to someone else, someone who might have no vested interest in his safety or success. It is an example that I remember always—when something is important to me or my career, I take charge and do it myself or at least get closely involved with it. Regardless of how much people might love me or care about my well-being, their passion for my career will never equal mine. Bill Elliott and his family knew that, too. Also, Bill didn't have to worry that an employee who was paid to do the setup might quit and take his secrets to another team, leaving him high and dry. It happens. A good chassis man leaves one job for another, and his old team, once highly successful, is suddenly struggling while his new team reaps the benefits of his experience and his setup notebook. Bill shrewdly controlled his own destiny. It's a pearl of wisdom that everyone should cultivate.

Once George sold the monetarily struggling team to the well-financed Harry Melling, it took off. They captured their first win in 1983, in a season-ender in Riverside, California; then they followed up with three wins in 1984. But the best came in 1985, when they set tongues wagging *and* complaining to NASCAR, beginning in Daytona for the season-opening Daytona 500. The Ford Thunderbird, sponsored by Coors and driven by a nondrinker, was so superior to the other cars, particularly the other Fords, that it looked as though the rest of the teams had retreated to an off-season of snoozing hibernation while the unassuming Elliott boys had worked without sleep for the previous two months. With a jaw-dropping, record-setting qualifying speed of 205.114 mph in Daytona, the Elliotts instantly became the darlings of Ford Motor Company, the idols of a new racing generation, and a storybook tale for sportswriters who are always yearning for a good angle. From the moment that the checkered flag flew in the sea-drenched air to signal for Bill to qualify for the 1985 Daytona 500, life would never be simple again for these men who had never known anything but a simple life. Fame may sound glamorous, but the transition is hard to make.

As the grind of 1985 churned toward the Southern 500 in Darlington, where Bill would attempt to become the first driver to win the Winston Million, life became increasingly difficult and tense. It was mostly work and very little joy or laughter. The media frenzy and the fans around Bill had reached such an enormous level by the time the Southern 500 arrived, that twin mountains, otherwise known as South Carolina patrolmen, were installed at his side. Everywhere he went, the troopers shielded him from unwanted attention and provided a solid barrier between him and the outside world. Bill's racecar was secured in a special roped-off section of the garage and no one except team members and NASCAR officials was allowed within the ropes. Regardless of what some might say, I do a fairly good job of playing within the rules. So despite my friendship with the Elliotts, I stayed away, like the other reporters. Bill met with us in an informal press conference once a day to share information and provide quotes.

One day, I was walking past the roped-off area when Bill caught my eye. He was sitting on one of the four-foot-high worktables, watching as the crew worked on the car. On each side were the ever-faithful state troopers. Bill waved, and I waved back. Then he grinned and wiggled his forefinger, motioning me toward him. I scooted under the rope and scampered over.

"Hey!" I exclaimed brightly, glad to see my friend. No sooner were the words out of my mouth than the twin mountains, who hovered over a foot taller, accosted me. Each one grabbed an arm. They picked me up, several inches off the garage floor, and one, stern and unsmiling, said, "Ma'am, you're in a protected area. No one without special clearance is allowed in here. We need to remove you."

My feet were dangling and kicking in midair as I protested with great embarrassment. Everyone within sight of the spectacle had stopped work and was watching me being bodily removed from close proximity to the *star*.

"But he invited me over here," I proclaimed, slinging my head toward Bill. "He motioned me over here." I looked over to see Bill doubled over with laughter. Needless to say, I was not amused. "Bill, tell them that you told me to come over here!" I demanded. "Tell them right now."

He stopped laughing and suddenly looked bewildered. "What are you talkin' about?"

"Bill!" I screamed, all patience gone.

He held up his hands. "I ain't got no idea what she's talkin' 'bout. I didn't tell her to come over here."

That was all the troopers needed to hear. They dragged me away and set me down outside the roped-off area.

"Now stay put," the stern one said, while Bill returned to choking gales of laughter. I realized that I had been set up and that I had paid the price for Bill's need of merriment in a strained situation. I was furious.

I put my hands on my hips and promised, "Bill Elliott, I'll get you back for this!" I started to storm off but turned back to sneer, "*I'll* be pulling for Earnhardt on Sunday! I hope he kicks your butt!"

Dale Earnhardt did give it his best shot that Sunday and came closer than anyone else to spoiling Bill's big day. But an equalized tire put him out of contention, and Bill cruised into Victory Lane, where counterfeit dollar bills rained down in abundance and "Million Dollar Bill" gave the media another great story to write. Success rained on Bill Elliott, and just as it is possible for too much rain to fall on a thirsty cornfield, too much success stormed into his life at once.

In some ways, success is more difficult, more unfair, than failure. Success can weaken our character and our resolve whereas failure can strengthen them. Success delivers a momentary buzz, but that initial high dies quickly in the face of extraordinary physical and emotional demands, with increased scheduling, appearances, and constant attention. Suddenly and unexplainably, a life and soul once owned by one person are now owned by many. To complicate the formula, the voracious appetite of ego feeds incessantly on a gourmet diet of success, plumping up the individual with self-importance. When the focus shifts to the person, it is harder to concentrate on the mission. Unless a person is solidly grounded and surrounded by caring friends, a once normal world is thrown off-kilter and a once bright future can be warped beyond repair. Success has probably destroyed more people than failure. How we deal with success defines our true character and broadcasts that discovery to a large audience.

Failure is a great teacher, turning mistakes, misunderstandings, and miscues into powerful lessons. Success, however, is full of lessons that we tend to ignore and overlook because we believe that if we have succeeded, there is nothing left to learn. Watching the Elliotts, I saw rapacious success try to gnaw their flesh, chew them into pieces, and spit them back at the mountain earth of their raising. Fame, and the startling suddenness of it, almost devoured Bill Elliott and his family. More pompous, less stable individuals would have succumbed to the false allure and instant celebrity. People of lesser character would have been infatuated with who the world *thought* they were rather than who they *knew* they were. But it wasn't easy to stay grounded. It was a constant battle against two enormous forces—the pull of celebrity versus the draw of home and the common life it represents.

"What nobody realizes is that success just came too fast for us," Bill told me, shaking his head with weariness. "We went straight from being nobodies to the top. That year, 1985, was both the best and the worst thing that ever happened to me."

The Elliotts handled stunning fame with graciousness and something of an aw-shucks attitude. This isn't to say they weren't proud of their accomplishments, for they were. And rightly so. The

Elliotts became instant media darlings, crowned royalty of the racing world, because they, as characters, were interesting and their story was sensational. But all this came with a price. Suddenly, everyone wanted a piece of them, especially of Bill, who developed ulcers and aged noticeably.

Bill earned two new monikers—"Million Dollar Bill" and "Awesome Bill from Dawsonville." The latter was truer than the former, because he was still one of the lowest-paid drivers on the circuit and the bulk of his winnings went to the owner, as is customary. The Winston Million had earned him less than a quarter of a million. So in 1986, Bill announced that he was fair game for any team owner looking for a good driver and willing to pay the price.

By then, I had left the newspaper world and gone into sports marketing in Indianapolis, specializing in Winston Cup racing. One team owner for whom I was working decided that he wanted Bill Elliott for his driver, and knowing that roots run deep with hometown folks in the South, he asked me to fly home and talk to Bill about the possibility. Bill and I had agreed to meet at the Gainesville airport. I was flying in from Indy in a private jet, and he was flying in from Dawsonville in a small single-engine plane he owned. As long as I have known Bill, he has been as avid about his aviation as his racing. It's hard to tell which one he loves more. I was the lone passenger on the small corporate jet and as we circled over Lake Lanier and prepared for the approach to the airport, I looked over at the lake and sighed deeply. It felt good to be coming home, particularly in such grand style, for the first time since I had left the newspaper. I settled back and relaxed in the seat, surrounded by a new set of Louis Vuitton luggage. I hugged myself and felt cozy, warm, and successful. The plane landed, and I had to wait only a few minutes before Bill buzzed in in his tiny plane.

"Hey!" he said without wasting time on any niceties. "You got a car?"

I froze for a second because the small airport did not have rental cars and our meeting was to be held several miles away.

"Oh, no," I groaned. "I didn't think about it. What can we do?"

"That's OK," he replied, walking past me and motioning for me to follow. "I got a car that I keep here. We can use it."

By the time I got out of the door with my designer luggage, he was already at his "airport car." When I saw it, I stopped and asked with disdain, "What's *that*?"

The car should have been parked at the junkyard rather than at the airport. It was at least twenty years old, a dingy green Dodge with a faded vinyl roof that was peeled off in most places and curled up in others. It was nothing short of ghastly. And I, the new executive, who had just arrived in a private jet with an expensive wardrobe tucked inside a set of Louis Vuitton luggage and thought I was the epitome of class, was not going to set foot in such a vehicle.

"You're kiddin', right?" Disgust clouded my face.

"No." He was tickled beyond words at my haughtiness. "This is my car and it's what we're goin' in."

"*I'm not!* No way am *I* getting into *that* car. That is the most disgusting car I have ever seen!"

"Well, you can just suit yourself. You can ride in this car or you can walk. It's up to you." He smiled like a man who knows when he has an ace. It was a blazing hot June day. I had lived away from Georgia long enough to forget how brutal the summers can be. I twisted my mouth and wiped the droplets away from under my eyes.

"Well?" he prodded.

I knew I had no choice. I had a job to do, regardless of the indignity I was forced to endure. Irritated, I grabbed my luggage, stomped down the steps, and stormed over to the car. I threw the bags in the backseat and as I slid in, he grinned and remarked slyly, "I knew you'd see it my way. Oh, you better roll down your window. This car ain't got no air conditioning."

"*What!* It's almost a hundred degrees outside and we're riding in a car that doesn't have air conditioning?"

"Beggars can't be choosers," he replied, still grinning about the situation. "Uh-oh. We're outta gas. I better pull into that station and fill up."

He pulled into a self-service convenience store and when he got out to pump gas, I decided to go in and purchase *The Times*, my old newspaper. I was coming out of the store, glancing over the front page, when a visibly awed fan did a double take at the famous NASCAR driver pumping gas into the horror of a car.

"Bill Elliott?" he asked, more to himself than to Bill.

Bill, the reluctant star who would have preferred racing without fame had he been given a choice, smiled and nodded.

A "golllleeee" smile covered the guy's face and he said, "I thought you only drove Fords! Whatcha doin' with that Dodge?"

Bill looked up to see me coming through the doorway and quickly replied, "Oh, this ain't my car." He nodded toward me and grinned. "It's *hers!*"

Needless to say, that fixed my little designer wagon.

Bill, like many of the older die-hard racers, just wanted to race. He never wanted celebrity. But when he discovered that one came with the other, he dealt with it in an admirable way. So has Richard Petty, who never fools himself into thinking that he alone is responsible for his success. Although Petty is stock car racing's greatest icon and therefore attracts a lot of attention everywhere he goes, he never shirks from what he views as a responsibility to his public.

Fortunately, I got past that period of stupid self-importance in my life. I learned from people like Bill and Richard—and from a couple of other drivers who weren't so gracious—that humility is the most important attribute we can possess. It's critical to maintain close ties to our true roots. If you get too impressed with yourself, you've lost the battle. You might as well pull up a chair, put up your feet, and savor your past accomplishments, because there won't be any future ones. Self-importance is self-indulgent at its worst and self-destructive at its best because it allows us to rest on our laurels rather than striving for greater success. We can always do even better if we continue to focus.

But just for the record, in case that guy from the convenience store is reading this, that was *not* my car!

7

A WISCONSIN YANKEE

IN A SOUTHERN COURT

My first date with Alan Kulwicki taught me an unforgettable lesson about human nature: one beer can have a powerful impact on a relationship.

Just one beer too many crumbled Alan's carefully constructed and maintained wall of protection, leaving him unshielded and vulnerable. Since I was a teetotaler then, I was completely clearheaded as he told me things that I am certain he regretted the next morning. But the private anguish that he spewed forth like poison released from his soul gave me the key to understanding the most misunderstood man I have ever known. Without the revelations provided courtesy of that one extra beer, I don't believe there would have been a second date for the southern belle and the Yankee racecar driver.

Several months earlier, I was covering a race at an old short track in Jefferson, Georgia, which the manager Rob Joyce was attempting to resurrect from a grave of weeds, kudzu, and dusty red clay. Being from the Midwest, Rob brought an unfamiliar series to the track for a race: American Speed Association. The ASA was as hot in the Midwest as All Pro or NASCAR's Busch Series was in the South. Eventually drivers like Rusty Wallace, Mark Martin, Dick Trickle, and the series champion Alan Kulwicki would ascend from ASA to the lofty heights of Winston Cup racing. But when I covered that race in 1984, neither I nor most of my readers had ever heard of ASA or any of its stars. I was the only reporter in the press box that day when Rob strolled in and pulled up a chair beside me. He gave me a quick rundown on the drivers, their accomplishments, and their personalities. He made no secret of the fact that he was pulling for his good friend Alan Kulwicki. "He's the greatest," Rob said. "No one works harder than Alan does and no one deserves success more."

Alan won the event that day, and when I introduced myself to interview him for the story, I met more than just a race winner. I met a man who would become one of the greatest instructors in my life education. I often think of Alan, and of the adversity and challenges he overcame to become an unlikely champion in a sport that struggled to understand him as he struggled to understand it. He was a man who epitomized, at various times, both the dark horse and the underdog.

Alan was the only racer I knew before his involvement in NASCAR—the others were already involved in the sport when I met them. As both luck and fate would have it, I was there, firmly entrenched, when Alan moved south with a car full of belongings and a heart full of dreams. For the first time, I was in a position to help a newcomer as others had kindly helped me. I introduced him to key media and opinion makers in the sport while he made me his personal pupil in his class: *Dream Chasing When You Don't Have a Snowball's Chance in the Southern Heat 101.*

It's interesting to see the circumstances that bring two people together at an important juncture and lead them to parallel courses of travel, growth, and education. A friend recently told me, "A coincidence is God wishing to remain anonymous." As much as Alan Kulwicki was destined for stardom, I was destined to be his star student and to learn almost as much from the road he traveled as he did.

A few months later, Alan returned to race at the Jefferson track and I decided to include him in a pre-race story I was doing, since he had won in his previous outing there. I went over to his small pull-behind trailer in the pits and reintroduced myself. "Yes, I remember you quite well," he said as he wiped the grease from his hands then reached out to shake my hand. I chatted a few minutes, asked some questions, and then prepared to leave. He stopped me at the door of the trailer as I started to step down to the grass.

"I've thought of you several times since I was here. I was hoping that I would get to see you again this weekend." Flirting didn't come easy to Alan, so he approached the arrangement of a date as he did everything else—straightforwardly with no nonsense. "If you don't have previous plans, would you have dinner with me after qualifying tonight?"

I was flattered that he had remembered me and had even thought of me in the months since we first met, so I agreed. In those days, a team of guys shared the same vehicle, so Alan rode with me in my new sports car while his crew took the truck back to their hotel. I don't remember much about dinner or the conversation later over beer and ginger ale, but I'll never forget the forty-five-minute drive as I took him to his motel. It was then that that one additional beer made the difference. He was slumped in the passenger's seat, tapping his fingers against the gearshift, when he asked, in a very low-energy way, "Have you ever come close to getting married?"

"No," I replied, surprised by such a question out of the blue. "I'm only twenty-two. It's not as though I'm an old maid or anything. Have you?"

He shook his head and looked out the window into the dark Georgia night. "No. I'm not sure if I'll ever get married."

"Why not?"

He turned his attention back to the gearshift and fiddled with it, never looking up. "Well, when I was in the second grade, my mom died. Since my dad traveled a lot, my little brother and I went to live with my grandmother. When I was in the seventh grade, my little brother died. He was a hemophiliac. When I was in the eighth grade, my grandmother died."

"Oh, no!" I cried out. Tears misted my eyes for the sad, lonely life of this guy I barely knew. "That's terrible!"

He shrugged as though to convince me that what mattered a lot really didn't matter at all. "Aw, well, it's okay. I just don't know if I'll ever fall in love and get married because it seems that everyone I love just dies and leaves me."

That confession bonded my heart to Alan's then and there and made me his friend for the rest of his life. Alan's vulnerability, which I would soon learn was hidden from most people, pulled me closer to him; frankly, without that admission, I probably would not have dated him again. From the beginning, it was apparent that we were an odd pair, a mismatch of personalities and philosophies. Alan was cerebral, serious, quietly ambitious and trailed by a lurking darkness that never let him completely escape its shadow. On the other hand, I was fun-loving, frivolous, gregarious, and never looked much further than the current day. My life had been as charmed as Alan's life had been cursed. As a result, I acted my age while Alan always acted many years past his actual time on earth.

That was the first time I realized that the hand of death can snatch away not only life from those it takes, but also youth from those left behind. For the next four years, I would date Alan Kulwicki off and on, usually more off than on. We were more friends than lovers, but I did try hard, at least at the start, to love him with the heart of a girl who believes she can save a man. I thought he needed permanent romantic love or else his life would be incomplete, but I was wrong. On the day that Alan, still a bachelor, crossed the stage at the Waldorf-Astoria to accept the trophy that recognized him as the best of the best—the 1992 Winston Cup champion—his life was complete. Apparently, God agreed, because four months later, almost to the day, the reigning champion died in a fiery plane crash in the mountains of East Tennessee. I cried and ached for the deep personal loss, but I was immensely grateful that he had achieved the pinnacle of his grandest dreams. Alan died having gained everything he truly wanted in life.

Nothing ever came easy for Alan. He rarely got a decent break, but the more obstacles he encountered, the more determined he became. I saw him through some very low points when he could barely keep his chin up; but although he had no idea where to turn or what to do, I never once heard him talk about quitting. *The Power of Positive Thinking* was one of his favorite books, as it was mine. It was one of the few things we truly had in common, and I was surprised when I learned how much he loved that book. Alan, the mechanical genius, was a serious scientist, so I expected him to base his philosophy of life on tangible evidence. I was wrong. Of course he practiced positive thinking. How could he possibly have weathered the storms, at times furious and ceaseless, if he did not believe in the possibilities of a mind that thinks positively? I am only surprised now that I was surprised then.

Alan had rotten luck, especially at the beginning of his Winston Cup career. Once, while I was still a sportswriter living in Gainesville, he moved temporarily to Greenville, South Carolina, and lived in a motel while he tried to run three or four Cup races with a nightclub owner named Big Daddy. His first attempt was a race at Richmond, Virginia; but as was often the case with Alan, when it rained, it poured. It rained out qualifying at the track that weekend, forcing NASCAR officials to fill the field by owner points. Of course, Alan's was a new team that had no points; but there was one position left vacant, and NASCAR was going to fill it with one of the two rookie teams that had hoped to make the field. The team with the earliest postmark on its entry form would be awarded the starting position. Alan's entry form had been mailed just one day later than the other team's, so his team packed up and headed back to Greenville. Alan was so bummed when he returned that it broke my heart.

I had such a huge crush on Alan at the time that whenever he called and my roommate, Karen, answered the phone, she was overjoyed. If anything, Karen is even more bubbly than I am, and her exuberance on the phone always left the quietly sincere Alan puzzled. He couldn't understand why she would exclaim excitedly, "Oh, yes! Yes! Yes, she's here! Just a second. I'm so glad that you called!"

That day when he called, she was dancing around the living room with uninhibited joy, distracting me from the somberness of Alan's tone and his disappointing news from Richmond. "Will you hang on for a second?" I asked him; then, covering the receiver, I said to Karen, "Will you please contain your enthusiasm and go upstairs? This is not a happy call."

Until then, I had known only the great success and happiness of the Elliotts. I was soon to learn, however, that most racing careers have more trials and tribulations than triumphs—although the highs are so grand and glorious that they sustain the dreams through the lows.

I was living in Indianapolis when Alan called to share the most monumental decision of his career. He had decided to sell his ASA team, pack up, and move from Wisconsin to North Carolina to place all his chips on a Winston Cup gamble. I swallowed hard, knowing what a big step that was for a man who was making a very comfortable living in ASA.

"That's wonderful," I said, but knowing that he could hear the hesitation in my voice, I asked, "Are you sure this is what you want to do?"

"Yes, I am," he replied with firm resolve. "I've thought a lot about it and I really want to be in NASCAR. I'm a big fish in a little pond, but I'd rather be a little fish in a big pond like Winston Cup."

There were times, quite frankly, when Alan looked more like a fish out of water. He was markedly different from the other Winston Cup competitors. He had a college degree in mechanical engineering at a time when most of the drivers were proud to have simply finished high school. He was serious, studious, and a loner who formed friendships slowly. He owned his team, often acted as his own crew chief, and drove the car. But the most critical hurtle he had to overcome was that of being a Yankee: his way of doing business and interacting was different from that of the backslapping good ol' boys of the South. It was the kind of fraternity for which he was ill-suited. Of all the dream chasers I've known who became dream capturers, Alan Kulwicki was the most courageous warrior turned victor. I watched him battle against greater odds than anyone else, including the Elliotts. They were, after all, true members of the culture who were embraced and accepted by the sport. For all the later nonsouthern drivers, like Jeff Gordon and Tony Stewart, Alan was a pioneer, the trailblazer who broke through subliminal barriers and doors.

Alan and I were different in many ways—intellectual, cultural, philosophical, religious, educational. The toughest difference for me was our varying approaches to everyday life. I was spontaneous, free-spirited, and capricious. He was methodical, grave, and carefully calculating. I laughed easily while he laughed rarely. His sense of humor was low-key, dry, and so intelligent that it frequently went over my head. The differences would drive us apart, and eventually I began to turn down more dates with him than I accepted. In Daytona in 1989, he motioned me over to his garage stall and complimented me on how I looked that day. Then he asked, "Why don't you go out with me anymore?"

I screwed my face into the pitiful expression of a child whose mama insists that she must eat her broccoli before dessert. I prefaced my reply with a half-whining, half-crying sound and then sputtered, "Because, Alan, you're *soooo* boring!" I knew him well enough to know that I was not hurting his feelings because he realized his light-hearted limitations. His dark, almost black eyes didn't blink as he waited for me to continue. He knew me well enough to know there was always more.

"I love you. You know I do," I went on. "But I feel so silly and frivolous when I go out with you because I'm always giggling and you never think anything's funny." I leaned close, our noses almost touching, and playfully batted my eyelashes. "Why do you have to be so boring?"

"Now, I cannot be boring," he carefully replied. "That is scientifically impossible. I'm a racecar driver, and anyone who goes 200 mph and takes that kind of risk cannot be boring. You must have me confused with someone else."

Alan was used to my wisecracks, and he was always such a darn good sport about them. Once, I rushed over to him in the garage and, dancing around excitedly, I squealed, "Alan, I've got the *funniest* story to tell you! *Wait* till you hear *this!*" I paused for dramatic effect, giving myself just enough time to absorb his emotionless expression and remember who I was talking to. I had wasted far too many funny stories in the past on Alan Kulwicki. So I soothingly assured him, "But don't worry. I'll tell you *when* to laugh!"

Even *he* had to smile at *that*.

He was always a good sport, unruffled by any criticism or helpful suggestion. Of course, there soon came a time when Alan could and did have his choice of women. Once his star began rising, there were women everywhere. I was happy to see my old friend and former flame enjoying life both on the track and off, but I couldn't resist teasing him.

"Just remember," I often reminded him with a broad smile. "That *I* dated you when you were a nobody." I winked. "Therefore, I should always have a special place in your heart."

He pretended to be perplexed. "Are you saying that these other women want to date me because I'm a Winston Cup driver?"

"Because you're a Winston Cup *star*," I corrected him.

"Wellll, I don't know about that. I think perhaps they date me because of my vibrant personality." Of course, with his so-dry-it-cracked sense of humor, he delivered that line with a solemn look on his handsome face, and I cracked up. That was an endearing quality of Alan's—he didn't joke around a lot, but he didn't mind being joked with.

Alan loved to be recognized and enjoyed his celebrity as it increased, but not in the self-absorbed manner of Tim Richmond. To Alan, it was a small compensation for all his hard work and sacrifice. It was the bit of encouragement that got him through times of disappointment. One day we walked out of the media center together in Atlanta and passed by a large group of fans who were on the other side of the garage fence. Alan was dressed in a black polo shirt, monogrammed with his sponsor's name, and a pair of dress slacks. We were talking as we passed the crowd but a couple of rather fast-looking women caught our attention as they yelled out, "Hey! Would y'all help us? Please!"

They looked so desperate that we paused for a second. One woman, a blonde with her fingers laced through the chain-link fence, asked pleadingly, "Would you please tell Alan Kulwicki to come out here?"

Alan and I both looked puzzled. "Alan Kulwicki?" I asked.

She nodded vigorously. "That's right. Could you please tell Alan Kulwicki to come out here to the fence. He's expectin' us."

Alan walked over to the fence, and I followed him. "I'm Alan Kulwicki," he said in a soft, matter-of-fact voice.

Those two women started laughing uproariously. "*You're* not Alan Kulwicki!" the other, a sassy-looking redhead, snorted. "You're too little to be Alan Kulwicki. We know him *personally* and he's big and tall." I didn't know what was going on but I started laughing because the perplexed look on Alan's face was priceless.

"But I *am* Alan Kulwicki," he insisted in a frustrated tone. As they continued to shake their heads and chuckle, he turned to me pleadingly. "Please tell them who I am."

I put my arm around his shoulders and leaned toward the fence. "I promise on my own life that this is Alan Kulwicki. I promise."

Now, these women thought that we were trying to pull something on them, and they were going to have none of it. Of course, it didn't help that the others hanging on to the fence did not recognize him either. At the time, Alan was still running in the middle of the pack and therefore did not get a lot of face time on television.

So the women continued to shake their heads with resolute firmness.

"*You* are *not* Alan Kulwicki!" the blonde insisted. "Look, we met Alan Kulwicki at a bar last night, and he told us that if we would come to the garage gate today and ask for him that he would come out and get us."

Just as Alan opened his mouth to reiterate his claim, one of the women, with a huge smile across her face, exclaimed excitedly, "Look! Over there's Alan Kulwicki!"

Alan and I spun our heads around in the direction of her pointing finger and saw, standing several feet away in the garage, Michael Waltrip! Instantly, I knew that Alan had been the subject of one of Michael's pranks. I cannot begin to tell you how funny I thought it was, especially since Alan could not comprehend what had happened. He was always so serious that it would not have occurred to him to pretend to be someone else while out for a social evening. Another prankster in Michael's category, like Kenny Schrader or Kyle Petty, would have figured it out instantly. As Alan carefully pondered the situation, I started laughing. That only further mystified him. Knowing that it would take him a while, I just shook my head and walked off, still laughing, leaving him to disentangle himself from the snare. As I passed Michael, I threw a thumb over my shoulder toward Alan and said, "I think your presence is being requested over there at the fence." When he looked over and recognized the women who were talking to Alan, his face completely paled and his jaw sagged. I still don't know which was funnier—Alan's befuddlement or Michael's reaction at being caught red-handed!

Okay, so Alan didn't trip through life with humor and frivolity. But after such a scarred youth, who would? He had traits more admirable and important. He didn't use the tragedies of his youth as an excuse to live a nonproductive life. Instead, he pulled himself up and used the strength he had gained from those setbacks to accomplish a heck of a lot in his short span of thirty-eight years. While I'm grateful for his love and friendship, I'm more appreciative that he left an even greater impression on my life. He taught me the importance of being brave enough and bold enough to follow your grandest dreams, even when it means stepping from a place of security and comfort into the unknown. He left the familiar surroundings and financial security of Wisconsin life to take a chance because he had great dreams and grand objectives. Imagine what gumption that took. At best, it was intimidating; at worst, terrifying. Still, he refused to let normal human emotions deter him from his dreams.

Alan was the deepest thinker I have ever known. He used positive terms to "outthink" and overcome his problems. He analyzed adversity and setbacks and then set about to solve them. He didn't take them as a sign that his dream was no more than pie in the sky. As he encountered difficulties, he simply devised ways to dispose of them. When I remember his early years, I am simply amazed by the incredible spirit and diligence of that remarkable man.

He was committed and dedicated in every detail, including his Saturday-night pre-race dinner—always pasta and 7UP. He believed in boosting his energy with complex carbs long before the practice became popular and trendy. He chose 7UP because he didn't want to put caffeine in his body on the night before a race; it might interfere with a good night's rest. Then, from Saturday evening until race time on Sunday, he drank copious amounts of water in order to thoroughly hydrate his body. This routine was light-years ahead of what his competitors were doing. His first Winston Cup sponsor was a steakhouse chain, so prior to the Saturday evening meal, we often ate at its restaurant if there was one in the town where we were racing. We ate free on coupons the chain gave him, and to Alan that was the grandest and most thrilling perk he could receive.

"Oh, no! Not there again!" I'd moan if I found out we were eating there two nights in a row.

"Why not?" he'd ask, amazed at my reluctance. "I've got coupons!"

"I don't care. I'll buy."

"No, no, no." He'd shake his head firmly. "Free food is part of my sponsorship deal and if we don't eat there then I am not getting the maximum value of my sponsorship." Of course, there was always a table full of his crew guys across the room who were also eating on complimentary coupons.

Through Alan, I came to realize that a happy, fulfilling life is not acquired by timid souls. It is created by those who are brave of heart, strong of spirit, and stubborn of mind. It takes fortitude of the grandest kind to choose the life we want rather than settling back meekly and letting life choose for us. Too many people allow ho-hum lives to choose them, and then they grouse about the dullness of their existence and lament the dreams they left scattered behind in their youth. They let family and financial obligations engulf them, overwhelming them with responsibilities. I saw Alan make tough choices and fight incredible adversity and overwhelming odds. But when he was down on the ground, fighting to stand again, he was at peace in his heart because he had chosen the right path. Alan Kulwicki showed me and the rest of the world that if you work long enough and hard enough and refuse to be sidelined by adversity, you *can* capture your dreams.

I made a profound self-discovery a few years ago during a heart-shattering time in my life—I had divorced, my father was dying, and my career had been shaken to the core. I don't exaggerate when I say that my life had suddenly and inexplicably crumbled into pieces around my feet. I was enshrouded with troubles and sorrows, and, quite honestly, I wanted nothing more than to crawl into a corner and hide away. Alan had been dead for about two years, but one day, while searching for a book I needed, I ran across a magazine with his picture on the cover. It was a salute to his life and career. I thumbed through the publication, solemnly reflecting on his life as I had known it. I thought of all the adversity he had faced and the setbacks he had met with absolute determination, and I knew that none of the troubles in my life could match the severity of those Alan had encountered. Everything began to pull itself into the proper perspective. I slowly realized that I was viewing all the upheaval at that point in my life as an ending rather than a beginning. For the rest of the day, I pondered on that and asked myself a question: "If I knew I was dying, would I be happy with the choices I've made? Would I have regrets about things I have not done, dreams I have forsaken?"

Think about that. It can change your life. It certainly transformed mine. For I decided that I wanted to live as Alan had lived—doggedly pursuing my dreams at every corner. Over the years, I had been so busy making a living that I had not made the life I truly wanted. I had let life lead me. Quickly, I modified my thinking and my attitude. Like Alan, I began to step over obstacles and put together the life I really wanted even though I'd been willing to settle for less. Thanks to his inspiration, I now realize that we don't have to settle. We only have to work hard and refuse to be sidetracked.

This reminds me of the rodeo cowboys who lasso calves in competition. Have you ever tried it? I have. A friend of mine tried to teach me how to twirl a lightweight rope over my head and then toss it several feet away to land on a stationary wooden post. I couldn't do it. I had to keep moving closer to the post until I was only a couple of feet away, and even then it was difficult. Now, imagine chasing a calf while both of you are running, then being able to toss a piece of string over the calf and rope it in. That was Alan and his Winston Cup dream. The target kept moving, he kept trying, and finally he lassoed the dream, complete with the Winston Cup Series championship.

From Alan, I learned that our dreams don't stand still and wait for us. They're moving targets, so roping them takes practice, perseverance, and resilience after countless failures. But, of course, if it were easy, we would all be living our dreams, wouldn't we? Alan was the best teacher possible because he refused to let his dream outrun him.

Well taught, my beloved professor. Well taught.

BOBBY ALLISON, MUFFLER
BEARINGS, AND ME

chewed my lower lip anxiously and, with a worried heart, turned to walk away. Again I had interviewed Bobby Allison for pressroom quotes, and again he had given me nothing more than "yeah," "fine," "maybe." The situation was getting dire, and I knew that, thanks to Bobby, my job—my first in the sport since I had left the newspaper business—was in jeopardy.

I enjoyed the Winston Cup circuit so much that when I was offered an excellent opportunity to move into motorsports marketing and travel on the circuit full-time, I couldn't resign from my newspaper job fast enough. Although it was a bit of a challenge to change from a reporter to a publicist, I was gaining ground and momentum. My one problem was Bobby Allison.

I was the publicist handling the Buick Motorsports account, and Bobby was Buick's biggest star, a legend of grand proportions. So it was important that we have a good working relationship, but—trust me—he did not make it easy. After a few months of trying every trick I knew—charm, flattery, toughness, assertiveness, flirtatiousness—I was still backed into a corner, because nothing was working. One of my tasks at every race was to gather quotes from my drivers, type the quotes up, and distribute them to the media. It was the hopeful intent that reporters would use my quotes in their stories, giving my drivers and Buick important press coverage. While other Buick drivers gave me very good quotes, our superstar would just say "yes," "no," "don't know," and "we'll see." I was failing miserably at my job, and there was considerable pressure from my bosses to get Bobby into the press more.

That afternoon in Charlotte as I stepped down from Bobby's race hauler and forlornly walked away, my heart was in my stomach. All the Buick executives were coming to town that weekend, and without a doubt they would be scouring the newspapers for mention of their product and drivers. Fretful thoughts were running through my mind when I heard Bobby holler, "Hey, Ronda!"

I was about twenty feet away when I turned back to see him standing at the door of the hauler, the top of his driver's suit unzipped and dropped to his waist. He tugged at the neck of his white T-shirt and grinned merrily. "The guys are over there right now adjusting the muffler bearings, and as soon as we get them adjusted we're going to be *o-kay!*" He pressed his thumb and forefinger together and formed a circle as an illustration. Immediately, my entire body began to twitch with excitement. That was the first time in the months I had worked with him that Bobby Allison had given me an entire sentence.

"What?" I asked, quickly scurrying back toward him as I scribbled frantically in my notebook. "Muffler what?"

"*Bearings*," he repeated, grinning from ear to ear, obviously gleeful that he had brought such joy into my life, for there was no hiding the relief and happiness that spread over my face.

"Muffler bearings," I said slowly and carefully as I wrote it down.

"That's right." He nodded and his eyes twinkled brightly. I

thought it was mighty sweet of Bobby to realize the peril I was in and to come to my rescue just in the nick of time.

Few times in my NASCAR life was I more excited than I was when I hurried to the pressroom to type up my first great Bobby Allison quote. With great pomp and circumstance, I paraded around the media center and handed my quote sheets to each reporter.

"There's an excellent quote from Bobby Allison in there," I happily informed each reporter. "Be certain to pay special attention to it."

Not only did I have a great Allison quote, but I had saved my job when it mattered most—when the Buick executives were in town for a rare appearance at a race. My happiness and excitement increased the next morning when I picked up a newspaper and saw that my Bobby Allison quote about muffler bearings had been used! Life, I thought as I drove to the track, could not be much more wonderful.

When I got to the track, I cruised through the Winston Cup garage, which was quiet, since Grand National practice was about to begin. Allison's crew chief, Bobby Hudson, was working under the hood of their racecar. Since Bobby was the current points leader, it was parked next to the defending champion Dale Earnhardt's car. In the nearly deserted garage, Earnhardt and his car owner, Richard Childress, were leaning against their number 3 car when I stopped by to speak to Hudson.

"So," I began, smugly pleased that I could now discuss racecars expertly. "Did you get the muffler bearings adjusted appropriately yesterday?"

Hudson glanced up with a puzzled look. "The what?" he asked in his usual soft voice.

"The muffler bearings," I repeated casually and confidently. About that time, Earnhardt slid down the front of his racecar and doubled over in laughter. Childress, I noticed, had a straight face but was trying to avoid choking on a grape that he had just popped into his mouth. Earnhardt was laughing obnoxiously; this told me that somehow I was the butt of a joke.

"Dale Earnhardt, what are you laughing at?" I sneered, greatly annoyed.

"You! You are the *biggest* dumb ass I have ever seen!"

I glared at him. "Shut up!" I turned back to Hudson, who asked, "Who told you about muffler bearings?"

"Bobby."

"Allison?"

I nodded. He shook his head slowly. My heart began to beat faster, the way it does when your life starts to flash before you.

"Why?" I asked. My mouth was suddenly dry.

His eyes were sympathetic as he spoke. "There's no such thing as muffler bearings. Racecars don't have mufflers and mufflers don't have bearings!"

The color drained from my face and I felt sick. "Oh, no!" I was almost faint from the knowledge of how much trouble I was in as I remembered that the quote had found its way into the newspaper! Apparently, the reporter who had used it was a novice and knew as little about racecars as I did. Or perhaps *he* was smart enough to know it was a joke and had used it as such. Either way, I was directly responsible for Bobby Allison being quoted in print about "adjusting muffler bearings."

"Where's Bobby Allison?" I demanded.

"In the Grand National garage," Hudson replied. As soon as the words were out of his mouth, I was off and running in my skirt and heels. I arrived in the other garage in record time to find Bobby—wouldn't you know it?—surrounded by his brother Donnie and every Buick executive from Michigan. But I didn't care. Nothing was going to stop me as I ran up to him, grabbed him by the chest of his driver's suit, and shook him frantically.

"Bobby Allison, how could you?" I wailed. "How could you do this to me?"

His eyes twinkled even brighter than the day before as he grinned and asked *innocently,* "Why, Ronda, what are you talking about?"

I put my hands on my hips and moved my nose within inches

of his. "You *know* what I'm talking about! The muffler bearings!"

"What about them?" He was still grinning and twinkling.

"There *is* no such thing!"

"Now, Ronda," he replied patiently, looking at me as an adult does a child. "Who told you *that*?"

I heaved a heavy sigh of aggravation. "Your own crew chief, Bobby Hudson, told me!" I was still steaming.

Without missing a beat, Bobby turned to Donnie and said, as if a big mystery had just been solved, "Well, see there, Donnie. Now we know why we're not running any better here than we are. My *own crew chief* doesn't even know about muffler bearings!"

I folded my arms and gave him a look of resigned exasperation while the Buick execs and everyone standing within earshot howled. Amazingly, though, that prank earned more respect for me from the Michigan folks than anything else I could have done. They were impressed that the king of Buick liked me well enough to pull such a devilish stunt. When I saw the reaction, I relaxed and laughed too, realizing that I would, in all probability, still have a job when I went to bed that night. That humiliation was the turning point for me and Bobby Allison. From that moment on, he gave me great quotes and we became good buddies.

When I left that job for another publicity job, Bobby gave my replacement such a difficult time that the poor guy finally begged me to speak to Bobby on his behalf.

"Bobby," I said when I cornered him in the garage during the week of the Daytona 500. "Why are you giving John such a hard time?"

He looked defiant and pulled back. "Because he ain't you and I ain't gonna talk to him."

"He's better and more experienced than I am; and if you talk to him, he'll do a much better job for you."

He shook his head obstinately and argued while I tried to reason with him. When I left, I assumed I had gotten nowhere. But later John laughed and said, "Whatever you said worked, because things were much better after that."

Bobby won Daytona that year (1988) with his son Davey running second. Despite the fact that he was no longer one of my drivers, I was cheering wildly as he crossed the finish line. The next week in Richmond, I ran over to hug him and tell him how thrilled I was that he had won.

He grinned broadly. "And everything would have been perfect if you had been in Winner's Circle with me instead of that ol'-what's-his-name!"

I shook my head and chuckled, realizing that it was harder to get rid of Bobby Allison's loyalty than it had been to get it.

Bobby Allison is a true hero in the old-fashioned sense, from the days when heroes were larger than life and had uplifting, positive ways meant to inspire and set examples—back before the days when it was acceptable to leave a trail of parties, women, booze, and drugs in the wake of fame and still be exalted as an example of heroism. The heartbreaking challenges for Bobby began with his career-ending crash in Pocono in June of 1988. For days, he lingered between life and death with a severe head injury.

"When I drove by the crash and saw that he wasn't moving, I prayed, 'Dear God, please let us keep him a little longer. Please don't take him now,'" a somber Davey told me a couple of weeks after the accident.

Davey's prayer was answered, but it was a long road back for his dad, who had to learn to walk and talk again and to remember. More painful even than the excruciating recovery was that the lively core of Bobby's existence had been torn away and completely destroyed. He would never race again. I have rarely known a man who loved racing more. Bobby would race five nights a week, flying himself to tracks all over the country, and then run Winston Cup and Grand National events on the weekends. He lived to race, and racing rewarded his faithfulness by providing a good living for him and his family. We were all grateful that Bobby's life was spared, but it broke my heart to see his anguish when he occasionally visited us at a track where we were racing.

"Davey, doesn't it just kill you to see his heart breaking like that?" I asked, impelled by my own torment as I watched Bobby looking forlornly at a row of racecars.

Davey's eyes moistened and he nodded. "Yeah," he said softly, "but I'm pretty selfish because I'm so glad that I've still got my dad."

Being the fighter that he is, Bobby became a team owner and eventually healed enough that the doctors let him return to piloting—his second love—though not to racing. On August 13, 1992, Bobby's world crumbled further when his youngest son, Clifford, was killed in a racecar crash in Michigan. Bobby was devastated then but his spirit was completely ravaged and left for emotional salvage when, on July 13, 1993, our beloved Davey died from head injuries suffered the previous day in a helicopter crash at Talladega. In exactly eleven months, the Allisons had lost two of their four children and both of their sons.

I remember vividly the weight of Bobby's body as he leaned into my arms as we stood in the altar of the St. Aloyuish Catholic Church in a surburb of Birmingham during the wake. Davey lay in a gleaming cherrywood coffin a few feet away as Bobby's tears soaked the shoulder of my dress.

"Bobby, he loved you so," I whispered through my own tears. "You were his hero."

He straightened up, pulled back, and looked me straight in the eye. "*He* was *my* hero. He was the greatest son that a man could ask for."

Tightly, I clasped both of his hands in mine. "You know what I'll never forget? The day that you crashed into the fence at Talladega and when I found you two, Davey was staring at you with absolute adoration. You were his idol, and I hope that you will always remember that."

The next two years brought further deterioration of the glorious life that had belonged to Bobby Allison for so long. Unable to find sponsorship, his race team folded; his adored wife, Judy, and he divorced and the family compound in Hueytown, Alabama, was put up for auction. Still, Bobby fought on valiantly. A few years ago, I ran into this hero of mine in the garage at a Talladega race. We embraced, and his first question was, "Seen any muffler bearings lately?"

As we talked and reminisced, the conversation turned to Davey, and Bobby said with a big smile, "I want to show you something." He reached into his back pocket, pulled out his billfold, and flipped it open to show me a photo of the two brothers, Davey and Clifford, with big toothy grins and their arms flung around each other. I smiled. "Doesn't that look just like both of 'em? Just like they were when they were clowning around with each other?" he asked, a beatific smile on his face. He looked at the photo fondly, longingly. "This is my favorite photo."

As I looked at the remnants of what once was, my throat began to close, and my nose burned as it always does just before my eyes fill with water and the tears fall. I was overcome with emotion, not only for the loss of my precious friend Davey, but mainly for all that Bobby had lost. I dropped my head and looked away, for I did not want to be responsible for further sadness. But Bobby knew that I was not strong like him. And then he, who should have been comforted by me, reached out and put his arm around my shoulders and said in a sweet, bright, comforting tone, "Now, don't cry for me. You see, I'm the luckiest man that God ever made."

I swung around and looked at him, this modern-day Job, with disbelief in my eyes. I couldn't fathom what I was hearing.

He smiled, his eyes illuminated by a wisdom that only sorrow can impart. Using his forefinger to emphasize, he began, "I've had a wonderful life. I made a very good living doing what I loved better than anything and it made me famous and put me in the record books. For thirty-five years, I had a wonderful wife who stood beside me *and* I had the love of two of the finest sons a man could ask for. Sure, I've lost a lot. But, at least I had it." He paused for a second, then winked. "And that's a *whole lot more* than most people can say." He ended with a firm nod of his head.

Bobby's optimism paid off. About six weeks or so after he and Judy attended Adam Petty's funeral together, they remarried. A cheer vibrated through the racing community as a bit of Bobby Allison's former happiness returned to him.

From this champion of valor, I learned that if we are to triumph over a life that sometimes seeks to defeat us, we must *choose* courage. Courage doesn't come by chance. I know it was not easy for Bobby to focus on the good in his life and accept the bad, especially when such cruel blows had come so close together. Like any man with the misfortune to be in his position, Bobby shed many tears and whispered many prayers. He must have uttered anguished cries—"Why me? Why my boys?" But that's not the point.

The point is that, as difficult as life was, he picked himself up from a crumbled heap and consciously chose to carry forth with a life positive in its reflections. That's remarkable. That's the act of a true hero. From Bobby's example, I learned that the mind can be a powerful ally or a destructive adversary. It can lift us to great heights of success or kick us into the pits of failure. For how we believe is how we behave, and that determines if we are covered in a cloak of bitterness or sheltered by an umbrella of hope that protects us until the sun shines again.

I pray that more sun will shine on the graying head of the man who has taught me about courage *and* about muffler bearings.

LIKE FATHER, LIKE SON

Few things gave Davey Allison greater glee than to tell the story of me and the muffler bearings. Repeatedly, he subjected me to writhing embarrassment as he told the story in my presence. After a year or so and dozens of occurrences, I was ready to squelch my prolonged agony. Like a child, I decided to tattle on Davey to the one person whose authority he always respected.

I found Bobby Allison on the racetruck, working on a carburetor. Well, I *think* it was a carburetor. I only know for sure that it *was not* a muffler bearing.

"Bobby," I began, twisting my mouth into a slight pout and casting my eyes downward sadly. "Davey's being awfully mean to me."

Bobby looked up and raised his eyebrows in the disciplinarian expression of a father about to spring into action. I knew when I saw that look that I had an ally.

"He is?" There was an undeniable sternness in his voice.

I sighed hurtfully. "He keeps telling the muffler bearings story. Every time I'm around, he finds someone who hasn't heard it yet and tells it again."

Bobby tried to keep from smiling, but his eyes betrayed him and I cut my eyes accusingly toward him. When he saw the look, he could no longer stifle his chuckle, slight though it was.

"Well, it *is* funny," he responded in both his and his son's defense.

"It's not funny after a hundred and six times of hearing it," I retorted.

Bobby knew that I was fibbing. Nonetheless, it softened him, and after a slight pause, I moved in for the bounty. "So I was wondering if you could help me." I bit my lower lip and then continued. "Could you tell me a good story on Davey that I could use the next time he pulls this little stunt?"

Bobby's eyes twinkled, and he grinned mischievously. "Sure, there's lots of good Davey stories."

Excitedly, I straightened up, stepped closer to my new best buddy, and put my hand on his shoulder in a gesture intended to seal our pact of conspiracy. "Oh, goody! I knew I could count on you!" I then stepped back, clasped my hands together under my chin as if in prayer, and pleaded, "Oh, please, tell me the very best story you can think of!"

Bobby stopped piddling as he began to think. "I know!" he exclaimed, snapping his fingers.

I listened with rapt attention as he told of the Saturday night when sixteen-year-old Davey debuted in the world of racing at Birmingham International Raceway. As you can imagine, it was an exciting night for the Allison clan. "I was in Martinsville for the race and I had a personal appearance that night, so I couldn't be there," Bobby explained. "And it absolutely killed me. I couldn't stand not being there for his first race, but as soon as I got back to my motel room, I called home."

When Bobby's wife, Judy, came to the phone, she was so ebullient that she could hardly talk, but Bobby could tell from her excited babbling that it had indeed been a red-letter night for the Allison family.

"Slow down!" Bobby instructed her.

She took a deep breath. "Well, he started seventh," she said more slowly, but then sped up dramatically. "And, Bobby, he finished fifth! You would have been so proud of him. He was great!"

Bobby began to laugh as he recalled the phone conversation. "So, I'm thinking, 'Hey, this is pretty good—he started seventh and finished in the top 5 in his first race. That's my boy!' Then I prompted Judy to tell me more about the race."

"Well, let's see," she continued, gathering her thoughts. "There were four—no, there were five—cautions, and Bobby, guess what! Davey only brought out *three* of them!" I joined Bobby in side-splitting laughter as he concluded, "I fell off my bed laughing because that's so typical of a mother's pride. It didn't matter that Davey had spun out and caused three of the caution flags; it only mattered to her that he didn't cause *all* of them!"

I clapped my hands and gleefully stomped my feet. I knew I had a story that would stop Mr. Davey once and for all. The next week, we were in Darlington to race and I popped into the infield media center where I discovered Davey, sitting on a stool and holding court with a few reporters gathered around him. As soon as he saw me, his eyes lit up and I knew what was coming. He grinned mischievously and asked, "Have y'all heard the story about Ronda and the muffler bearings?"

As hard as it is to believe, there were a couple who had not heard the story, so Davey launched into a terrifically embellished version. I listened patiently and joined all of them in laughter at the story's conclusion.

"Isn't that the stupidest thing you ever heard of?" I asked amid the laughter. They all agreed that it was, in fact, unmatched in its stupidity. I then smiled and innocently asked, "Have y'all heard the story of Davey's first race, when he was sixteen?"

The smile immediately vanished from Davey's face and his eyes widened in undisguised apprehension. Slowly and with great relish, I began to tell the story, which, at its conclusion, met with as much hilarity as the story of the muffler bearings had. Davey, however, was not laughing, nor did he show the slightest sign of amusement. He was, after all, a hotshot newcomer and everyone marveled at how he good he was from the get-go. I supposed he wanted everyone to think that he was race-perfect from his first lap. As the laughter died down, Davey said rather curtly, "Well, I gotta get back to the garage." He walked past me silently with a grim expression, but I smiled up at him sweetly. The antidote worked—Davey Allison got a taste of his own medicine, and he never again told the story of the muffler bearings in front of me, and I doubt that he ever told it privately. I don't think he wanted to risk my hearing about it and retaliating again.

Davey had burst gloriously onto the Winston Cup scene, beginning in the summer of 1986 with a substitute ride for Neil Bonnett in the Junior Johnson car, which turned out to be a fabulous showcase for his talent. In 1987, he turned up in Daytona to drive for the Ford team that Robert Yates would eventually buy and stunned the sport by earning the outside pole, next to the pole-sitter and eventual race winner Bill Elliott. Davey was born to be a star, and by the time Daytona's SpeedWeeks celebration ended, no one doubted that he was a fresh breath of Alabama air. The famed Alabama gang had a new member, who would become their biggest media star to date and the one who would rally a new generation of fans into the NASCAR stable.

Practically from the start, Davey and I were pals, with affection and admiration for each other. The spring Talladega race in 1987 produced some stellar moments on television that would be replayed and remembered for many years. There was one moment, though, that was not televised, yet it would be remembered, at least by me, for a long time. On qualifying day, Davey and I were talking in the garage during one of those rare, blissfully quiet moments when cars are either going through inspection or rolling onto pit road so that there aren't any engines running. Suddenly, I saw

Davey's eyes dart to the right, felt a stinging slap on my rear end, and heard an ear-splintering smack echo through the aluminum-topped shed. Davey and I both jumped a foot and I screamed, my heart pounding rapidly from fright. I had no idea who or what had hit me until I turned to see an ashen-faced Rusty Wallace, who had scared himself even more than Davey and me.

"Are you all right?" Rusty asked in a panicked voice. I had never seen him unsettled, but his little prank had clearly backfired.

"Ouch!" I whimpered, rubbing my right hip where he had slapped me and trying to catch my breath after the stinging and the fright. The loud pop and my scream had brought the garage to a stop as all the guys turned to see what was going on.

Davey, too, was white and very alarmed. "Are you okay?"

I nodded but turned to the culprit. "Rusty Wallace, I am going to kill you! What were you doing?"

"Honest, I didn't mean to hit you so hard. I was just going to sneak up behind and scare you. I don't know what happened. I'm so sorry."

"Man!" Davey exclaimed, shaking his head. "I saw it coming and it still scared me! That was a hard hit."

I was still rubbing my injured hip, but I couldn't be mad at Rusty, although I tried hard to pretend I was, especially when I saw such startled fear in his eyes. It had been an accident. Apparently, the angle at which he brought his hand down and the light cotton fabric of the slacks I had on combined to make a thunderously loud and painful smack. That night, when I was toweling off after a shower, I caught a glimpse of something in the mirror. After further inspection, I rolled my eyes in resigned exasperation. The next morning when I saw Rusty for the first time, he was talking with Davey. I marched over to him.

"Rusty Wallace, I'll have you know," I began in a scolding tone, with one hand on my hip and the forefinger of the other one wagging in his face, "that I have your handprint on my rear end!"

Startled, both snapped their heads back in wide-eyed surprise.

"Where you hit me yesterday! I oughtta bop you upside the

head. It left a big bruise in the shape of your hand! It is a perfect handprint which, I might add, is going to be there for at least a week!"

"No," Rusty responded, shaking his head. "I don't believe it. You'd better show me." He threw back his head and laughed at his own cleverness while I glared at him.

"Maybe he could autograph it for you," Davey suggested helpfully.

I turned my glare toward him. "*You* stay outta this!" I turned back to Rusty. "And *you* owe me a big favor for this!"

Rusty paid his debt the next time we returned to Talladega. My old pal Chip Tarkenton, who was a television sportscaster in Birmingham at the time, called to ask an urgent favor—he needed a celebrity racer for a late-night telecast. All my drivers and Davey, my next choice, were committed elsewhere but Rusty, without hesitation, agreed to make the one-hour drive to Birmingham for the show. What I appreciated more than anything else was that he did not have to be coerced into it or reminded that he owed me a favor. It's funny how you remember little kindnesses, isn't it?

The biggest news of that spring race, however, was not the gingerly way I had to lower myself into a seat and then shift my weight to my left side. By the time the day ended, there would be bruises much more serious than mine. Halfway through the race, Bobby Allison's Buick lifted as he came into the tri-oval on the front straight. The air churned under the car, whipped it into the air, and slammed it straight toward the grandstands. I was in the press box, almost directly in front of the incident; and although I have seen many terrifying things in the course of a race, nothing has ever scared me more. The 3,400-pound racecar soared straight toward a section of spectators. As I watched in what seemed like a time-suspended moment, Bobby's car started to fly over an 11-foot-high wire fence that sat atop a 5-foot-high concrete wall. But, mercifully, before it tumbled into the horrified crowd, it caught on the top edge of the wire and fell back onto the track in a splintering, ripping crash. My fear for the spectators quickly turned to fear for

Bobby. I was terrified that he had not survived the horrendous crash. I flew out of the press box and rushed back to the infield and the garage. Meanwhile, the race was red-flagged to attend to Bobby and any injured spectators (there were only a few minor injuries from flying debris) and to repair the sturdy fence, which had been torn apart.

It took me a while to find Bobby. I'll never forget what I saw. He was in the family compound area, sitting in a folding lawn chair. He was still white and trembling with shock. Kneeling beside his dad and clutching his hand was an equally shaken son. Even today, many years later, I remember clearly the look of worship, fear, and adoration in Davey's dark-brown eyes. It was a touching scene.

"Bobby, are you all right?" I cried out as I ran up to him.

"Yes, Ronda," he replied softly, his voice quivering. "I am. It was a scary ride but thank God, I'm all right."

Davey glanced up at me briefly when he heard my voice, but then his eyes quickly returned to Bobby, and nothing else would pry them away from his dad. He stared at him intensely as if he were afraid that if he diverted his eyes that Bobby would vanish. I stayed for a few minutes and then said, "I'm going back to the media center to let everyone know you're okay. Is there anything else you need? Anything I can do for you at all?"

Bobby shook his head. "No, I'm fine. Thank you."

"Thank you, Ronda," Davey said, without breaking his stare from his father's face.

Apparently, Davey recovered quickly because when the race was restarted a couple of hours later, he delivered one of the best press stories of 1987. He won the first race of his Winston Cup career, after only a handful of starts, at his home track, on the day that his father's spectacular crash had stopped the race. As the crowd stood to cheer, it was an unforgettable moment of triumph, capped off by a front-page photo of father and son embracing in the Winner's Circle.

That spectacular crash would lead NASCAR to institute the restrictor plate rule, aimed at slowing down the racecars on the superspeedways of Talladega and Daytona. With restrictors on the carburetors, the production of horsepower is limited, so speeds are reduced. It has slowed the speeds on those tracks by 15 or 20 mph, which is a major reason that Bill Elliott's speed records will, in all likelihood, never be broken. It is ironic that in the first race with the restrictor plates—the 1988 Daytona 500—Bobby Allison, the man responsible for the rule changes, was the victor, with Davey following him across the line in second place.

When Bobby was critically injured in Pocono, Davey, without hesitation, took over as the head of the Allison family, looking after the parents who had once watched over him as well as his siblings and their children.

"It's the hardest thing I've ever been through," Davey confided to me a couple of weeks after the accident. "I'm so tired that I just want to sleep for two weeks. But I'm so thankful that I've still got my dad that I won't complain. I'll do whatever I have to do."

Sudden fame was a challenge for Davey. From the beginning of his meteoric rise, it appeared that his marriage to his lovely high school sweetheart would be a casualty. I was walking to my gate at the airport in Bristol, Tennessee, one Sunday afternoon when Davey slipped up behind me, threw his arm around my neck, and whispered "Hey" into my ear.

He followed me to my gate and suddenly, out of the blue, began talking about his personal troubles. I was saddened because I liked both Davey and his wife enormously and I honestly had no idea that their marriage was in trouble. As he talked, I could tell that Davey was extremely unhappy.

"I'm sorry that you're having such a hard time, but I hope that everything works out for you," I intoned sympathetically.

"Oh, it's gonna work out. I promise you that," he said firmly. "Life's too short to be unhappy, and I'm not gonna be. Besides, it's an occupational hazard for me. I can't risk bein' so distracted by my personal life that I lose focus in the racecar. Not even for one second."

"Do you have any idea as to what you're gonna do?"

He shook his head. "Naw, I'm still thinking. But to be honest, I just hate to start over financially. We had to struggle for so many years and now, finally, I'm making good money and things are comfortable. I'm not ready to go back to being poor!" He punctuated the statement with a small chuckle, then ran for his gate.

That conversation was not mentioned again until a few months later, when I was crossing the garage and heard someone call my name. I turned to see Davey hurrying toward me.

"Guess what," he said, catching up and walking beside me.

"What?"

"I'm getting a divorce." He smiled as if the weight of the world had lifted from his shoulders. I stopped and looked at him with surprise. In the Winston Cup garage, no racecar has ever traveled as fast as a rumor. Yet I had not heard one rumor in the normally gossipy garage, so I had assumed that things were working out for Davey.

"Are you serious?"

"Sure am." He looked different. The dark scowl and cloudiness had lifted from his face and eyes. I smiled.

"I thought you didn't want to be poor again," I said in a teasing tone.

Seriousness filled his face. "Well, you know I thought about that and I decided that while I'm in a good financial position now, I'm not as well off as I'm going to be. So, I'd rather split what I've got now than what I'm *gonna* have."

At the moment, I thought this was the most amusing philosophy I had ever heard, and I threw back my head and laughed heartily while Davey puzzled over what was so funny. But over the years, I have mused over that fresh approach and I think it is one of the most commonsensical things I have ever heard anyone say. I have given that advice to many people in marital unbliss since that time, and I have always credited Davey.

Davey lived as if he knew he had only a short time on earth. He made every day count and made the kind of decisions that gave him the most peace and pleasure. He didn't waste time and lived each moment with gusto. He never strolled. He always walked at a hurried pace as if he had too much to do and not enough time. As it turned out, he didn't have enough time. But not a moment was wasted. When he wasn't racing, he was fishing, flying, hunting, or doing anything else that gave him pleasure. A hunger for adventure led Davey, an accomplished pilot who flew himself all over the country, to take helicopter lessons, although that decision would lead to tragedy.

Like Davey, I am determined to live life to its fullest and not waste one precious moment. Wonderful, happy lives that are fun and exciting don't just run to us, flop down into our laps, and exclaim, "Here I am! Enjoy!" You have to go after the kind of life you want, realizing that it isn't a sprint event. It's a long, grueling race that you have to take one lap at a time, and it requires both focus and patience.

My life is a solid balance of work and play. Sometimes I want to play too much; other times I want to work too much, so I have to force myself to be disciplined and achieve a balance. A key, too, is to find a job that you enjoy. Another key is to keep, or at least recapture, the excitement of childhood when you viewed everything with wonderment and enthusiasm. Remember how excited you got when you were going to a circus or a ball game? How you looked forward to it for days? Yet, as you grew older, you saw things in a more mature way, and gradually things that were once fun lost their luster and excitement. Before you knew it, you accepted life on that basis and then it didn't sparkle anymore. But Davey had an incredibly childlike interest and was always animated, hopping around with anticipation over flying with the Blue Angels, fishing with the revered television fisherman Orlando Wilson, or meeting one of his favorite country music singers backstage after a concert. He was an inspiration because he reminded me that we may age in years, but we don't have to grow old in attitude. We can act mature, be responsible, and still view life and all it offers through a child's precious eyes.

Joy of life is contagious. If you're excited about life and all that it holds, the people around you will get caught up in your joy, and the sparkle of your life will add glitter to theirs. It's a wonderful contribution to humanity, and just think—it's a simple key you hold in the palm of your hand.

Davey Allison knew from early childhood that he wanted to be a racecar driver. He didn't make alternative plans or choose another vocation as a backup. He threw everything he had into creating the kind of life he truly wanted. He was a real go-getter, always hustling, always running enthusiastically toward a fun, happy, fulfilling life. What a brilliant accomplishment—to die with no regrets, leaving no desired stone unturned. Please let Davey's life be the example to you that it is to me. Consciously craft the life you want and take full advantage of every day, because we never know how many days we'll have. As Davey showed us all, it's a smart idea to wrap our days with the joy and enthusiasm of a child.

PASSION PLUS ACTION
EQUALS EARNHARDT

Four cars were coming from three directions and trying to squeeze through the one-car gate opening on Talladega's back straightaway. The race on the track had ended, but the race to get home had just begun. Since I was approaching the gate from the straight-on position, I had the advantage as I headed toward the airport. In my rental car, I was jockeying for position when I felt a nudge on my back bumper from the fourth car that was coming from the same direction as I was. I looked in my mirror to see some idiot—drunk, I assumed—trying to wedge his large sedan between my car and the wall. He kept pushing and I gripped the steering wheel tighter, muttering under my breath, "You can't get that car in there. What are you tryin' to do?" I hate to admit this, but I'm quite sure that I probably used a couple of words that I had learned in the garage and on pit road—the kind of words that the driver or the crew chief uses over the team radio when the tire changer doesn't tighten a lug nut and the team gets a penalty.

To my further annoyance, the menacing car and its driver kept coming, rudely pushing, continuing to intrude into space where there simply was *no* room. I tried to block and protect the position that was rightfully mine, since *I* had patiently waited in traffic until it was my turn to cross the track. I was absolutely infuriated when the car and its overbearing driver managed to push past me and then found a clearing to zip off to the right and out of the traffic jam in which I was still ensnared.

But the driver couldn't be content with the mere satisfaction of knowing that he had won. He had to gloat. Before he made his final escape, he pulled up beside me, blew the horn, and waited for me to turn and acknowledge that *he* was the victor and *I* was the loser. I took a deep breath to abate my anger and turned to see that the offender was none other than an exuberant Dale Earnhardt, with his window rolled down, hanging out and cheering wildly that he had done the impossible—*and* that he had beaten me. Winning, of course, was the most important. Dale's wife, Teresa, was in the front seat beside him, laughing at him and his heroics, and three crew guys with big, goofy grins were in the backseat, waving merrily at me. Earnhardt lifted his fist in victory, then gunned the throttle and took off to weave his way around the traffic jam on the grassy field en route to the private airport about a mile away. Once I knew it was Earnhardt and not a drunken race fan, I was not surprised that within a matter of minutes he had nudged, pushed, and cleverly maneuvered his way through the jutting disarray of hemmed-in cars. As for me, thirty minutes later I was still landlocked while Earnhardt and his passengers were airborne for North Carolina.

The next week in Pocono, he sidled up to me in the garage, nudged me with his elbow, and smiled smugly. "Beat'cha, didn't I?"

I rolled my eyes and shook my head. "You know, you didn't have to muscle your way around those cars. All you had to do was pull up beside 'em and let 'em see that you're Dale Earnhardt, and they would have been fallin' all over themselves to get out of your way.

The next morning, they'd have been bragging to all their friends about letting Dale Earnhardt get in front of them in traffic. That would have been the simple thing to do."

He drew back and looked at me in stunned disbelief. His blue eyes clearly registered no comprehension of doing anything the "simple way" or being given anything that he had not worked to win. Finally, he folded his arms across his chest and shook his head. "Huh!" he huffed. "That wouldn'ta been no fun!"

Dale Earnhardt was a competitor like no other I have ever known. He was as passionate about winning on the day he died as he was when I first met him seventeen years earlier. That's quite a statement in a sport where riches spoil and the money keeps coming regardless of whether you finish first or thirtieth. The hectic pace that the drivers keep up eventually wears them down, and that—coupled with a privileged life of jets, private motor coaches, and huge homes—often kills the killer instinct. The drive that brought them into the top race circuit in motor-sports is subliminally parked. But not for Earnhardt. Never Earnhardt. He was fiercely competitive in all he did, whether it was a championship race, a fishing trip with his buddies, or a not-so-casual game of scissors, rock, and paper.

A few years ago, a friend, the Nashville music executive Don Light, asked me to fly from Nashville to Bristol, Tennessee, with a group of record label executives who were considering a racecar sponsorship. We flew in a Falcon jet owned by the former driver and team owner Dick Brooks. The Falcon is an incredibly fast plane, so the time from takeoff to touchdown on the other side of the state was only about twenty minutes. At the track, Richard Childress, Earnhardt's car owner, asked, "How did you like that jet? Fast, isn't it?"

I nodded in astonishment. "We were here in less than twenty minutes."

He chuckled. "I know, and it's killing Dale that Brooks has got a faster plane than his. Brooks told him, 'I might not beat you on the racetrack, but I'll beat you home every time!' "

Needless to say, Earnhardt did not rest until he had a jet that was as fast as any. He could not stand to be outdone. In Richard Childress, he had the perfect accomplice, for the two men were identical in their drive to be the best—always, not just for a year or so. In watching those two and the team they built into a multi-championship contender, I discovered the importance of synergy between the principals. Earnhardt was a smart man—that's why he stayed with Childress for seventeen years. He could have left and named his price anywhere, or he could have driven for a team he owned. But he knew the critical importance of a team that clicks together perfectly, where everyone is the best at the job he does. Earnhardt knew better than to tamper with success.

With Childress and his team, he had found the best. He never let ego interfere with making strong, practical decisions. When it became popular for stars to own the teams for which they drove, Earnhardt shrewdly resisted, mindful that he already had a great car owner. Instead, he started race teams and hired others to drive for him. It is extremely difficult to do both. Ricky Rudd, only half joking, said that being a team owner was what had turned his hair prematurely gray. Like Darrell Waltrip, Bill Elliott, and others before him, Ricky was only too glad to turn over the headache of team ownership to someone else and return to driving full time.

Earnhardt always combined action with passion, and that was why he succeeded. He didn't just think about what he wanted or liked to do—he went out and did it. Dale Earnhardt did what everyone should do—he took what he loved doing more than anything else in the world and made a living at it.

"I can't believe that I get paid to do what I'd do for free—race," he once said.

One January while the Chevys were in Daytona for a test session, I was walking through the garage when I heard someone call my name and I looked in that direction. "Hey, come over here," Earnhardt hollered with a jerk of his head. He was leaning on the handle of a jack, watching as the crew worked on his car. As we shot the breeze, talk turned to business, farming, and the chicken houses that he was building. I listened, somewhat surprised, to the business strategy that he was developing and his plans for his financial future. My surprise came from learning that Earnhardt cared about something other than racing; to be frank, it was somewhat unusual to find that in a driver.

"Darrell Waltrip is my hero," he said candidly. My eyebrows shot up in shock. Those two were the most formidable nemeses on the circuit, always trying to one-up each other.

"*Darrell* is your *hero*?" I repeated, thinking I had misheard when someone fired up an engine.

He nodded emphatically. "Sure is. He's the first driver who came into this sport and treated it like a real business. He took the money he made here and made other money with it. He's been very smart, and I want to be like him. I want to take the money I make from racin' and invest it. That's why I'm gittin' into the chicken business."

I was seeing a side of Earnhardt that I didn't know existed, and I was impressed. I also thought he was underestimating how well he had already done.

"But you've done very well with the money you've made," I protested. "Look at all you have now."

He pursed his lips tightly and shook his head firmly. "But I ain't done all I can do. I'm just gittin' started, and I'm gonna do much better."

Well, guess what. He did. Earnhardt built an empire, using his initial race winnings as the core funding; within a few years, the money he made as a racer was chump change compared with what he was pulling in as a souvenir wizard, team owner, car dealer, chicken farmer, and real estate mogul. As was his style, he did not quit until he had set a new standard for all racers, present and future, to follow.

But he wasn't always that dedicated. Retired car owner Bud Moore, for whom Earnhardt drove in the early years, worked hard to corral the free spirit. "Dale used to do just as he pleased," Bud told me several years ago. "If he had a sponsor's commitment but the weather was pretty and he wanted to go fishin', he went fishin'. It took me some doing, but we got that worked out where he realized that sponsors come first."

That's a perfect example of Earnhardt's discipline. Once he focused, he could not be shaken or redirected. I have often heard others say that the most naturally talented drivers of the modern era were Earnhardt and his buddy Tim Richmond. Some venture further to say that had Tim lived, he would have proved to be better than Earnhardt, his favorite competitor. Harry Hyde, Tim's crew chief, used to say, "Tim would rather race Earnhardt than eat when he's hungry!" To anyone who knew how much Tim loved food, that was quite a statement. Of course, such speculation is useless, but I will offer this opinion for what it's worth. The Tim Richmond I knew, a young man born to tremendous privilege, did not have the focus and discipline of the steely-minded Earnhardt. He also lacked the blue-collar, poor boy hunger that was such an impetus for Earnhardt. Tim was astounding on the track, particularly after he teamed with Harry Hyde, but it's hard for me to imagine that Earnhardt could have ever had an equal in every aspect of his professional life, let alone a superior.

Earnhardt is my role model for how success springs up and blossoms beautifully when passion is combined with action. Aspiring writers frequently ask me for advice on how to be published. They insist that writing is their passion and they want to write for a living, but very few will persevere and follow through. Their passion is worthless without action. In the same way, many people struggle to make a living at a job in which they have no interest and for which they have no passion. Every penny earned is a chore, and while it pays the rent, it does not accumulate into great wealth or bring happiness.

Passion combined with action, however, is potent, as dynamic as the Earnhardt-Childress union. Earnhardt often bemoaned the fact that he never finished high school. He was, however, one of the smartest men the sports world has ever known, and as much a hero in the business world as he was on the racetrack. This ninth-grade dropout showed by his success that smarts and savvy don't always come from thick books and highfalutin degrees. Sometimes they come from just plain hard work and firm determination.

IF YOU'RE EVER IN A
WRECK, I'LL BE THERE

It was the first time I had ever been to a bus stop. But there I was, on the outskirts of Indianapolis, waiting for a friend. I sat in my car and watched with interest as an odd assortment of people disembarked and was amused to see that the oddest in the crowd was my friend Linda McReynolds—because she was the most out-of-place. She simply didn't seem to be the Greyhound type.

Traveling by bus seemed like a good idea at the time. Her mom lived about three hours from Indianapolis, and Linda, the wife of Larry McReynolds, who was soon to be a superstar crew chief, had flown from their home in South Carolina to visit her. She then decided to take the bus to Indy so that she could fly with me on a corporate jet the next day to a weekend race in Michigan.

She waved when she spotted my car, opened the door, threw her bag into the back, and climbed in. As soon as she closed the door and began to buckle her seat belt, I wrinkled my nose and screwed up my face in distaste.

"Whew!" I said. "You *smell* like some of those people *look* who just got off that bus." The smell that had suddenly saturated the air was a mixture of smoke, perspiration, various foods, greasy hair, and dirty laundry.

She lifted her left arm, sniffed her shirt, and winced. "Ugh!" She shuddered. "Get me to a hot shower as soon as possible or *I'm* going to be sick." She motioned to the bus and solemnly vowed, "That is something I'll never do again. Buses aren't for me."

Several years later, I chuckled about that when I was stepping down from an elaborate motor coach worth several hundred thousand dollars, which is now home at the racetrack to the McReynoldses. Linda, it turned out, really is a bus person. She's just a high-class, luxury bus person, the kind of bus that has gold bathroom fixtures, a king-size bed, mirrored walls, and big-screen television. When Linda rode the Greyhound, we were all poor, struggling upstarts. We didn't know how bright our futures would be, but we had high hopes.

A few years ago, I ran into Linda and Carolyn Yates, wife of team owner Robert Yates, at a private party for charity at the Wildhorse Saloon in Nashville. Carolyn and Linda, who was wearing a Rolex covered in diamonds, had commandeered one of the team's planes and flown, on a whim, to Nashville for the party. Despite her dramatically improved fortunes, Linda is still the same beautifully sweet friend I have always known. I had to ask, though, "Is it as much fun as before?"

She shook her head, brushed a wisp of blond hair behind her ear, and pressed her lips wistfully. "No. We make more money now than we did then—but we had more fun then. It's a lot different. I miss the old days."

I liked her answer because it revealed that she was still the same simple woman who had slept on my sofa the night she had firmly vowed that she was "not a bus person." Larry, who was crew chief for Dale Earnhardt, Davey Allison, Ricky Rudd, and other top drivers, is now a television announcer for Fox Sports. He, too, is still the same person, with a kind heart and a sweet personality.

I learned a lot from folks like the McReynolds who were my confidants in the days of our erstwhile youth and have maintained the bonds of friendship even when we were separated by distance or by fame and fortune. They remember their friends, including me, from the salad days. As I always tell Richard Childress, "Remember, I was your friend back in 1985 when y'all were blowing all those engines and falling out of more races than you stayed in! I loved you guys before the rest of the world cared!"

My friends, famous or not, rich or not, young or not, are precious to me, and I cherish each one of them. I learned a lot about being a good friend during my years on the circuit because I had great teachers—wonderful friends who went above and beyond the call of duty to help me. I once left a company I was working with over a conflict of ethics. I was jobless for six months, and then one night the phone rang. It was Carolyn Rudd, Ricky's sister, offering me a job and doing it as if *she* needed *me*, not vice versa. Many months earlier, although I barely knew her, Carolyn had a beautiful card of encouragement hand-delivered to me in Riverside, California. Somehow, she sensed my need for a friend and rose to the occasion. Through Carolyn, I got to know her best friend, Judy Parrott, wife of veteran crew chief Buddy and mother of championship-winning crew chief Todd. Judy has a beautiful, calming effect on everyone around her because she doesn't overreact. She meets every situation with humor, grace, and compassion. Carolyn and Judy befriended and loved everyone in their path, and through them I learned the importance of giving and caring.

When I first came into the sport, I was only the second woman to cover it on a regular basis. Deb Williams, the grand dame of the garage and the first woman in the NASCAR press box, welcomed me with open arms. She could have closed me out and protected her turf. I had certainly seen enough male reporters do that to me in other sports. Instead, she welcomed, encouraged, helped, and, eventually, grew to love me as much as I do her. She was raised in the mountains near Asheville, North Carolina, where friendship and loyalty are second to nothing. When my dad was critically ill and in need of massive blood transfusions, she called to offer her blood. When he died, she came down from Charlotte immediately and spent the night with me.

When people like Deb Williams reach out to you, sooner or later it becomes your turn to reach out to others. By the time Beth Tuschak of the *Detroit News* and later *USA Today* showed up to cover races, I was a publicist. Still, I embraced and helped her as Deb had taught me. Since there were only a handful of women on the circuit at that time, we formed a tight circle and supported each other. Both Deb and Beth were part of my wedding when I married—Beth caught the bridal bouquet—and although the marriage didn't last, our friendships certainly have.

I always remember how people like the Elliotts and Lunsfords helped me early in my career and gave my professional life a solid start. I'm always mindful of that, and I try to do the same in every way I possibly can. It's very important to me that my early benefactors know how much I appreciate their mentoring and friendship. Recently, I told Bill Elliott how much his family had meant to me and how grateful I'd always be. He blushed and treated me to his famous aw-shucks look, which I hadn't seen in years. "I didn't do nothin'," he protested modestly. "It was mostly George and Dan."

"But you used to give me quotes and stories that you didn't give to anybody else."

He threw back his head, laughed, and then nodded. "Now I *did* use to do *that!*"

Because of great friendships like this, I know the value of people who care deeply. I tried to be that kind of friend to Tim Richmond when most of the world turned its back. I will always have respect for Rick Hendrick because he compassionately stood by Tim until the bitter end. He never forsook or denounced him. It was a beautiful lesson in the etiquette and responsibility of true friendship.

One of the most important things we can do in life is nurture friendships and form unbreakable bonds with good, solid people who will return our friendship. Without good friends, life and its accomplishments mean very little. It's an empty existence. Regardless of how busy I am, I make a conscious effort to routinely telephone all my good friends. I'll tell you this—there are a few friends I *wish* I could call now.

I have also learned this about life: we're all a reflection of the friends we have, deeply influenced by their attitudes and their actions. It's important to be around good, positive-minded, generous people who take life and squeeze so much out of it. Those who are filled with light and illuminate those along their path. Negative people who routinely lament about their agonies, complain constantly, and refuse to take control of their destiny are not welcome for long in my life. I have little patience for people who would rather complain than attack problems constructively. I realize that we all have bad days or bad experiences that knock the wind out of us. I'll be the first to stand by my friends and love them, encourage them, and pray for them during these times. But people who wallow in self-pity and bitterness are harmful to those of us who want to make the best out of bad situations. In the interest of self-preservation, you have to distance yourself from self-pitying people, or pretty soon you'll start thinking and acting like them.

I try to surround myself with people who love life and boldly stand up to its challenges with resilience. As Bobby Allison once said to me, "If I asked God why he let bad things happen to me, I'd also have to question why he gave me so many good things. If I'm not willing to question the good in life, I certainly can't question the bad."

THINGS AREN'T ALWAYS
AS THEY APPEAR

From the corner of my eye, I saw the deep scowl on Dale Earnhardt's face. I thought that if I didn't acknowledge him that I could sneak by, so I looked straight ahead and kept walking. I was already in deeper than I wanted to be.

But no such luck. He saw me.

"Hey!" he called in a gruff voice. "Come here!"

I hesitated and took a deep breath, as though that would help, as if it could possibly calm the beast. He saw my reluctance and glowered at me, and when Earnhardt glowered, I always cowered.

"*I said 'come here,'* " he commanded. Slowly, I dragged myself over to where he was sitting—on the back of his Busch Grand National trailer in the garage of the Charlotte Motor Speedway. He scooted over and patted the place next to him. "Sit down." I did. He looked straight ahead for a minute while I tried not to squirm like a child who is anxious to dispense with a scolding. When he spoke, he still didn't look at me.

"I guess Bill's pretty mad at me, ain't he?" He paused and then cut his steely blue eyes sideways toward me to ascertain my reaction.

"Huh!" I snorted, thinking there could not possibly be a more ridiculous question in the world. "I think we could accurately say that that's an understatement." Sarcasm dripped from every syllable.

His jaw visibly tightened, and he knitted his eyebrows together in a deep frown. In a tone as close to defensive as Earnhardt could ever get—for he never defended, never complained, never apologized—he retorted, "Well, I can't help that. That's just racin'."

For the past few days, a war had raged between the Earnhardt camp and the Bill Elliott camp. It had started on the racetrack while a huge crowd of fans and a television audience watched. Then, when the media encouraged them, they continued the fight in the press. This had happened in the 1987 Winston, NASCAR's version of an All-Star race, in which only race winners from the previous year could participate. It was a short 135-lap race divided into three segments with high monetary stakes—no championship points, but the winner took home a check for $200,000, a lot of money at a time when other races paid the winner as little as $50,000 or $60,000 (a win at the Winston now earns $500,000). Earnhardt had driven even more aggressively than usual that afternoon, tangling with Bill and Geoff Bodine as the trio headed into the first turn. That nudge from the 3 car, in which the other two cars struggled to keep from crashing, was the match that started the fire. Heads got hot, tempers flared.

Then the simmering situation between Bill and Dale erupted into an explosion when Earnhardt passed Elliott for the win by dropping off the track and taking a 100-yard sideways shortcut on the grass below the apron on the front straightaway. The smoking tires on Earnhardt's car chewed up the impeccably manicured grass, sending pieces of the perfect turf spinning through the air as the back end of his car swung wildly. As only he could do, Earnhardt held on, whipped the car back up the track in front of Bill, and took the win—but only after carrying Bill up to the wall, causing a bashed-in fender and a cut tire.

All the fans were on their feet, a few cheering for Earnhardt but most booing him. There was no middle ground, and there were no disinterested spectators. While the fans chose sides, those of us on pit road jumped up on the three-foot-high pit wall to see what would happen next. Earnhardt took the checkered flag, and the normally cool-headed Bill took his revenge.

It's hard to get Bill mad. Usually he just doesn't care enough to get angry, but there on the back straight on the Charlotte Motor Speedway he let his rage boil over. He caught Earnhardt on the cooldown lap and rammed his car hard from behind. The crowd cheered, but NASCAR officials frowned, later imposing a fine of $2,500 for both Bill and Earnhardt. When fans in Georgia raised enough money to pay Bill's fine, he wrote a check for the same amount to the state's drug abuse program and personally presented it to the state's governor—who was one of the fans who had chipped in.

After the race, Elliott groused that Earnhardt "like to have wrecked me and several others on the track. We're not kids and we're not Saturday night wrestlers." For his part, Earnhardt quickly put the press in line by saying, "The whole deal is between Bill and me and nobody else. If he wants to say anything, I'll stand flat-footed with him any time." Tim Richmond, who ran third, said it was worth the third-place finish to be behind the action and enjoy the entertainment.

And, of course, I wound up right in the middle, my loyalties severely tested.

The Earnhardt-Childress team and the Elliott team, without dispute, were my favorites on the circuit, each team filled with good friends. I decided to try to walk the straight and narrow, right down the middle, knowing that Earnhardt's 3 team probably expected me to side with the Elliotts. Secretly, I did. Not because they were better friends or because they were "home folks" but because I thought that what Earnhardt had done was risky and unfair. On the other hand, his gutsy move was nothing short of spectacular and was the kind of daredevil entertainment that helped to draw more fans to the sport. Earnhardt was the absolute best when it came to injecting excitement into a race.

So when Earnhardt said tersely, "That's just racin'," I replied before I could bite my tongue, "I *think* that Bill's idea of racin' is *on* the *track* and not *through* the *grass*."

I smiled innocently, or at least I tried to fill my feeble smile with innocence. Earnhardt was not fooled. He glared at me and shot back, "I knew you'd side with him."

Subtly, though, I saw the crusty front, the false bravado, crumble and beneath it, ever so slightly, I glimpsed a vulnerability so oddly out of place that I wanted to blink and shake my head to clear it of an image so foreign and unfamiliar. A wounded look clouded his eyes, although he tried to mask it with a mean scowl. Suddenly, I realized that Dale Earnhardt did care. Regardless of what he said, despite how he acted, he cared what people thought of him; he cared if he had been perceived as a bully or had played unfairly. My heart melted as he perched his elbows on his knees, leaned forward, and dropped his eyes to the ground between his legs as though he were immensely interested in the asphalt.

"I'm not taking sides," I said softly, feeling an overwhelming urge to put my arms around him and comfort him. But I kept my hands folded in my lap. Wordlessly, he looked around at me. "You know what I always tell people about you?" I asked.

"What?" His voice was low, and the tone sounded bruised.

"That although you're the guy who always wears the black hat, you've got the biggest heart of any person I've ever met. Bill's a nice guy, but I doubt that he's ever given away all the money and stuff you have. He doesn't instinctively see the deep hurt and desperate need in others the way you do. That doesn't mean he's a bad person; he's just different from you. If people knew the inside of Dale Earnhardt, they'd be shocked at what a softie the tough ol' guy is."

He blushed slightly, shrugged his shoulders awkwardly, then

changed the subject. I rarely had frank conversations with Earnhardt. Normally, he was playfully tormenting me about something and I was fighting hard to stand my ground. When he first discovered me, he would tease me continuously, so I did everything possible to avoid him. He would affix that penetrating stare directly on me, well aware of how it made others squirm, and then say anything he darn well pleased. More than once, he stopped me to make some aggravating remark; then he'd snigger and swagger off. I quickly discovered that the only way to deal with him was to look him straight in the eye, screw up all my courage, and pop back with something tart and, I hoped, witty. I knew that if he ever figured out how uncomfortable he made me, he would be relentless, so I fought back feebly with every fiber of my body. A few times, my comebacks were so unexpected and so clever that the Intimidator would throw back his head, laugh hard, and just walk away, shaking his head.

I eventually learned, however, that the only thing predictable about Earnhardt was his unpredictability. One thing he enjoyed teasing me about was my chest. He often had some aggravating comment to throw at me as he passed me in the garage. One year for the championship banquet at the Waldorf in New York, I wore a lovely little strapless sequined number that I had ordered from Neiman-Marcus in Dallas. The key word in that sentence is "little." The dress, in retrospect—retrospect being an hour after I had dressed for the banquet—was a poor choice, for it was mostly cleavage and little dress. My friends quickly christened it the "bunny dress," for I looked exasperatingly like that sex symbol of the 1960s. I didn't know until that evening that strapless dresses aren't for ample-bosomed women, since they won't stay put. They slip lower with each movement. I have never spent a more uncomfortable evening.

"Nice dress," Alan Kulwicki commented at the banquet. "You wear it well."

My face reddened and my eyes narrowed. "Alan," I retorted sharply, "*I* am not wearing this dress. *It* is wearing *me*." Trust me, I was not bragging.

My embarrassment looked as though it might extend into immortality when the next issue of *Winston Cup Illustrated* ran a color photo of me in the bunny dress in its banquet spread. And, of course, the photo was shot from an upward angle. When I saw it, I again reddened and immediately thought of Earnhardt. "Oh, no," I thought miserably. "I'm gonna catch hell for this when I get to Daytona." I knew he was going to have a field day with it, so for the remainder of the off-season—six agony-filled weeks—I dreaded the jabs and teasing I would get when I saw him. Given the choice, I would have much preferred a root canal treatment without Novocaine than what I was certain awaited me in Daytona. Trying to anticipate his remarks, I worked hard on comebacks. But as I explained earlier, Earnhardt could not be predicted. I spent the first few days of SpeedWeeks avoiding him. Then, one day, unexpectedly, he swung out from the side of the 3 truck and our eyes met. Inwardly, I winced. Outwardly, my body tensed. I swallowed hard while my heart sped up. But not a word said he. Instead, he merely cut his eyes over at me, tilted his head, grinned, and shook his finger at me. He kept walking and never mentioned it.

Earnhardt taught me that people and situations aren't always as they seem, that it's unfair to judge people by preconceptions or public personas. You can cause yourself a world of hurt over misjudgments and wrong assessments. Remember the Elliotts in 1985? The racing world overlooked their potential because it was hidden by a slow-talking, country-boy naïveté. Watching Bill blister the Daytona track at a record-setting speed, one rival crew member commented, "How can someone who talks that slow go that fast?" That's the power of being underestimated. When no one expects a challenge from you, that lets you work full-force without scrutiny or stress. What could be better? The Elliotts were smart enough not to let the other teams know that they could outsmart them all. They used the miscalculation of the other teams to their advantage. Dan Elliott knows what an edge you get when people underestimate you. "It's the best ammunition you can have," he has always said.

I've embarrassed myself a few times because I stupidly judged people by what I had read in a newspaper or heard from others.

One particular incident stands out painfully in my mind, and although I cringe when I remember it, I don't ever want to forget it, because the lesson was so powerful.

Bruce Jenner, the great Olympian, was trying his hand at road racing, and he showed up at Watkins Glen, New York, one year. I believe he ran a Trans Am race on Saturday before the Sunday Winston Cup race. Bruce and Carolyn Rudd were friends, so she introduced us and we talked briefly. Actually, I talked, because he didn't have a lot to say. I *assumed* that this was because he was arrogant, conceited, and self-absorbed. After all, that's what the tabloids wrote (I, of course, read them only when I'm standing in line at the grocery store) and perhaps I had heard one or two comments to that effect. I was unimpressed. And it goes without saying that he apparently had the same opinion of me. A couple of days later, I saw him again, at the airport in Elmira, and he just looked at me. No greeting, no smile, no acknowledgment that he knew me from somewhere, anywhere.

He was standing a couple of people in front of me as we passed through the metal detectors at the tiny airport. Two young women were checking carry-on bags as they came through the X-ray machine. When they recognized Jenner, they started to flutter, and of course, I rolled my eyes to think that they would be impressed with him. Wordlessly, he picked up his bag and strolled out to the tarmac. The women started nudging each other and giggling. They were still jabbering excitedly when my bag rolled through.

"I can't believe that we just got to see Bruce Jenner in person!"

"I know!" exclaimed the other, who then said to me, "You're going to be on the same plane with him. Aren't you excited?"

I rolled my eyes again. "No. Trust me. It's no big deal."

They stared at me as if I were an idiot, which I was. I just didn't know it yet.

"What do you mean by 'it's no big deal'?" the first one asked.

"I've met him. He's arrogant and he thinks a lot of himself," I replied in an authoritative tone.

They both looked crestfallen. "Oh, no!" they said in unison.

"Oh, well," one said, shrugging her shoulders as she handed me my carry-on. "I guess if you're that good-looking, rich, and famous, that happens."

The plane was nearly full. As usual, my carry-on was so heavy that it was difficult to raise it over my head and stash it in the top compartment. I struggled for a few minutes, trying to push other bags aside and make room for it. Suddenly, from the corner of my eye, I saw Bruce Jenner jump up from his window seat several rows back. I glanced around to see that he was looking directly at me as he used his long legs to crawl, with a strong effect of urgency, over the two people sitting beside him. Then he came hurrying up the aisle straight toward me. With a sudden thud, my heart fell to my stomach as I realized that he was coming to help me, *me* who had just made such unwarranted, unkind comments about him.

"Oh dear God," I prayed silently and frantically. "Please, *please* don't let him be coming to help me. Please!"

I know that God heard my prayer, but he ignored it. He chose that precise moment to teach me a big lesson that I will never forget. Jenner smiled sweetly and solicitously as he reached me. I will always remember the obliging look of kind courtesy on his face.

"Here," he said gently as he took the bag from me. "Let me help you with that." Effortlessly, he reached into the overhead compartment, rearranged other bags, and placed my bag in a perfect-size hole. I wanted to die, or at least to crawl under the seat and never emerge again. Adding to my rightly deserved discomfort were the people standing behind me in the aisle who had overheard my unnecessary, unkind remarks. I glanced around, red-cheeked, to see one man looking at me with a raised eyebrow and an expression of reprimand. I returned his look with one of appropriate chastisement. It wasn't a facade. It came from the heart.

My luggage properly stored, Jenner turned and looked down at me. "Is that it?" he asked.

I nodded, then swallowed to push down the knot in my throat. "Thank you very much."

"Anything else I can help you with?"

"No, that's it. Thank you."

"Okay." He looked directly into my eyes and smiled warmly. "Have a good flight." As he returned to his seat, I sank into my seat and slunk down, withering in embarrassment. Solemnly, I did repentance for the entire trip. Let me tell you something—had I not actually seen Bruce Jenner boarding the plane as I popped off my big mouth, I would have sworn that he heard me and was retaliating in the most perfect way possible. But I *know* that he didn't hear me. He was simply following his natural instinct of courtesy and compassion. After that experience, I promised myself that I would never again judge someone I didn't know, based on the opinions of others.

The bottom line is this—regardless of who people are or what the situation is, unless you know them well or are personally involved, you just don't know what you don't know. Images and perceptions can be, and usually are, mighty wrong. It is best to reserve judgment and to give everyone the benefit of the doubt. I'm an expert on this because lessons learned the hard way are the lessons you don't forget.

WHAT GOES AROUND
COMES AROUND

The feeling of generosity and kindness that permeates the world of NASCAR is a throwback to the days of old, when folks, unasked, stretched out a helping hand to neighbors in need. I spent almost a decade—the most formative years of my young adult life—covered by a warm cloak of love and compassion where tough men put aside friendship for a few hours on Sunday to compete fiercely on the track, then, amazingly, share information among themselves the following week.

Without hesitation, team owner Leonard Wood might wander over to Bud Moore's trailer and explain that he and his team were having trouble with too much down force on their newly redesigned Ford. Bud would commiserate and then share information on his own team's experiences. Later, if the Wood brothers' team benefited from a new discovery, Leonard would saunter back over to Bud's hauler and share the information. It was constant give-and-take; folks were always helping the same folks they were trying to beat. I never saw one Winston Cup star worry about a new driver or team that came into the sport. Instead, they all sought to help the newcomer with sage advice, remembering when they were once new and others had helped them. The only repayment they expected was for that person, in turn, to help someone else. It became an ongoing cycle that keeps giving and giving.

When I left the Winston Cup circuit, finally tired of the constant travel and endless nights away from home, I entered the world of corporate communications. I considered myself worldly, having worked in the midst of celebrities and enjoyed a lifestyle that had enabled me to travel extensively. I quickly discovered that I was as naive as a young girl who had never left the farm. I was not prepared for the greed, viciousness, and back-stabbing that I found in the corporate world, where people advanced by destroying their coworkers rather than by their own merits. It was a dose of reality that I found extremely hard to swallow. I was astounded to discover that people who competed against each other in NASCAR were more of a team than people who worked together in the business world.

It was a brutally cold winter's day in Richmond, Virginia, when Dale Earnhardt stood up at the pre-race driver's meeting and said simply, "Fellas, Ernie needs a set of tires for the race today, so I'm passin' the hat and we're all gonna help him." He dropped a handful of large bills into the hat and then passed it around himself. He wanted to make certain that everyone contributed to struggling driver Ernie Irvan's hardscrabble effort. Ernie was struggling in the world of big-time racing and Earnhardt, the multichampion, undaunted and unafraid of any competition from anyone, reached out his hand. Earnhardt was incredibly kind and compassionate. The inside of that man was completely at odds with his tough exterior.

The first time I saw that soft side of Dale Earnhardt was toward Kenny Schrader, who had recently moved to Charlotte to devote his attention to a full-time Winston Cup career. Like most new racers, Kenny was struggling financially. He was aided by his wife, Ann, who worked as a registered nurse to supplement their meager income. Kenny had managed to work out an endorsement deal with a mobile home manufacturer, and he was purchasing a small piece of land for his new home. I was standing a few feet away in the Darlington garage when Earnhardt approached Schrader. He was awkward and a little gruff as he narrowed his eyes and said, "Heard you're gittin' a place to live." Schrader nodded and told him briefly about it. Then Earnhardt asked, "You got the money? 'Cause if you don't, just come by the truck and see me and I'll write ya a check to help ya out."

Schrader, obviously humbled by the unsolicited offer, replied, "Naw, I'm OK. I've got it handled."

"Okay, but if you run into any trouble, just let me know and I'll take care of it." Earnhardt then walked off to his racecar and left me, the eavesdropper, wide-eyed and open-mouthed. I told that story several years later in front of Schrader, who wisecracked, "Yeah, but did ya hear the interest rate he was gonna charge me?"

He was teasing, of course, for he knew that Earnhardt was the kind of friend who offered help rather than waiting to be asked for it. I replayed that scene in my mind several times when I realized that Kenny was the first person to see that Earnhardt was dead. It was a horrible shock for Kenny, who wrecked with Earnhardt, then jumped out of his car and ran over to check on his good friend. He knew from the moment he saw Earnhardt that one of the best friends he had ever had was gone.

One year I was working on a fund-raising committee for cancer research. We were racing in Sonoma and I decided that, to jump-start the project, I would ask the drivers and team owners for help. I started on the 3 truck with Earnhardt and Childress.

First, I listened to Earnhardt gush shamelessly over the latest antics of his daughter, Taylor Nicole, then I said simply, "Listen, I need some money for a cancer fund-raiser I'm working on." I held out my hand. "So, fork it over."

He gave me that famous look—squinted one eye, lifted the other eyebrow, tilted his head, and stretched his mouth into a tight, straight line. I didn't flinch. I just looked him straight in the eye, waiting to answer any question he had about the charity project. But there were no questions. Wordlessly, he reached for his billfold, pulled out several large bills, and handed them to me. After that, it was a cinch to get money from the other drivers. I just told them that Earnhardt had been the first one to step up to the plate and contribute. The Elliotts sent a large check from the racing team, and Ernie and Sheila Elliott matched it with a personal check. Sadly, a few years later, they would personally know the devastation of cancer when their son, Casey, the handsome, personable heir to the family's racing throne, died of it. He was only twenty-one years old. George, the patriarch who had launched the dynasty, died of cancer in 1998, seven years after the death of his beloved Mildred. George's death came only six weeks before the death of my own father. Losing two of the most important men in my life in such a short time was excruciatingly sad.

Without question, the folks on the Winston Cup circuit are generous with money and contribute heavily to many organizations and causes such as breast cancer research, scholarship funds, and the Make-A-Wish Foundation. The Alabama Institute for the Deaf and Blind in Talladega has for many years hosted an event called Race Fever during the May weekend when the series is in town. As part of the event, the school auctions off race memorabilia including autographed drivers' suits. The first Race Fever night raised $12,000, and now it easily brings in $250,000 each year, thanks to the generous support of the race community.

On my first visit there with Bill Elliott, I surprised him by using a few signs I had just learned. I signed a greeting and my name, delighting the children, who quickly answered in fluent sign language. An astonished Bill recovered instantly and quipped, "Leave it to Ronda. She'll figure out a way to talk wherever she goes!"

From my racing friends, I advanced in my understanding of the responsibility that comes with success and privilege. It's this simple—when we are blessed, it is our responsibility to give back to society. But giving money is only a small part of generosity. My fellow sportswriters repeatedly shared their notes, quotes, and information when I was brand-new to covering the sport. Then, men like Harry Hyde, George Elliott, Richard Childress, Bud Moore, and others repeatedly and patiently answered my questions about racecars, engines, rules, strategies, and tracks. They certainly had better things to do, but you would never have known it. Harry Hyde always went one step further and colored the details with great stories like the time he made his driver stay out on the track and told him that they would pit him as soon as Harry and the crew finished their ice cream bars. They used that one in *Days of Thunder*.

It has always been easier for me to write a check for a good cause than give my time and energy. I have always been in awe of the good people who chair committees and donate their talents and hours for nonprofit ventures. Many times I have thought, "I wish I could be more like that, less selfish and more willing to invest my time." Then I stumbled across the solution—find a cause that you're absolutely passionate about. When I was asked to join the board for the University of Georgia library, I didn't have to think twice. I love libraries, particularly those dedicated to assisting patrons and preserving history.

Speaking of history, my NASCAR friends demonstrated to me the importance of paying homage to the legends and accomplishments of those who have gone before us. The sport is built by the efforts of many, and today's participants are generous enough to express appreciation to pioneers like Lloyd Seay, Curtis Turner, Joe Weatherly, the Flock brothers, Lee Petty, Raymond Parks, Smokey Yunick, Fireball Roberts, and others who planted the seeds of the fruit that is being harvested in great abundance today. Admirably, the sport's army continues to recognize those warriors from the past.

While some of the other racing series struggle to maintain market position, financial stability, and a constant influx of newcomers—IMSA, for instance, is completely defunct—NASCAR continues to flourish and prosper. Here's one of the reasons: from even the earliest years, stock car folks have looked after each other. If a potential sponsor came to Dale Earnhardt or Richard Childress and their cars were slap-full of names, they would help place the sponsorship money with a racer who was struggling. This was done solely in an effort to help others. But here's what happened: it strengthened the sport by providing financing to more cars and increasing the number of competitors and therefore the level of competition. I know of another series that quite frequently doesn't have enough cars to fill the field. In other words, it falls short of the number required to complete the starting spots, so there's no need for qualifying. Part of the thrill of NASCAR racing comes from seeing which cars are fast enough to make the field and which ones will have to go home. NASCAR competitors never thought of the far-reaching effects of their generosity. They thought only of helping their friends. And look how far that spirit of kindness and generosity has gotten them and their sport.

Darrell Waltrip was always one of the most colorful and most controversial figures in the sport. When I first came into the sport, he was loudly booed at drivers' introductions. The crowd would go nuts, booing and jeering DW as they would later do with Earnhardt and Jeff Gordon. The drivers, like Earnhardt, may try to act as if they don't care, but they do and it hurts, no matter what they say. The happiest I've ever seen Darrell, other than when he won the Daytona 500, was when he briefly (for two years), unseated Bill Elliott as the fans' Most Popular Driver. Bill has had a practically unbreakable hold on that honor, winning it fifteen times in seventeen years, but Darrell surprised everyone, particularly himself, by winning it first in 1989.

While it's hard on the drivers to be vocally disliked by the fans, it's even harder on the wives. I remember a story that spread quickly through the garage in Darlington. Betty Jo Yarborough, Cale's wife, approached a sniffling Stevie Waltrip, who was crying about the unkindness of fans during the introductions for a race there. Betty Jo, a veteran of such abuse, put her arm around Stevie and said,

"Honey, don't cry when they boo. Cry when they stop caring enough to boo. That's when you're *really* in trouble."

When I was working with Mark Martin and we lost the points lead for the championship to Earnhardt in Phoenix, one race shy of the season's end, I came out of our truck and ran straight into Stevie. "Where's Mark?" she asked. "I want to talk to him and tell him that when Darrell won his first championship, we lost the points lead, too, before the last race but we came back to win it. I want to give him a word of encouragement."

See how the circle of goodwill continues to grow and spread?

Another element of generosity is that of forgiveness. Winston Cup folks know a lot about that because tempers can flare in the heat of battle. Of course, NASCAR doesn't hesitate to facilitate forgiveness by having a little "sit down" between the principals in the NASCAR trailer. Still, the drivers, owners, and crews realize that it doesn't help anyone to nurse a grudge. Besides, one thing you learn quickly in a sport where people travel often between teams is that the person you hate today may be your boss tomorrow. It happens in every industry and field because all companies draw from the same pool of talent. So it's better to keep all bridges safe and standing. The year that Bill and Earnhardt got into it in the Winston, Rusty Wallace and Kyle Petty wound up in a fistfight in the garage over something that had happened between them on the track. Kyle's dad, Richard, stepped in to break up the fight, but the anger soon dissipated anyway. "We've been too good friends for too long to stay mad and let something like this come between us," Kyle explained with perfect logic and with the generosity of spirit that promotes forgiveness.

As my daddy always said, you can help people only when they *need* help. The other times when you think you're helping, it's usually done at your convenience. The mark of a true friend is seen when helping isn't convenient.

NASCAR people also offer random acts of kindness like the one that Mark Martin's dad, Julian, offered me once. I was newly married and had been away from home for several days, so I was anxious to get home as soon as possible. We were racing in Rockingham, which is a couple of hours by car from Charlotte. When the race ended, I would have to drive to Charlotte, take a flight to Atlanta, and then drive another hour and a half to get home. Julian, a pilot, had flown his own twin-engine plane to Rockingham and landed across the street at the drag strip. When Mark fell out of the 400-lap race about 100 laps into it, Julian, knowing I was anxious to get home, approached me and offered to fly me to Charlotte so that I could catch an earlier flight. I was delighted! So was Jack Roush, who also hitched a ride with us, in order to catch an earlier flight to Detroit. That offer got me home seven hours earlier, which, at the time, was equal to a week at least! When Julian, his wife, and his daughter were killed in a plane crash a few years ago, I thought of that bit of kindness that had meant the world to me, and how that one small act made his death feel so personal to me. Julian Martin, for one Sunday afternoon, had touched my life in a generous, sweet way. While I ached for Mark over the loss of his beloved father, I hurt for the world over the loss of such a fine person. If we can all leave such random acts of kindness scattered behind us, imagine what a strong legacy we can leave. A person's life isn't truly measured until it is over, and then the real test comes from the number of people who can remember a kindness from that person that touched their lives. A lot of remembrances from a lot of people are indicative of a truly full life.

A few years ago, the series was racing in Daytona in July. Dave Marcis, who has always had a close relationship to Earnhardt and Childress, had rented an engine from the Childress organization for the race. He practiced all day, but just before qualifying, something in the engine broke. As soon as Childress realized what had happened, he hurried over to the stall to check on Marcis and the engine. Now, engines blow all the time, so, ethically, Childress was under no obligation. But he knew that making the race was important to Marcis because for a low-budget team like his, every dollar counts. Marcis would have had all the expenses but none of the payout. The problem was that whatever engine went into the car had to pass through NASCAR's inspection or it couldn't be used for qualifying. Time was ticking away.

But Childress had a solution: "We'll pull the engine outta Dale's car, since he's already qualified and it's already been through inspection." The Childress team helped to install the engine in Marcis's car and then, just in time, he rolled out onto the track. He not only made the race; he earned one of his highest qualifying positions of the year. True friends like Childress don't walk away when problems arise. Instead, they're generous with their time, and they help to find a solution.

From many of my racing friends like Earnhardt, Childress, the Martins, the Pettys, and the Elliotts, I learned how to behave when life blesses you. Good follows good and bad follows bad. The seeds of kindness, compassion, and goodwill produce a harvest of the same. As my daddy liked to say about the importance of sharing blessings, "It isn't an option. It's an obligation."

LIMOUSINES IN THE INFIELD

It was well after midnight on a Saturday before a race at Charlotte Motor Speedway. Tim Richmond, his mom, Evelyn, and I had just left the Speedway Club, where we had had dinner and watched two shows by country singer Louise Mandrell. Suddenly, Tim had a bright idea.

He leaned forward and told the limousine driver, "How 'bout making a round through the infield?" The driver nodded. "Yes, sir. Be glad to." He turned the stretch limo in the appropriate direction while I looked at Tim as if he had lost his mind.

Once, at Darlington, *USA Today* had asked me to go to the infield and do a sidebar story on the fans. In addition to having my first run-in with a mound of stinging fire ants, I learned that the infield could be quite a rowdy place. Many of the fans started partying on Friday, and by Sunday life in general and the race in particular were clouded by an alcoholic haze. With that in mind, I did not think it was wise for one of the sport's top stars to showboat through the maze of trailers, campers, and campfires. It occurred to me that Tim could possibly start a riot—the friendly, enthusiastic kind, but a riot nonetheless.

Regally, he settled back against the seat and smiled contentedly. "I want to see my fans." In other words, Tim wanted to see how many homemade signs proclaimed him the best or favorite driver. I looked at Evelyn and shook my head, but she shrugged nonchalantly and looked out the window. She was fully accustomed to Tim's impulsiveness—plus anything her Timmy wanted was fine with her. He could do no wrong.

Tim Richmond loved being the center of attention. While he was the most controversial figure in the sport and people often disagreed on their opinions of him, this is one thing that no one ever disputed. To his credit, he wasn't the kind of star who enjoyed his celebrity part of the time, then was annoyed by the attention and autograph seekers at other times. He was always happy to oblige fans and never acted as though they were out of line if they asked for an autograph in the middle of dinner. He adored being adored and for him twenty-four hours a day, seven days a week were not too much.

Tim's devotion to his fans was legendary. Once he had held up the start of a race at Daytona because he would not stop signing autographs and go to his car. Harry Hyde, his crew chief, was screaming at Carolyn Rudd over the radio to get Tim to the car because NASCAR officials were furious. Finally, Carolyn told Tim to get to the car; she would handle the remaining autograph seekers. She promised a couple of people that if they would give her their names and addresses, she would mail signed photos to them. One rather large woman didn't take kindly to Carolyn's offer and gave her such a furious shove that it sent the tiny, white-clad Carolyn spiraling backward into a mud hole. When she finally got to the car, where Tim was buckling himself in, he cut his eyes over to her, covered in mud from head to toe, and snarled, "Where in the hell have you been?" Tim believed that the world should always, without fail or excuse, revolve around him.

Earlier that evening in Charlotte, I was waiting in the lobby of my hotel for Tim and the limousine. A guy, apparently a race fan, came up to me and started hitting on me during most of my forty-five-minute wait. After thirty minutes of a nonstop monologue, during which I mostly tried to ignore him, he finally said, "Hey, baby, it looks like you're being stood up tonight. So why don't you just go with me?"

I pursed my lips tightly. "No, thank you." I was getting very aggravated. First of all, I hate it when people are late. Second, I hate obnoxious guys like that jerk who won't leave a woman alone when she makes it abundantly clear that she's not interested. By the time the white limo pulled up to the Hilton, I was shaking with fury. Almost before the car had completely stopped, Tim jumped out and came hurrying in. As the automatic double doors parted, he held out his arms and immediately began his defense—blaming it on the driver's tardiness—when he saw the anger flashing in my eyes and my arms folded across my chest.

Mr. Obnoxious, completely astounded, shouted, "Oh, my gawd! It's Tim Richmond! This is who you've been waitin' on? Tim Richmond?" He rushed to the beaming Tim, who loved nothing more than to be recognized—and, of course, to have his name shouted in the middle of a hotel lobby was even better. Mr. Obnoxious grabbed Tim's hand and began pumping it furiously. "Man, I can't believe this. You're my favorite. I don't pull for nobody else but you. I really like the way you gave Earnhardt hell in Pocono a couple of months ago."

"Yeah, that was a pretty good race." Tim nodded, always in agreement with anyone who thought he was great.

"Hey! Can you wait here and let me go get my buddies outta the bar? They ain't never gonna believe this unless they see it with their own eyes."

In a moment's time, four members of Tim's adoring public presented themselves in a stampede of enthusiasm. They gathered in a circle around him and excitedly began to sing his praises. Tim was in heaven, but I was closed out of the tight-knit group that engulfed him.

I heard Mr. Obnoxious say, "I can't believe that I was actually hittin' on Tim Richmond's girlfriend. Man, you gotta know that if I'd known she was yours, I'd never said a word to her. But wait till the guys at home hear that I tried to pick up Tim Richmond's girlfriend!"

Tim looked up from an autograph he was signing and said casually, "Oh, she's not my girlfriend." He looked at me, and a sinister smile spread over his face as he realized that this was the perfect opportunity to dish out my comeuppance. He continued, "So, you can have her if you want her." He placed his hand on Mr. Obnoxious's shoulder and looked back at me to assure himself that enough steam was boiling out from my ears. Apparently there wasn't, so he stoked the fire further. "But buddy, I gotta warn you—she's a helluva lot of trouble."

Infuriated, I turned and stomped toward the door. "Hey, where are you goin'?" he called after me as the double entrance doors slid open. "I got you a date here."

"I don't need your help!" I stormed back.

"Well, I beg to differ but the way things have been going for you lately, I think you *do* need my help in getting a date."

I refused to answer as I walked out the door. The limousine driver opened the car door for me, and I angrily clumped inside and sat down in the seat facing Evelyn. She smiled warmly and asked, "Where's Tim?"

"Inside, signing autographs for his adoring public," I snarled sarcastically.

Evelyn nodded and commented, "He loves his fans and his fans love him."

After a few minutes, Tim popped into the limo and we were, at last, on our way to the Speedway Club. Tim's tremendous appeal was further substantiated that evening when he was met by cheers and applause when we entered the dining room—late, of course. As it turned out, he was a bigger attraction than Louise Mandrell. For the entire evening, he graciously took time for everyone who approached him. I especially remember a family of three from Ohio who were big fans of his. The teenage daughter worshiped Tim and had her room plastered with his photos. Tim spent a generous amount of time with them, between shows and then at least half an hour after the last show.

So, after an evening of playing to his fans, it was really no surprise when Tim instructed his driver to cruise the infield. Whenever he saw a Tim Richmond banner, he'd say, "Hey! Stop here." Then, dressed in a suit and tie, he would jump out, run over to his adoring public, and thank the fans for their support. At our last stop, nine or ten people were sitting around a campfire, enjoying the mild, starlit evening. The white stretch limo first caught their eyes and they begin pointing, talking, and laughing. Wide-eyed, they watched as the car pulled to a stop a few feet from their perch, then absolute shock filled their faces when their favorite driver emerged, ran over to them, introduced himself, and shook each person's hand. He talked for a few minutes, signed autographs, and then headed back to the car. He stopped at the door of the car and turned back. "Hey, guys! Thanks for your support!" He playfully pointed his finger at them. "Now, don't let me ever hear that you've been pulling for Earnhardt!" They all laughed as the amazing interlude came to a close when the car slowly pulled away.

At the time, Tim's evening with his fans meant nothing to me. But in recent years, I have developed a strong appreciation for him and other drivers like him, who take a moment from their lives to give fans a great moment in their lives. Richard Petty is like that. At the beginning of his career, he deliberately developed an elaborate, beautiful signature for autographs. It is so fancy that it takes him a good fifteen or twenty seconds to write. He has given so many autographs that he has probably spent a full year of his life just signing his name! But I once heard him say, "If people care enough to want my autograph, then I want to give them one that's special and a nice keepsake!"

What a great attitude! Richard and the entire Petty family handle fame so well and so graciously. The constant demands of fame are never treated as an inconvenience. There are few people more famous or recognizable in the United States than Richard Petty. With his cowboy hat, sunglasses, and brilliant smile, he is an icon who is recognized even by folks who aren't racing fans. Imagine five decades of being stared at, being hounded, shaking hands, and signing autographs. Many people would tire of it after a couple of years and perhaps become reclusive. Not the King. He doesn't thrive on it as Tim did, but he certainly accepts the responsibility that comes with his phenomenal career. He and his wife, Lynda, have done a fine job of teaching their children, too, to respect the fans who are responsible for the wonderful lifestyle they have. Kyle, a carbon copy of his dad with the dark hair and that smile, is always enthusiastic and friendly to fans.

"I'm bad about remembering people when they come through an autograph line," Kyle once remarked. "People can come through my line, and if I met them five years before at another personal appearance, I remember them. I'm bad about that."

"You're *bad* about that?" I asked, teasingly. "Or you're *good* about that? I think that's a great trait because it makes people feel so good."

He shrugged modestly and grinned. "Yeah, I guess so. I just have a crazy mind that remembers people and they can never believe that I recognize them from years before."

Most of the NASCAR stars I have known were like that— friendly and willing to show their appreciation to the fans who pay the bills. It's elementary to say that you should always be kind and gracious. But remember that there are times when it's not easy— the driver's just fallen out of a race or dropped in the points standings, the sponsor's not happy or there isn't a sponsor to help foot the bills, or fatigue or illness is making life difficult. But as Mark Martin once commented, "You have to hide your grumpiness or shrug off a bad day because that might be the only time a person ever sees you, and you don't want that fan to go off and talk about how rude you were."

Dale Earnhardt, a man who was deeply grateful for his life and the opportunity to race for a living, said, "Them people in them stands make this possible for all of us. If it weren't for them buyin' tickets and souvenirs, wouldn't none of us be here. The best thing I can do is give 'em a show and treat 'em right." He staunchly believed that he had an obligation to entertain his fans.

I have watched these remarkable heroes for years, but I really came to appreciate them when I was thrust into a very minor version of this kind of spotlight with my first book. Their examples helped me enormously to stay focused and remember to be grateful to each person who spent hard-earned dollars to purchase my book and enable me to make a living by doing what I love. I always remember my friends like Earnhardt and Petty, who taught me to "give 'em a show and treat 'em with kindness, because if it weren't for them, where would you be?"

Regardless of what business you're in, always remember that somebody's money somewhere makes your livelihood possible. The most gracious thing we can all do in life is to have an attitude of gratitude and treat our customers, clients, fans, or patients with thoughtfulness and kindness, just the way Richard Petty treats his fans.

Gratitude is also important because it joyfully permeates our being and draws more good things to us. It's like an incredibly powerful magnet. Don't wait, however, for these things to fall into your lap—go out and use that great attitude to make them happen. It's simple—to have more for which to be grateful, we must first be grateful for what we have.

THE MEASURE OF SUCCESS

John Jarrard could barely contain his glee. In fact, he did not contain it at all—he let out a whoop and a holler that pierced my eardrum. I pulled the phone away from my head until the cheering was over. When it stopped, I deadpanned, "So, I take it that you're excited?"

"Excited? Huh, yeah, I think you could say that," he replied, laughing. "I can't believe I'm going to Talladega! Man, this is great!"

"But remember," I intoned, "you have to sing for your supper."

"Not a problem, I promise."

I first met John when he was a struggling songwriter hoping to make it in Nashville one day and I, a college student, was working part time at a radio station in our hometown. Over the years, we occasionally crossed paths, although he had moved to Nashville to follow his dreams and I moved around the country on a regular basis. By the time I placed this particular call to him in the spring of 1988, John Jarrard was one of the hottest songwriters in Nashville, having already chalked up number one hits for Alabama, Don Williams, Conway Twitty, and others. This was, however, just the beginning of a momentous career in which he would continue to churn out hits and become a wealthy man, not just in dollars but in the way that counts most—he was able to follow his dream *and* make money at it.

With his talent and incredible perseverance, John led a charmed life, but fate pulled one cruel trick on him. When he was in his mid-twenties, he lost his eyesight in a demonic battle with diabetes. He still had partial sight when I met him, but it had already started to disintegrate, and within a couple of years it was gone completely. John was unfazed by what he saw as a minor inconvenience and continued to pursue life in an enthusiastic, happy manner. A friend of mine, a preeminent music executive in Nashville, told me that he used to look out his window and see John tapping his way down Music Row with his white cane, knocking on doors and pitching his music to record executives. Loss of eyesight could not halt the vision he had for his future.

John, too, was one of the biggest stock car fans I have ever met. He loved racing as much as he loved music—maybe even more. And if you had asked him, he probably would have said that the song of which he was the proudest was not his platinum George Strait hit but rather the one he had written to commemorate Dale Earnhardt's third championship in 1987.

So, as we prepared for Race Fever Night at the Alabama Institute for the Deaf and Blind in 1988, it occurred to me that we should ask John to perform some of the big hits he'd written. He could inspire the school's children with his accomplishments, give the crowd some of Nashville's top-quality music, and pay a visit to the racetrack. It was a win-win for everyone.

John was all atwitter that night as we waited at the motel for my date, Alan Kulwicki, to pick us up. "I can't believe that I'm actually goin' to meet Alan Kulwicki," John kept saying with a smile that stretched from ear to ear. "Man, this is just too much."

Reactions like that always amazed me because I had long before reached the point of taking my racing friends for granted. What really astonished me was that John, the hit songwriter, who rubbed elbows with the biggest stars in Nashville, was still fired up over meeting a NASCAR driver.

Alan arrived and was immediately thrilled that John was so excited to meet him. So, in high spirits, we climbed into a brand-new Thunderbird and headed to the school. Now, Alan was a superb driver on the racetrack, but he wasn't quite as good on a backwoods highway. He tended to let the car drift from side to side as though he refused to be corralled by such a small area; he was used to having the full width of the track. (Riding with Tim Richmond, on the other hand, was like gliding on smooth silk. I have never ridden with a better road driver than Tim.) But that night, Alan was talking and as we traveled the rural highway, he kept drifting over the yellow line. I kept touching his arm or knee and whispering urgently, "Alan, watch it!"

Finally, I said over my shoulder to John and his wife Beth in the back seat, "John, are you getting motion sick back there?" Alan was not amused.

John, however, saved the day with his quick, heartfelt reply. "I can't see it but I can feel it and all I can say is he's Alan Kulwicki and he can drive any way he wants. I'm just happy to be here in the same car with him!"

John was a big success that night and an even greater inspiration as he played his guitar and sang his hits. Earlier, I had told him the story of being at dinner with Darrell and Stevie Waltrip a couple of weeks earlier in North Wilkesboro, North Carolina. As we left the restaurant, Darrell, a big country music fan, was singing John's latest hit, "She's Not in Love Any More," then a current top-ten record by Charley Pride. That night, as John concluded his miniconcert, he told that story to the audience, all the time grinning beatifically as though it were the greatest accomplishment of his life. "I've had songs recorded by people like Alabama, Conway Twitty, Don Williams, and other big stars," he said. "But, folks, you *know* you've made it when *Darrell Waltrip* sings one of your songs."

That story still delights me because it reminds me that we all have different measures of success. The confident person measures his success by what is important to him, not others. What might be considered losing to one person is winning to another. When Dave Marcis, a grizzled veteran, was approaching sixty, he was thrilled to make the field without using a provisional start (a position earned by a driver's performance the previous year and used when his speed isn't fast enough to make the field or he wrecks his car). Jeff Gordon, on the other hand, would be loath to take a provisional or even to qualify thirtieth. Over the years, I watched Kulwicki, the Elliotts, Dale Jarrett, Davey Allison, and others come into the sport and work their way to the top, one level at a time. First, they started out, just hoping to make the field. Then, they wanted to make the field *and* finish the race. I remember Alan finishing twentieth in one race, his best outcome to that point, and being as thrilled as when he later won his first race in Phoenix. They peel through the different levels until their goal is to win the race and, eventually, the championship.

This was a great lesson to a youngster like me. Until those years of observation, I thought you just barreled out of the starting gate with anything you did and went straight for the top. But as I watched those who were destined for stardom chip through smaller goals to large ones, I realized that the true path to great success is a journey of failures and small successes strung together.

While I was working on this book, John Jarrard died from complications of his diabetes, a disease that took his sight, kidneys, legs, and a finger but never his dignity, optimism, or confidence in himself. Since compiling this book required conjuring up my memories of Alan, Davey, Tim, Earnhardt and others who have passed away, I was already pretty glum about the great people I have known, loved and lost. I couldn't believe that I would have to write about yet another friend now departed. Yet, as I mulled over John and the contribution that his life made to my education, I realized that with his death, he had taught me one last wonderful lesson—it isn't the quantity of our years that matter, it's the quality. John was a small-town boy who followed his heart and dreams to Nashville and to spectacular success. Nothing came between him and his dream. The same can be said about Alan, Tim, Davey, and Dale.

But still the best lesson I learned from John Jarrard was measuring success on our own terms rather than society's—knowing, for example, that being a stay-at-home mom who raises well-balanced adults who contribute significantly to the world can be as important as being a researcher who is looking for a cure for cancer. We should all take a moment to stop and celebrate those moments of success that mean so much to us. Most important, we should take joy in what we see as success even if the rest of the world doesn't see it our way.

LAUGHTER IN THE FAST LANE

I only made Alan Kulwicki laugh once. The other times, the best I could get was a slight, tight smile, so small that it was barely noticeable. That's why the memory of that one laugh is so vivid. Oddly enough, I wasn't even trying to be funny, because with Alan, I had long before given up on that.

Alan loved classy things. He wore Italian leather shoes and always carried a spiffy leather briefcase even when, for him, every penny counted. I love expensive sunglasses and always have several pairs. On that historic laugh-making day, Alan stopped to talk with me, and the first words out of his mouth were, "I like those sunglasses. Very nice." He nodded with approval.

"Thank you." I smiled pretentiously then continued, "They're Laura Biagotti." At that time, she was a little-known Italian designer and had just launched a line of sunglasses. But to illustrate that you can take the girl out of the country but not vice versa, I mispronounced her name, calling it Bia-*ja*-ti. It sounded more exotic that way. Of course, I could have said that to any other driver or crew member in the garage, and no one else would have called me on it. But Alan knew better.

He looked mildly puzzled. "Bia-*ja*-ti? Hmmm," he murmured thoughtfully. "Are you sure that's how you pronounce it? I thought it was Bia-*gaw*-ti."

"Alan," I replied, quickly and evenly, putting my hands on my hips. "It doesn't matter how you *pronounce* them as long as you can *afford* them!"

That's when he laughed. I was so excited that I danced around, then grabbed him by the shoulders and jabbered happily, "You laughed! You really laughed at me!" After my singsong recital and jig, he was still laughing when he walked away. For my part, I thought seriously of having a T-shirt printed up that boasted, "I Made Alan Kulwicki Laugh!"

Two things are mighty important to having a successful, happy life, with the emphasis on "happy." And, not surprisingly, they both have to do with laughter and fun.

First, choose a job that is fun. Life is too short to have to "work" for a living. I've had a couple of jobs that were nothing but work and misery, in which I considered the completion of each day to be a hard-earned triumph. There have also been many times that I was so busy having fun with my "job" that I either forgot my payday or didn't have time to spend the money! I was fortunate to be a sportswriter while still in college, then stumble into sports marketing. Imagine being paid to be at Winston Cup races when other people are spending their hard-earned money and using their leisure time to be there. I watched many people like Dale Earnhardt and Kenny Schrader, who would rather race than eat or sleep, have fun making a living—and a darn good one, too. It's that simple. Determine what you love to do, then figure out a way to make a living doing that. Look at all the people who make annual six-figure incomes by fishing! Those are the people who turned their hobby into their job.

Regardless of what you do, have fun doing it and always find a way to laugh. Humor is the best stress reducer in the world and helps us to survive trying times. Those of us who were involved with the Darrell Waltrip–driven, Rick Hendrick–owned Tide team of 1989 have found ways to laugh at something that was far from funny when it happened.

That year turned out to be one of the best of Darrell's career, beginning with a Daytona 500 victory in February. In May, we were in Charlotte for the high-paying Winston, and Darrell was the one to beat that day. His car was perfect, and his driving was flawless. We were all starting to gear up for a coveted trip to Winner's Circle as Darrell headed for the white flag. When he came out of the fourth turn, though, a hard-charging Rusty Wallace caught Darrell's car in the rear quarter panel and sent him spinning across the track and down through the grass on the front straightaway. It was close to a replay of the incident between Elliott and Earnhardt a couple of years earlier, except that this time no one saw it coming. I tensed up as I felt a wave of rage sweep through our pit.

"Oh, no," I mumbled under my breath, knowing that I was about to face the toughest challenge for every publicist—damage control. Darrell Waltrip was colorful and often irrepressible. As a reporter, I had loved that, always knowing that I could count on Darrell for the kind of quote that would spruce up the blandest story. As a publicist representing his sponsor, though, I often cringed at those colorful remarks. Isn't it funny how something we once loved can turn on us?

That day, while the crew members geared up to face off with Rusty's crew, I took a deep breath, then took off in a hard run to the garage—yes, I had on high heels—knowing that my one chance for deliverance from disaster was to get to Darrell before the press did. That was a challenge, because ABC Sports was carrying the race live for the first time, and more electronic and print media were present than ever before. While Rusty took the checkered flag for the victory and Darrell seethed (rightly so), I raced against time. Amazingly, I made it to the garage just as Darrell's brightly colored car headed toward the garage stall. I was the first one to reach him.

Someone tossed me a bottle of Gatorade, and I reached in to release the protective window net as Darrell took off his helmet. As I thrust the bottle toward him, I stuck my head in the window and frantically pleaded, "Please, *please* be careful what you say. Calm down some before you get outta the car." Though his jaw was clenched in anger, so tightly that the muscles were twitching, he stared straight ahead and nodded silently.

For years, I have watched fictional television portrayals of people being mobbed by media after leaving a courtroom, a ballpark, or the like. I used to shake my head in amazement and say, "In all my years as a reporter or publicist, I have never seen that happen." After that day in Charlotte, I can say this no longer. While I was pleading with Darrell to calm down, I was being crushed against the racecar by a mass of reporters and television cameramen. There were at least forty of them, trying to get to Darrell, and the only thing between them was a five-foot-two slip of a girl. I felt the raw-edged bones of my hips grinding painfully against the car. After a couple of minutes, Darrell took a deep breath and said, "Okay, I'm ready." He handed me the bottle of Gatorade, and I turned, as best I could, to the churning mass and commanded, "Okay, stand back and give him room to get outta the car!"

They moved back slightly as Darrell pulled his six-foot-one frame through the window. He took back the Gatorade and swallowed another sip as the reporters screamed questions, the most prominent being, "What do you think about what Rusty did to you?"

Darrell then uttered what has become one of the most famous quotes in Winston Cup history, "I hope he *chokes* on that $200,000!" (Several years later, when Darrell retired from racing, Rusty presented him with a bag of fake money and quipped, "Well, I *didn't* choke on that $200,000!")

No sooner had those words left Darrell's mouth than two huge North Carolina state troopers mercifully appeared to escort him back to his hauler. As each trooper took an arm, Darrell—thank God—remembered me. He reached behind him, grabbed my hand,

and, as they pulled him through the restless crowd, brought me with him. Within seconds, the troopers delivered us safely to the Tide truck, where Darrell, followed by a couple of team people, immediately retreated to the closeted lounge at the back of the truck. The reporters had followed us. Standing at the front of the media mob was Dr. Jerry Punch, one of the sport's favorite television broadcasters. Although Jerry, an emergency room doctor who moonlighted on weekends as a racing announcer, was well-known for his role on ESPN, he had just signed a new deal with ABC, and this race was his first outing with the network. He stood there with an ABC mike in his hand and a cameraman at his side. There is no one better liked or more respected in the sport than Jerry. He has long been one of my favorite people. So it was hard to say "no" when he motioned me over and asked if he could talk to Darrell.

"I'm sorry, Jerry," I said in a low voice. "But it just isn't a good idea." Jerry nodded and smiled faintly. I knew he understood. But, apparently, his new bosses didn't, for I looked over to see Jerry pressing his finger on the earpiece that connected him to the broadcast producers. He listened intently, then said a few words into the radio. I knew exactly what was happening. The people on the production team were telling Jerry that they needed to hear from Darrell before they had to switch to golf. Poor Jerry was in the toughest of spots. He was too nice to intrude, yet he was being pressured by his new bosses. It's hard to be a great reporter if you're a good-hearted person, the kind who is thoughtful. You want to back away and leave people alone in times of emotional distress. It was a tough decision, but Jerry did what any paid professional would: he attempted to do his job. He motioned to his cameraman, and they gingerly stepped up on the truck. I shook my head but didn't say a word or try to stop him. I knew he had a job to do. I didn't interfere, because of our friendship and my respect for him. Jerry and his cameraman had inched a few steps past me when a key member of the team, who could be very volatile, saw the intruders. While the camera was rolling, he lost it. He ran over to a cabinet, jerked open the door, and pulled out a swaybar, a metal bar that is used in the setup of the car for weight transference. The particular one that the crew guy was holding was about three feet long and a solid inch in diameter, and it weighed probably twenty or twenty-five pounds—in other words, a deadly weapon. He drew the bar back over his head and charged toward Jerry and the cameraman, screaming profanities and, in short, telling them to get off the truck. It didn't take a lot of persuasion. The television guys scrambled away quickly, and poor Jerry looked heartbroken because he had upset someone.

Mission accomplished, the guy, still holding the swaybar, looked over at me and angrily shouted, "Keep everybody off this truck! Everybody!"

I replied dryly, "Oh, I don't think you have to worry about that anymore!"

Immediately, I began to worry about what the corporate executives were going to say. Keep in mind that the incident was captured on video for posterity, and for future broadcast use and it wasn't exactly great public relations. I formed my argument—I was not big enough or strong enough to deal with a crazed madman who was wielding a swaybar. I always believe in being prepared for the worst but praying for the best; usually, I settle for something in between. Sure enough, one of the Tide executives did have a comment about it. He was the same one who always teased me about how quickly I slapped one of our Tide hats on a driver, owner, or crew member when the cameras approached. Perhaps you've noticed how drivers are always wearing hats embroidered with the names of their sponsors? Well, there often is someone like me lurking nearby to ensure that they have a hat on at the right moment. When I was working with both Tide and Folgers, I always had one hat of each threaded through my belt loops. Tide is a Procter and Gamble product, along with practically every detergent on the market. One big competitor, however, that Procter and Gamble doesn't own is Fab, which is owned by Colgate-Palmolive.

"Ronda, could I talk to you about the excitement on the Tide truck after the Winston?" the P&G exec asked.

I swallowed and immediately began sputtering my defense.

"Wait a minute!" He held up a hand and laughed. "I don't expect you to take care of a madman."

I blinked hard. You never knew what to expect from the corporate folks. "You don't?"

"Not at all." He smiled warmly, and I relaxed. Then he continued. "I was just wondering if the next time one of our guys goes crazy and tries to kill a cameraman and reporter live on television, could you possibly put a *Fab* hat on his head?"

What a wonderful way to defuse a tense situation—find a way to laugh about it.

A beautiful April day in Martinsville, Virginia, provided me with two entertaining, even hilarious memories. The first was the most embarrassing thing that ever happened to me. My underwear fell off in front of an audience that was 99 percent men.

One of my Buick drivers, Morgan Shepherd, had won the pole for the event, and with Morgan's previous track record at Martinsville, I knew we had a good chance to win the race. As a result, I was feeling quite good as I pranced into the track that morning. I was passing the small booth where team credentials were being picked up by a long line of guys when suddenly I felt something around my ankles, only a moment before I tripped. I had on an ankle-length, straight, pale-yellow skirt that was translucent when the sun hit it just right, so I had put on a half slip that day, then pulled the form-fitting skirt over my head and hips. Apparently, the skirt was so straight that when I pulled it down, it dragged the half slip past my hips. Every time I moved, the slip edged lower toward my feet. When I looked down, my slip was bunching around my ankles. It was half on, half off, still clinging above my knees but pooling on the ground around my feet. I looked around quickly, but there was nowhere to hide—plus there were men everywhere, and they were starting to look, point, and laugh. I was horrified. Desperate, I spotted an old station wagon parked next to the credentials booth. I staggered around to it, but it gave me coverage from only one direction. A woman was passing by and I stopped her—"Ma'am can you help me? Would you stand there and shield me a little?" She did, as I yanked the slip off, accompanied by cheers and cat-calls. I heard about that for weeks in the garage.

What happened later that day was one of the funniest things I ever saw. I had gone over to the hospitality area, which was on a hill directly behind the back straightaway, to have lunch with my colleagues and watch the race. Between the hospitality area and the back straight were railroad tracks. There were three or four of us from our office having lunch and socializing when our pilot drove up in a rental car. The hospitality parking area was a long distance away, so he decided to make his own parking space: he parked directly on the tracks.

"Bud, *what* are you *doing*?" someone asked, calling him by a nickname I had given him.

Bud cupped a hand to his ear—he was half deaf anyway—and responded over the roar of racecars, "What?" He was walking rapidly toward us, so she waited until he was closer to ask, "Why are you parking on the railroad tracks?"

"That's the only place to park. Besides, I'm parking close by so all of you won't have so far to walk to the car when we leave." His goofy smile widened. "Do you know how far hospitality parking is from here? But don't you worry—I'm taking care of you."

"What if a train comes?" I asked.

"Aw, there aren't any trains going to come through here on Sunday." Where he got this information, I have no idea.

One of our bosses, a tough man unforgiving of mistakes and human error, was absorbing the situation. At best, he was always skeptical. At worst, he was cynical.

"Bud, I'm telling you," he began in a no-nonsense tone, "that rental car had better not get hit by a train. If it does, you're fired!"

"Boss, don't you worry. A train isn't going to hit that car. You can trust me. I know what I'm talking about." That was when I began to worry. I loved Bud. He brought laughter to some of my darkest days. But, in all honesty, Bud *never* knew what he was talking about.

When we had finished eating and Bud was helping us clean up the table, for some reason I happened to turn my eyes toward the tracks. I was so horrified that it took a second to get my voice.

"Bud!" I finally managed to scream. "There's a train coming!"

Bud's goofy smile instantly disappeared when he saw the train about a hundred fifty yards away, a train with a warning whistle that we hadn't been able to hear over the whirl of race engines. He dropped a handful of dirty plates and napkins and took off running to that rental car while our boss was hollering, "Bud, I told you about parking that car on the tracks!"

Now, wouldn't you think that *if* someone was going to park smack in the middle of some train tracks, he wouldn't lock the car? And if he *did* lock the car, he would not drop the keys in his deep pants pocket from which he could not retrieve them while trying to outrun a train? Well, if you did think that, it is because you don't know Bud. I was surprised that he even knew where the keys were. He slid to a stop at the door of the car and began frantically digging for the keys. He found them. He dropped them. Then he fumbled so badly as he tried to get the key into the lock that it was like watching the Keystone Kops.

We were scared to death and screaming, "Bud, let it go!" "Get away from there!" "Bud, please! Please come back! The train is right behind you."

Like the rest of us, though, Bud was more scared of our boss than of several tons of speeding hot metal. He would rather have died than let the rental car be crushed after he was warned about it. By some miracle, he got the door unlocked, climbed into the car, and drove it off the tracks, just seconds short of being smashed to death. He parked the car several yards from the track, and when he emerged from the driver's side he was grinning with great satisfaction, his light-blue eyes twinkling with delight. He strolled toward us with a cocky swagger, his strawberry-blond mustache, which was always a bit too long and scraggy, twitching from the jumping nerve above his upper lip.

"I told you that I had this all under control," he said through quivering lips. With that, I fell to my knees, weak with relief, then collapsed in gales of laughter. With Bud safe from both the train and our boss, the entire scene became hilarious. We started laughing, and several years later we still laugh whenever we retell the story.

There have been many times when we had to laugh at mishaps and setbacks. Once, Mark Martin was the Winner's Circle driver for Sears Point Raceway in Sonoma. We were glad of that opportunity because it gave us exposure in the huge San Francisco market. The media representative for the track called me and asked if we would consider doing a press conference in Sacramento, which was a couple of hours away from San Francisco.

"No," I responded. "It's too far."

"Would you do it if I hired a helicopter and flew us there? It'll take only about twenty-five minutes by air." She kept pitching, and she was working so hard to make it easy for us that I gave in and called Mark to convince him.

"Listen, it'll add only a couple of hours to our day, and it'll give us great exposure in the state capital. It's easy. An absolute cinch." This was the year that Mark was a top contender for the championship, so there were a lot of media demands piled onto his already hectic schedule. Both Mark and I were trying to keep the commitments to a minimum and make the championship race the top priority. Mark, always amicable, heard me out, and although he protested slightly, he finally agreed. After a morning of television and radio in San Francisco, we met the helicopter in the parking lot of Candlestick Stadium. The flight to Sacramento was extremely interesting because a devastating earthquake had hit the city several months before, and the pilot flew us over the most heavily damaged sites. We landed at a softball complex where a car and driver were waiting to take Mark; his wife, Arlene; the track's media director; and me to the press conference.

The press conference was a bust. Only one guy from a radio station attended. I was more embarrassed than the track's media person, because I had talked Mark into it. Nonetheless, he remained a good sport and shrugged it off. This was very good, since the worst was still to come. When we arrived back at the softball complex, our helicopter was missing. The pilot was supposed to have waited there until we returned, but a couple of phone calls revealed that producer George Lucas had called for him, so he had flown back to pick Lucas up and left us stranded. We waited at that complex for over two hours while the San Francisco company scrounged up another helicopter and pilot for us. Arlene and I seethed, fussed, and fumed while Mark remained completely calm.

"Mark, aren't you upset about this?" Arlene asked.

He shrugged. "Naw. This is an absolute cinch. Just ask Ronda."

There was something so comical about the way he said it, that suddenly we burst out laughing as we realized how funny the entire situation was.

"Well, at least the pilot abandoned us for a famous movie mogul," I commented. "Think how much worse we would feel if he had left us for a nobody."

"Yeah," Mark agreed. "Instead, *we're* the *nobodies* he left for the *somebody*!"

Of course, from that point on, whenever I called Mark to pitch a "no lose" situation, he always asked, "You mean this is one of those deals that's a 'cinch' just like Sacramento?"

Of the drivers I worked with, no one ever made me laugh more than Kenny Schrader, a simple guy from a blue-collar Missouri background. Despite the wealth and fame that have come his way, Kenny has remained completely humble and unpretentious. He doesn't hesitate to make himself the butt of the joke, as he would do whenever I used what he called "them big words that I don't know." In one conversation, I had used both "analytical" and "equate." He interrupted as usual to say, "Okay, I don't know what them words mean. You're gonna have to wait while I get a dictionary."

He was hilarious about it. So, the next time I called I used another unfamiliar word. Kenny quickly stepped in and said, "There you go again. Is this gonna be another one of them conversations where we have to analytiquate?"

I fell off the chair laughing, realizing that he had combined "analytical" and "equate" to form a new word. It was actually quite brilliant. I love Kenny's blended word so much that I use it often. And know what? No one ever questions whether or not it's a legitimate word. God bless people like Kenny Schrader, who never take themselves too seriously.

I always considered Michael Waltrip to be the king of comedy. He was best friends with Kyle Petty, and together they were basically the court jesters. I was close to the Waltrips, including Michael's parents, and I suspect that one or more people in the family kept urging Michael, a fun-loving bachelor, to ask me out. Since Michael was handsome, personable, and a hotshot racecar driver, he was always popular with the ladies, beautiful ones. One year when we were in Daytona for the 500, I was sitting on the pit wall during qualifying when Michael meandered over and sat down next to me. We chatted for a long time and then he astounded me by asking me to be his date for a Pontiac dinner on Saturday night before the 500.

I shook my head and slapped my ear, certain that I was hearing incorrectly. I just looked at him, but he didn't flinch. Finally, I said, "And the punch line *is*?"

"No punch line," he replied quite seriously. "I want you to be my date on Saturday night. Will you go?"

I was still very skeptical, but Michael's personality is so charming that I knew I would have fun. So, despite my skepticism, I said yes.

"You're not gonna believe this," I announced to the rest of the Waltrips when I stopped by Darrell and Stevie's motor coach. "Guess who asked me out." They were as shocked as I was. But Michael's mama was very pleased and excited.

The night of the date arrived, and Michael called from the lobby. I was wearing a white, buttery-soft leather skirt and a black evening sweater accented with generous amounts of white mohair and rhinestones. When I stepped off the elevator, Michael's eyes widened.

"Wow! You look beautiful." From that first moment on, he was the most perfect date I have ever had. He was the kind of courteous gentleman who wins women's hearts in romance novels. He was a textbook example of the perfect way to treat a lady. I felt that I was floating through a surreal dream because it was a side of Michael that I had never suspected existed. At the cocktail reception we hooked up with Kyle and his wife Pattie, who was also intrigued with Michael's solicitous, thoughtful manner.

Michael placed his hand on the small of my back and leaned over to ask, "Would you like something to drink?"

"I'd like a glass of white wine, please."

"Certainly. Pattie, may I get you anything?"

She stared at him with a dazed look and mumbled, "Kyle will go with you and get something for me." As the duo walked off, she was still staring in disbelief.

"What," she asked, "is going on with him?"

I laughed. "I don't know, but I can tell you this—he is the most perfect date I have ever had. I've never seen a man more thoughtful or courteous." For the remainder of the evening, he was just as wonderful. When I excused myself from the dinner table to go to the powder room, he arose and helped with my chair. When I returned, he arose again and pulled out my chair. He opened the car door for me every time I got in or out. When we arrived back at the hotel in the beautiful Trans Am he was driving, he said, "Wait a second so I can come around and open your door."

The perfect date ended with the perfect first-date good-bye. He walked me to the elevator and, standing a respectful distance away, took my hand and said in a proper tone, "I had a wonderful time. Thank you very much for joining me tonight." Then, he leaned over and kissed me pristinely on the cheek.

Still tremendously amused and feeling that I was in a movie, I smiled and said, "Michael, I had a lovely time. You are the most perfect gentleman I have ever been out with."

"Really?" he asked, raising his eyebrows in thrilled surprise.

"Really," I said firmly with a smile.

He smiled proudly. "Thank you." He turned to leave. "Well, I'll see you at the track tomorrow."

"Okay. Good night," I said as he walked away. About twenty feet away, he stopped and turned back to me.

"Uh," he began in a wistful, timid voice. "Ronda, will you do me a favor?"

"Certainly, Michael. Anything. What is it?"

The expression on his face was completely earnest as he finally, albeit unintentionally, explained his real motive for asking me out. "When you get to the track tomorrow, would you mind finding my mama and telling *her* what a *perfect gentleman* I was tonight?"

I could only nod "yes" as I fell against the wall, doubled over with laughter, as my perfect date walked out into the starry night.

NOT FOR MEN ONLY

Mark Martin and I were sitting on the back of his race hauler in the garage of the Daytona International Speedway on a perfectly clear, pleasant February morning. It was a few days before the Daytona 500, which is, of course, the sport's biggest event. Although I handled the racing public relations for Folgers, and Mark and the Roush team were sponsored by this brand of coffee, we weren't talking business. We were chitchatting about life in general and watching the activity of a busy garage as team members, many carrying items like shocks, springs, and carburetors, scurried back and forth busily between haulers, racecars, and other teams.

From the corner of my eye, I saw Davey Allison, a couple of trucks away, dash out from the small alleyway created by his hauler and another truck. Davey, with rounded shoulders and a slight stoop that was identical to his dad, Bobby, was a young man in a hurry. Always. Although he was somewhat tall and fairly skinny, his stride wasn't long. It was a series of quick, shuffling steps that produced a small bobbing effect as he rushed through the garage. He spotted me and stopped suddenly as a wide, playful grin stretched across his face.

"Heeyyy Roonnnda," he drawled in a boyishly flirtatious tone.

I smiled coquettishly and playfully batted my eyelashes. "Heeeyyyy Daaavey." He had arrived in Daytona that year for the new race season, recently separated and soon to be divorced, so we had spent the previous week in a playful flirtation that we exaggerated comically. He hurried over to us, and Mark greeted him with his standard, "Hey, man!"

The height of the hauler put us level with Davey's chest, so he propped his elbow on my knee and leaned toward us.

"What are y'all doin'?" he asked.

"Aw, just watching all these guys try to figure out what's wrong with their cars," Mark responded. He stopped and chortled. " 'Bout what my guys are doin' over there. How you runnin'?"

Davey shrugged. "We changed the setup some yesterday, and it ran a little better in practice this morning."

The previous day Davey had shared with me an amazing trick he had learned, and I wanted him to show it off in front of Mark. I nudged Mark with my elbow and said with a wink, "Watch this."

I put my hand on Davey's shoulder and motioned with a throw of my head toward Mark. In the same soliciting tone that I use to coax my puppy, I urged, "Davey, tell Mark what I had on yesterday."

Mark raised his eyebrows and looked vaguely puzzled. I'm sure that he couldn't have cared less what I had worn the previous day. But that wasn't the point. After all, how often can a guy remember what someone else was wearing? How many times do guys even notice? Without a second's hesitation, Davey looked Mark square in the eyes and said, "She had on a yellow silk blouse, black pants, and a bright-blue coat that came down long."

Mark looked at me accusingly and remarked plaintively, "You rehearsed that."

I glowed at a stunned Mark with a "ta da" smile. Davey cocked his head to the side and announced, "And I can also tell you what you were wearing day before yesterday."

It was my turn to be skeptical. My smile vanished, and my jaw dropped. "You cannot."

"Can, too," Davey replied confidently. He paused for a second, squinted one eye as he looked skyward, and then described an ensemble. "Now, ain't that right?"

I was stunned. I certainly had an outfit like that, but I couldn't remember when I had worn it. "I don't know," I said slowly, shaking my head. "I don't remember."

"Yeah, you do," he persisted. "Don't you remember that we were over in the Grand National garage and that TV guy from Birmingham told you that he liked that color?"

I snapped my fingers. "That's right! That's exactly what I had on."

Mark, still bewildered, slowly shook his head in amazement. "Man, if you're paying *this* much attention to the setup on your racecar, we're all in *big* trouble on Sunday!"

And that, I surmise, is probably the reason that women had to fight their way into the NASCAR garage in the 1970s. It makes a lot of sense. A woman, especially one who is a rare presence in an arena of men, can be a distraction. Surely you've noticed. From the very beginning, NASCAR made it clear that they were serious about the business of racing, even if racing was a form of entertainment. The sport has always been ruled with a firm professional hand and a no-nonsense approach.

Consider, if you will, the letter I received immediately following the first Daytona 500 that I covered as a reporter. It was from the speedway's public relations office, and it requested copies of stories that I had written during the event. I covered many major sporting events, but I never received another similar request. It was clear that they wanted to make sure that my press credential had been used for the proper purpose—gathering news stories, not manhunting. The year was 1985, and since Bill Elliott had dominated

SpeedWeeks that year by winning the pole, one of the Twin 125 qualifiers, and the race, and he and I had also collaborated on a daily diary, I had plenty to send. In fact, it was a huge, bulging package with about three dozen stories—so much stuff that the speedway's public relations director wrote back and basically said, "Okay. Okay. Enough. I get the message loud and clear," and then he added graciously, "Please know that you are always welcome at this speedway and that you will always have press credentials."

By the time I arrived on the NASCAR scene, though, life for women on the circuit was a breeze. You can chalk this up to a handful of women such as my good friends Deb Williams and Carolyn Rudd, who blazed the trail and bulldozed through the walls of resistance. Today, women are crucial to the economy and the well-being of the sport. Dozens of women now travel on the circuit as publicists, marketers, and reporters, whereas in the earlier days there were only a few of us. If people ever dare to dispute the importance of women to stock car racing, they have to look no further than the grandstands, where almost 50 percent of the spectators are women. An estimated 60 percent of the sport's souvenir dollars are spent by women and these women are extraordinarily loyal in dragging their dollars to America's cash registers to purchase the products of NASCAR sponsors. The birth of stock car racing is owed, undeniably, to men, but its substantial growth has been fed and nurtured by the love and loyalty of women.

Deb Williams, who began her long and illustrious career in Winston Cup racing as a reporter with the now all-but-defunct United Press International, will always remember picking up her press credentials for a race in 1980. The pit passes stated clearly, "No Women Allowed in the Pits." Of course, being the little bulldog she is, she certainly didn't let that pass and immediately lashed out against the track manager. His response? "Oh, we're not talking about women like you. We're talking about the other kind of women."

He was referring to what I call "pit bunnies." Most people in the sport call them "pit lizards." It's the NASCAR version of "groupies," a small circle of women who follow the circuit from track to track and along the way garner enough clout with different teams to get credentials. I have no idea how they fund this kind of freewheeling lifestyle. After all, have you ever tried to get a room in a tiny town like North Wilkesboro where motel rooms are normally $40 a night but become $100 rooms with a three-night minimum when a Winston Cup race arrives? Regardless of where you live, you have to fly to at least half of the races. Then there is the cost of food. It's incredible.

Winston Cup wives don't much like pit bunnies, and some wives are even haughty toward them. But I actually liked most of the ones I've met. They almost always have a heart of gold, and they just want to be included in a glorious world with wonderful people. Of course, I have known men who did the same thing, becoming volunteer pit crew members. They take vacation time, pay their own expenses, and work gratis, just to be near the center of the sport. For a team owner, it doesn't get better than free labor that pays its own way to the races. Only in NASCAR.

When go-kart champ Ricky Rudd went NASCAR racing in the mid-1970s, his dad sent along Ricky's big sister, Carolyn, to oversee the race team. Since Carolyn was in charge of the finances, she would have to sign the tickets for gas and tires. "I used to have to wait outside the garage because women couldn't have garage credentials—someone would have to bring the gas tickets over to me and push them through the fence for me to sign," Carolyn explained.

Not only would Carolyn eventually get garage credentials any time she desired, she would work vigilantly to bring sponsors into the sport in the mid-1980s. When Folgers, owned by Procter and Gamble, became the first major nontraditional sponsor to enter Winston Cup racing, Carolyn played a pivotal role in the development and implementation of its marketing strategy. It was such a success that P&G soon followed with Crisco and Tide, the grandfather of all its brands. Until that coffee brand appeared, the traditional sponsors were mostly automotive products bought by men, such as filters and gas additives, as well as brands of beer. The first major step away from those products had been soft drinks such as Mountain Dew, which, ironically, sponsored the car owned by Junior Johnson and driven by Darrell Waltrip. Johnson, of course, had been a fabled moonshine runner turned stock car driver who was immortalized in Tom Wolfe's famous article for *Esquire* magazine in the 1970s. Johnson, who had spent time in prison after being nabbed by the feds for his moonshine endeavors, received a full presidential pardon and helped to perpetuate the legend of NASCAR. "Mountain dew" was another slang term for moonshine.

The NASCAR world I knew from the beginning was one of equality. In those days, it was only Deb and I among a regime of crusty, hard-talking, softhearted sports guys. But for me, the playing field was finally level. I had the same access to the drivers that every reporter had. Covering the Atlanta Braves, I had to wait outside the locker rooms until the players had showered and changed and were heading home. In the NASCAR garage, I could approach Richard Petty or David Pearson as easily as any of my peers. After having to work twice as hard for so long just to get the basic information for a story, I felt that the greasy, earsplittingly loud garage was my own personal paradise where drivers and crews welcomed me with patented Southern hospitality. One day I was walking through the garage in Rockingham, North Carolina, when I encountered team owner Richard Childress and photographer Dorsey Patrick, who had been one of the first women granted access to the garage. I stopped to talk to them, and Dorsey commented how hard Childress had fought for the inclusion of women in the sport.

"I'll never forget it," she said firmly. "He always believed that women deserved to be treated equally with men."

If anything, being a woman *helped* me on the circuit, because the guys would take extra time for me and would never consider waving me away when I needed an interview. Sometimes they would snap at male reporters and send them scurrying away and then, in the next instant, see me hovering nervously close by and wave me over with a big smile. The men, most of them gallant Southern gentlemen, seemed to have a primal instinct to help, protect, and respond in a courteous, thoughtful manner. They weren't territorial and weren't afraid that women would be the downfall of their sport. Instead, they were open-minded and intrigued by the new dimension of women in their world.

Early in my sportswriting career, I discovered that it was beneficial to dress as a woman and not a tomboy. I did not want to sacrifice my femininity to work in a man's world. I refused to compromise who I was. I also refused to give up my high heels! I found that men treated me with greater deference, respect, and generosity when I presented myself as a completely feminine woman. I believe that the innate chivalry in men emerges in a business world when they are reminded that they are dealing with a lady. But when a man sees a woman as "one of the guys," that's how she gets treated. The NASCAR garage has strict regulation for clothing, prohibiting shorts, open-toed shoes, and sleeveless shirts (not a big deal until you're in Daytona in the July heat). I adhered strictly to the dress code but improvised my own fashions, wearing jeans only during inclement weather. Of course, those long, straight skirts and three-inch heels could prove challenging at times when I had to race across the infield to reach a driver who had just crashed or race up through the grandstands to the press box. My most vivid memory of such a high-heel sprint is the Daytona Firecracker 400 in 1987.

I was the publicist for Buick Motorsports, over whose stable Bobby Allison reigned as king. One of my myriad responsibilities was to represent Buick in Winner's Circle and make certain that the driver and crew were photographed in Buick hats. I always left the box of hats on one of the race haulers and would retrieve them toward the end of the race, if needed, for Winner's Circle. Racers are notoriously superstitious, so it was forbidden to take the hats to pit road "in case" your car won. That, in essence, would jinx the car. Or that's what the team guys always said if they found a box of hats in the pits and our car had gotten outrun. It was just too much of a burden of guilt to bear, so I left the hats on the truck.

The Firecracker 400 is now a night event. But back then it was still run in the broiling July heat of the beachside city, and that clingy, wet steam was merciless. I was wandering between the pits of the various Buick teams, completely convinced that none of them would be going to Winner's Circle that day, when I stopped in Bobby Allison's pit with five laps to go in the race. I immediately noticed that the crew was tense and hand-wringingly anxious.

"What's wrong?" I asked one of the crew members.

"Nothin'. Just hopin' we can pull this off," he replied, not diverting his eyes from Bobby's red-and-white car zipping around the track. I looked at him as if he were an idiot, then glanced at the scoreboard, which showed Benny Parsons leading and Kenny Schrader running second. Bobby was nowhere in the Top 10.

I turned back and, shaking my head, said, "He's not gonna win. He's a lap down."

The crew member shook his head, still not looking at me as the scoreboard flashed two to go and Bobby passed Parsons. With that move, I and the rest of the spectators thought that Bobby had just moved to the tail end of the lead lap.

"He's not a lap down. He just took the lead. The scorers have got it wrong. He's about to win this thing!"

My heart stopped, suspended by fear, panic, and disbelief.

"Noooooo!!!" I screamed just as Bobby took the white flag to signal the beginning of the final lap. I couldn't believe the jam I was in. My job depended on whether or not I made it to Victory Lane in a timely manner with those darn hats. Bobby's pit was almost at the very end of pit row, which meant that it was a looonnnnngggg way to the garage and back to Winner's Circle, more than a mile. To complicate matters, I was wearing a straight skirt in which I could barely walk—but it looked good, so I tolerated it. It never occurred to me that I might have to run in it, or in the high heels I was wearing. Did I also happen to mention that it was hot enough to drop a champion racehorse on one of its best days? Quickly, my mind skittered through all these challenges and I reacted quickly. When the guy heard me scream "no" with such groaning desperation, he looked at me as though I were crazy for not wanting my driver to win.

"Are you sure?" I yelled in sheer terror. I wanted to make certain before I killed myself that I was dying for a winning racecar and not a losing one.

"Dead sure."

"Oh, my gawd!" I blurted as I turned to run. "Get on the radio and tell Bobby to take a slow victory lap," I hollered over my shoulder and took off as though I were trying to outrun a bullet.

I had gotten only about fifty yards when I heard an ear-splitting crash and turned to see Bobby taking the checkered flag while smoke billowed from the crashed metal of Parsons's and Schrader's cars. Those two, also unaware that Bobby was on the lead lap, thought they were racing for the win and had crashed each other within a few feet of the finish line. Schrader flipped spectacularly and skidded across the line on his roof in a made-for-television moment. Later, he would tell reporters that he had no idea that Bobby Allison was on the lead lap and that's why he had "let Bobby pass" without fighting for position. As soon as the two crashed, the yellow flag came out to fly simultaneously with the checkered and, thus, slowed down the field. That was a big miracle, because it gave me some additional time for my tottering sprint.

Unbelievably, I got to Winner's Circle only seconds behind Bobby, but I was a drenched, drooping mess with a soaked shirt, limp hair, and makeup that was running in dirty rivers down my face. I didn't look very good, but the hats were gorgeous (or so I thought) as they adorned the heads of Bobby and his crew. My job completed and saved, I found a corner of Winner's Circle and, without even the strength of a newborn kitten, sank wearily to the ground and then saturated my dry throat with a cold drink. Bobby spotted me soaking in my puddle as he was leaving for his post-race press conference. He stopped and grinned.

"You look like you've raced as hard as I have today."

"Harder," I muttered weakly.

"That so?" He arched his eyebrows and gave me that patented twinkle and glimmer.

I nodded. "At least you got to use tires in your race. I had to use high heels."

Femininity sometimes comes at the cost of comfort, and while sometimes it makes an easy job harder, it often makes a hard job easier. To this day, I practice what I learned in NASCAR—a well-heeled lady always gets the courtesy of gentlemen, so it's worth a little inconvenience.

TIM RICHMOND:

LIVING FAST, WITH SASS

Tim Richmond opened the door of his hotel room, dressed in a paisley print silk dressing robe. "Hey! Come on in," he motioned with a throw of his head. "I'm on the phone."

He ran his fingers through his longish light brown hair and padded barefooted across the carpet. His robe fell just below his knees, emphasizing calves so small that it seemed impossible to me there were any bones beneath the skin. They looked to be about six or seven inches in diameter and all I could think in my puzzlement was, "I have never seen legs so small in my life, not even on a pre-teen girl."

He flung himself down on the bed and propped himself up against a stack of pillows, leaning against the headboard as he talked to his sister in Ohio. They were discussing the latest drama of his life, which was unfolding here in Daytona Beach where the racing world was gathering for the prestigious 1988 Daytona 500.

A few days earlier, NASCAR had banned Tim from racing in the Busch Clash, a race reserved for pole winners from the previous season, after a drug test had yielded positive results. Indignant, outraged, and screaming that it was not true, Tim had retained lawyer Barry Slotnick and flown him to Daytona for a press conference to announce that Tim was filing suit against NASCAR. The ordeal made the front page or front sports page of every major newspaper in America. Eventually, a second test would prove that Tim was clean of any drugs and that his false positive had been due to the presence of over-the-counter medications. But Tim, too often a prisoner of a destructive kind of pride, did not surrender immediately. He continued with the lawsuit for several more months until NASCAR won a ruling forcing him to surrender his medical records. He steadfastly refused to do so, and the suit disintegrated. But on that February night, it was still a couple of days before the discovery of the false positive, and Tim was doing what he did best and most frequently—performing at center stage with all eyes drawn to him.

He was holed up at the Hilton, using one of his many aliases, protected by bodyguards and holding court for a small, select circle of friends. I had been one of the first summoned to appear before His Highness and, as usual, the prince knew he could count on me. I closed the door behind me, removed my coat, threw it over the sofa, then pulled the desk chair over next to the bed and listened as he talked.

Tim's sister, Sandy, asked to speak to me, and as Tim reached over to hand me the phone, his robe fell open several inches wide at the chest. I became transfixed by a perfectly round sore the size of a quarter, off-center on his right side. It looked like a burn, except it was precise in its roundness. Tim yawned repeatedly as I talked with Sandy, and when I hung up the phone, he stretched his arms over his head and arched his back. "I am so tired," he remarked lazily. "I slept all afternoon."

"You sleep the most of any person I've ever known," I commented dryly, thinking of all the times he had called me and said that either he had just awakened from a nap or he was going to take one.

"Yeah, I know." He shrugged and then spread his hands, palms up. "But what else have I got to do? I don't have a job, so I've just gotten lazy."

The previous year had been an emotional roller coaster for Tim, filled with tears, laughter, scandal, sympathy, and the kind of headlines that only the irrepressible star could generate. At the start of 1987, Tim had barely escaped death from a vicious double pneumonia that forced him to miss much of the first half of the season. Several pounds heavier, Tim had returned to run The Winston in Charlotte. He started second and finished third, but his comeback was bumped to the back pages, overshadowed by the more interesting story of the spectacular feud that erupted during the race between Dale Earnhardt and Bill Elliott.

But when Tim returned a month later for his first regular Winston Cup race, he took a back page to no one, winning in Pocono, Pennsylvania, the first time he strapped himself back into a racecar. He followed that stunning victory with another one the next week in Riverside, California. At one point in the Pocono race, he hunted down his favorite prey—Earnhardt—and toyed with him before snatching away the lead. The two competitors came down the front straight and Tim pulled up on Earnhardt's bumper so close that only the thinnest sliver of paper could have passed between the two cars. I have never seen such an amazing feat in a race. It took my breath away, and it grabbed the admiration of others who watched. In the stands and in the pits, people jumped to their feet for an exuberant standing ovation. Tim Richmond, the most dazzling of the NASCAR stars, was back in his best form. The Pocono victory was so emotional for Tim that he later admitted having cried when he saw the checkered flag. It was made sweeter when his close friends, including Earnhardt, joined him in Victory Lane. A smiling Bill Elliott, who lost the race to Tim by eight car lengths, pulled up beside him on the victory lap and saluted both his win and his bravado.

Tim was immeasurably talented. At thirteen, he learned to fly a plane. At sixteen, he was a championship high school track star and tailback whose jersey was reverently retired after four explosive years of weaving, dodging, and charging. By age seventeen, he had racked up a winner's reputation in the upper-crust world of horse shows, and at eighteen, he stepped into a sprint car that his dad had purchased for him. Then, one by one, he conquered Super Modified cars, Indy cars, and stock cars. He always firmly maintained that he could be a record-setting drag racer, too. There is no doubt in my mind that he was right. He was so athletically talented that nothing ever seemed challenging or difficult for him. Life came easy for Tim Richmond. It was death that came hard.

Life could also be tempestuous for Tim, because no matter how good his intentions were, he could never hold the car straight in the fast lane of his life. By the time we arrived in Watkins Glen, New York, to race five weeks after that Pocono win, he was on an obvious downward spiral. While a heavy rain fell in Watkins Glen, weather that would postpone the race by one day, talk from the idle racers centered on Tim's rumored incoherence. I heard the talk but didn't see Tim until early that evening in the lobby of the Corning Hilton. The elevator opened, and he staggered off, accompanied by two rather unsavory-looking characters. Seeing me, he grabbed me in his arms and whirled me around a couple of times.

Slightly alarmed, because it was obvious that something was awry, I immediately pulled back. I've never been around drugs of any kind, so I have no idea what a person who is high looks like. I do know that there was a strange, unfamiliar look in his eyes, and my intuition told me that something was very wrong. His companions did nothing to ease my uneasiness, so I turned down his slurring invitation for dinner.

The next week in Michigan was no better. I ran into him a couple of times at the Ann Arbor Hilton, where we were both staying. This time, his companion was a woman with breasts too large for her tiny shirt and hair too blond to match her dark roots. As he left the hotel on Saturday morning, he invited me to stop by the Richmonds' motor coach.

Later that morning, at the track, I found Tim and his mother, Evelyn at the Motor Coach, but no sign of the busty blonde. After a few minutes of conversation, Evelyn left to check on lunch for her spoiled-rotten son. Again, Tim looked strange, just as he had in Watkins Glen. His speech and his actions were slow, almost slurred, and he was somewhat silly and dazed. After fifteen minutes of useless conversation, I asked, "What's wrong with you?"

"Nothing." He flopped down on the sofa and grinned goofily.

I raised a suspicious eyebrow and used the warning voice of a mother. "Tim." He closed his eyes and ignored me, so I decided not to waste my time. "I gotta go. Qualifying starts in fifteen minutes. You'd better get dressed."

He grabbed my hand and pleaded in a childlike way. "Don't go. Please stay. I don't want to be alone. Wait till Evelyn gets back."

"Tim, get up and put your driver's suit on and I'll see you on pit road." He made a face at me and threw one leg over the top of the sofa. With my hand on the door to leave, I looked back to see him sprawled lazily with a silly smile and half-closed eyes. He stretched his mouth into a wide yawn, compelling me to speak again.

"You'd better get your butt up and get dressed. The clock is ticking," I warned.

"Okay, okay," he muttered, waving me away lethargically. "I can't change until you leave." Then he popped one eye wide open and grinned mischievously. "Unless, of course, you wanna help me."

"*No thanks*," I replied sarcastically as I pushed the door open. As I stepped off the bus, he was laughing and called after me, "I knew *that* would get rid of you!"

What would happen an hour later would make every sports page and broadcast in America. Tim, of course, paid no attention to my helpful instructions. Big surprise. He later told reporters that a friend had stopped by the bus to see him, and when she left, he had fallen asleep because he wasn't feeling well. He did not awaken until some time later, when he heard a furious banging on the locked door of the bus, accompanied by frantic screaming.

As it turns out, Tim had almost missed qualifying. With his car and crew ready and waiting on pit road, but no driver, NASCAR had finally given the team a five-minute warning, telling them to find Tim and get him to the car or he would miss that qualifying chance. They finally located him sound asleep on his bus. Of course, he wasn't even dressed in his uniform so they jerked him up, screamed at him to get dressed quickly, then threw him into a golf cart, which sped across the garage and into the pits. When the cart screeched to a stop next to his racecar, a harried, dazed Tim was fumbling with his shoes, trying to get them on. Someone handed him a helmet, and he staggered out of the golf cart and into the car, which he fired up and promptly took out on the track, accelerating to a speed close to 200 mph. His lousy performance would result in a starting position of twenty-fifth.

For the drivers and teams on pit road who saw the spectacle, it was nothing short of unsettling. Between this incident and his behavior at Watkins Glen the previous week, Tim had done an excellent job of spooking his fellow drivers, who were forced to rub sheet metal with him at heart-thumping speeds. An outcry went up to NASCAR from the garage participants, with many claiming that they did not feel safe racing on the same track with the unpredictable driver. Tremendous pressure mounted as Tim found himself in a corner, fenced in by suspicions and unfriendliness. He raced the next day and finished an unimpressive twenty-ninth, but after missing Darlington's Southern 500, he released a statement that, for reasons of health, he was resigning from the Hendrick Motorsports team.

Tim Richmond, one of the most talented drivers who ever sat behind the wheel of a racecar, would never race again.

Six months had passed since his resignation when Tim arrived in Daytona, to look for a ride for the Busch Clash. A record-setting pole in Pocono's second race of 1987 had awarded Tim the honor of racing in the prestigious matchup of pole winners. But NASCAR officials, wary because of the events at Watkins Glen and in Michigan, had instituted a drug-testing policy in January.

This wasn't a surprise, or even an irritant, to Tim. He was

expecting it and had discussed the possibility with me before he went to Daytona. Although I didn't hear from Tim until three weeks after the race in Michigan that ended his career—he had gone into seclusion and no one was able to track him down—I arrived at my hotel in Richmond, Virginia, in early September to find a message waiting for me. Restless and unhappy as he often was, he called me at least four times that weekend, just to talk. That was the beginning of a regular routine for us in which Tim would call and pontificate for hours in an undisguised effort to exorcise the demons that were feasting on his soul and robbing him of any peace. For the next year or so, he would call several times a week, often in the wee hours of the dark nights that haunted him most. The conversations were always lengthy, and I was not allowed to hang up, no matter how sleepy I was, until he had finished talking. Once, while I was in Dover, Delaware, for the fall race, he called and talked for four hours as we watched the entire Miss America pageant together, courtesy of the long-distance lines. Of course, he had acerbic comments to make about each contestant, for nothing or no one was ever perfect to Tim, including and most especially himself.

"You know what Rick (Hendrick) told me today," Tim asked during one conversation. "He said that I'm the only person he ever saw who runs away from failure more than he runs toward success. I never thought about it until he said it, but you know something? He's right." In a lonely, thoughtful voice he often used, he said: "I'd like to meet the person who really knows me."

Tim Richmond was an enigma to himself as much as to everyone else. You can ask twenty people who knew Tim, and you will get twenty completely different assessments. He specifically tailored his personality to each person he encountered, depending on how much he liked or disliked you. My specially tailored version of Tim Richmond was good—occasionally almost to the point of saintliness—witty, charming, considerate (for the most part), difficult, argumentative, kind, wounded, needy, lonely, sad, bitter, and self-protective. Above all, he was colorful and entertaining. I love to be around people who are not boring, so, despite the difficulty often associated with being his friend, I adored having him as my pal.

Somewhere around Christmas 1987, about four months after the ordeal in Michigan, Tim called me with a grand new plan. He always had a scheme that would interest him momentarily, then he would discard it and be on to something else.

"Guess what I'm going to do." He sounded smug.

"Knowing you, there's no way to guess. What?" I was sitting on the floor of my apartment, preoccupied with untangling Christmas tree lights.

"I'm going to run the Busch Clash!"

The jolt was so great that I looked to see if the lights were plugged in and if they had produced an electrical shock of some kind. They weren't and they hadn't. The shock came strictly from Tim's announcement.

"You've got to be kiddin'," I remarked in a "have you lost your mind?" tone.

His smugness turned to surliness. "Why? What's wrong with that?" he snapped.

I began to list the reasons, the top being that he was not a favorite of NASCAR's nor had he endeared himself to the other drivers, not to mention the fact that he didn't even have a car to drive. "Besides," I concluded, expecting my next statement to completely dash his plans, "they'll make you take a drug test before they let you drive."

"So?"

"So, are you willing to do that?"

"I certainly am." His tone was indignant. Now, keep in mind that I never saw Tim do drugs, had never heard him mention them, and—other than his erratic behavior at those two races—had never, in all our conversations or meetings, seen anything to indicate that he was a drug user.

"Let me tell you something." I could clearly imagine him on the other end of the phone, straightening his spine, pulling his shoulders back, and cocking his head to one side with one eyebrow raised and the other wrinkled. "If they want to do a drug test, I'll be the first one to step forward and drain the lizard! I'll even *volunteer* to do it."

"All right. As long as you know what to expect." Of course, Daytona was six weeks away, and I figured that by then he would have moved onto something else. But he did not forget. For the next few weeks, he plotted, planned, and prepared. His arrival in Daytona was the big news in both the garage and the media center. He was cool, calm, collected, and confident that it would be a triumphant return.

Then his drug test came back dirty.

Dark, angry skies and torrential cold rains covered Daytona that late winter day; the flood washed away practice and forced crews to huddle in their small garage stalls or retreat to their trucks. Under the cover of an umbrella, I was jumping ankle-deep puddles, dashing from the media center to the garage, when I saw Tim, waving from underneath a large golf umbrella, hurrying toward me. He was wearing a short black leather jacket with long fringe and straight black jeans that covered his long skinny legs.

I skipped toward him, grinning happily because I knew he was back where he belonged, where he wanted to be. "Hey!" I bubbled as our two umbrellas collided. His face was as dark and angry as the skies.

"My drug test came back positive." His voice was sharp.

My eyes bugged. I couldn't comprehend for a moment what he was saying. "What?" I asked, my smile replaced by a look of bewilderment.

He leaned closer until his nose was two inches from mine. Slowly, he repeated, "It came back positive."

My eyes narrowed. "Tim, you swore up and down to me that you were clean!"

With one hand clutching the oversized umbrella, he used the other to grip my shoulder. "Listen to me. There is no way. *No way.* Trust me when I tell you there is nothing in my system! *Nothing.*" There was a hidden meaning in that statement, which I would discover much later.

Although I talked to Tim on the phone a couple of times, I did not see him again until I was summoned to his hotel room a few days later. I didn't know what was up or what was true. But I did know that Tim was my friend, and although he could be as annoying as heck, I cared deeply, so I refused to forsake him when friends suddenly became few and far between. I had heard the ugly rumors about Tim concerning his health and possible habits, but I shrugged them off. I firmly believe that we should judge people by what we see with our own hearts and eyes and not by the gossip of others. With my eyes and heart, I saw a wonderful, compassionate friend.

Since I was one of Tim's closest confidantes at the time, I believed I would be one of the first to know anything worth knowing about him. As it turned out, I was among the last. That night at the Daytona Hilton, he was remarkably calm, after having been consumed for two or three days by raging anger. By then, he had moved into another phase—"they're all a bunch of stupid idiots," which he accented by shaking his head and rolling his eyes. We talked for about an hour, and then I left for a dinner engagement. Tim walked me to the door, hugged me, kissed me on the forehead, and clutched my hand tightly. "You've been a damn good friend to me. Thank you," he remarked gruffly, unaccustomed to being sentimental or complimentary. I wanted to say that he didn't make it easy, but I held my tongue. He changed gears as easily and quickly as he did on a race restart. "Now, get outta here. I'll talk to you later."

NASCAR reexamined the test results and announced that cold medicine and ibuprofen that Tim had been taking for a head cold had muddied the waters and caused the false positive results. NASCAR also stated that there was an extraordinary amount of these medications in his system. I was happy to know that he had been truthful with me about being clean, but something else nagged at my mind. I thought about his substantial weight loss and his skinny legs (he loved food and had always struggled with his weight), his extreme fatigue, and, most hauntingly, the burnlike sore on his chest. I dug in and started researching probable causes. Within three weeks, I was convinced that my dear friend was sick with AIDS. Six months later, a mutual friend confirmed my suspicions.

"Sweetheart, he's really bad," our friend said gently as I buried my face in my hands and sobbed the first of thousands of tears that I would shed for Tim Richmond. "He doesn't accept it, and he won't talk about it."

"But I'm one of his best friends," I wailed. "Why won't he tell me? I'll still love him. I won't turn my back on him."

The friend smiled cynically. "He doesn't believe anyone is capable of that kind of love and compassion. I'm sorry to say that, but it's true."

For the remaining twelve months of his life, I pretended that I didn't know that Tim was ill, and he pretended that there wasn't anything to know. I could have asked him outright, lulled into a false sense of security by the apparent closeness of our friendship, but I had seen too many other friends summarily dismissed and discarded from his life over violations much less imposing than the crime of prying into his deepest, darkest secret. He could desperately need a person one day, then coldly turn his back the next and never allow access within his hallowed circle again. His past was a graveyard scattered with the ghosts of former friends. I knew his remaining time was precious, not just to him but also to me. I did not want our friendship buried in that graveyard, for I would have been the one haunted by it, not Tim.

From the moment that Tim announced his resignation from Hendrick Motorsports, he was hunted by the press, determined to unravel the mystery of the flamboyant star and the sudden brakes he had put on the fame that he had courted all his life. He became, quite simply, what he had always wanted to be—the biggest story in the world of sports. A few weeks after the announcement in 1987, he called me one night at home from his parents' house in Ashland, Ohio.

"I've got a problem," he said.

"What's new?"

"Shut up with the wisecracks and listen to me." He explained that a reporter from *USA Today* was "stalking" him, "hiding in the bushes," and asking questions of people who knew Tim. Finally, the evening before, Tim had spied the reporter in a rental car outside their home. In typical Tim fashion, he had jumped into a car, accompanied by his parents, and taken off after the reporter. As Tim described the chase—two cars whipping, spinning, and fly-ing—I started laughing at the mental picture. I knew the reporter, one of the newspaper's very best, and the thought of him trying to flee from the hotheaded driver and his aging parents in the family sedan was just too much.

"So, I need your help," he concluded. "I want you to call USA Today and tell 'em to lay off me!"

I knew that trying to reason with an unreasonable man was senseless, but still I forged ahead. "Tim, fame is a two-way street. You can't court reporters and publicity in the good times and then run from them in the hard times. They don't forget. If you don't cooperate in some way now, they'll remember it when the good times roll around again. Besides, if you're gonna talk, USA Today is the best place to tell your story."

"I'm not doing it," he retorted firmly, in a tone that ended the discussion. "Now, call that idiot and tell him to leave me alone!"

I did call the reporter the next day, and his version of the mad-cap chase was as amusing as Tim's. Imagine looking into the rearview mirror of a slowpoke rental car to see that you're being chased at high speed, in the dark of night on an unfamiliar back road, by an angry rascal who is quite accustomed to trading paint at 200 mph with guys like Dale Earnhardt. Certainly, few things could be more daunting. "That guy's a lunatic!" he ranted. "He tried to run me off the road and kill me!" He paused, then added in a warn-ing tone, "Listen, there's more to this story than Tim Richmond's telling. I know he's your friend, but the guy's hiding something."

"I hope you're wrong," I replied in the tentative voice of a person who wants to believe the best but fears that the worst is hidden within.

"I don't think I am. But the story's dead anyway because I can't get confirmation from any reliable sources."

Tim was relieved that the hounds were calling off the search.

"That's because," he explained calmly, "there's nothing to find." He said this so convincingly that it was hard to believe otherwise.

Tim was a paragon of unpredictability and contradictions, so what happened next wasn't surprising. *USA Today* was turning five years old, and in celebration of this milestone for a little newspaper that the critics had scoffed at, a grandiose party was scheduled the following week in Washington, D.C. Everyone who had been associated with the paper in its first five years was invited, and Tim knew I was planning to fly to Washington for the party on Friday, then rent a car and drive to Dover, Delaware, for the weekend's Winston Cup race.

A few days before the party, Tim called and casually inquired, "Do you have a date for the *USA Today* party?"

"No, I'm going with a group of friends from the newspaper."

"Good. Because I'm going to be your date!"

"What!" I squealed into the phone. "Have you lost your mind? You can*not* be serious!"

But he was. After weeks of being a fugitive from the unrelenting pursuit of the press, after playing cat and mouse with one of the paper's star reporters and then, according to the reporter's version, trying to kill him, Tim had decided to turn the tables and was filled with glee at the prospect of sashaying into the *USA Today* party, on its turf, filled with every reporter, editor, and executive, past and present. But Tim always played on his own terms, and he enjoyed nothing better than being the star, the center of attention. He well knew that if he waltzed into the grand celebration, he—currently the most desired interview in American sports—would be a show-stopper.

"What's wrong?" he asked innocently. "I have a custom-made tux. I won't embarrass you." Wickedly, he added, "Can you assure me of the same? Just what are you planning on wearing?"

I couldn't talk him out of it, but in all honesty I didn't try hard. I knew that the folks at *USA Today* would be nothing short of thrilled to have him traipse into their snare. So, he proceeded with his plan—he hired a plane to fly him from Ohio to Washington, scheduled a limo, and had his tux pressed. After my arrival in Washington, I received a call from Tim, as planned.

"Hi, sweetheart," Tim said. The weakness and sweetness of his voice told me something was wrong. "Listen, I've got bad news. I can't make it this afternoon. I'm not feeling well, and the doctor doesn't want me to make the trip. I'm so sorry, because I really wanted to do this."

That was the one and only time that Tim ever admitted being sick to me. I suspect that normally when he didn't feel well, he just avoided contact with me. But in that case, he had no choice. I also knew it wasn't a ruse or a case of last-minute jitters. I could tell that from the sound of his voice. Of course, I had planted the seed in Tim's mind that he should tell his story to *USA Today* and it had definitely taken root. Though my reporter friends were disappointed at the no-show, the time was quickly approaching when they would hear Tim's version of his life.

A couple of weeks later, I was sound asleep in my hotel room in Charlotte when the phone rang at 4 A.M.

"Hello," I mumbled groggily.

"Wake up!" Tim commanded. "I've got to talk to you about my plan."

"Will you please stop calling me in the middle of the night?"

"Quit grumbling. This is important. I'm coming to Charlotte tomorrow for the race, and I want you to pick me up at the private airport and drive me to my house on the lake."

I sat straight up in bed. "What!" Tim had not set foot at a racetrack since the debacle in Michigan two months earlier, and to say that his unexpected return would be news was an understatement. But again his mind was set, and again, instead of running away, he was changing directions. Tim was always in a chase with his demons. Often they chased him, but sometimes he turned to chase them. He had decided to come to Charlotte, one of the sport's biggest weekends, and boldly confront the rumormongers, those who were still his friends and those who weren't.

My memories of that weekend will be forever engraved in my

mind: Tim screaming about the poor quality of my driving and insisting that I pull over on the interstate and let him drive; Evelyn, deeply concerned, calling me to ask about Tim's spirits; Pattie and Kyle Petty, Barry Dodson, Tim's former crew chief, and Harry Hyde showering Tim with friendship and affection in the garage area; his lump-in-the-throat emotion at the tender kindness bestowed upon him by Humpy Wheeler, president of the speedway; the exultation of the fans who were fortunate enough to catch a glimpse of the star; the security guard who handed me a message on Sunday morning from Tim with instructions to meet him outside the garage gate next to the credentials window at 10:30 A.M.; then finding him there surrounded by a small group of fans—mostly females—signing autographs and having him turn to me, stretching out his trembling left hand and whispering, "Look at me. I'm a nervous wreck." He was scared to come back, afraid of how he would be received, terrified of the "friends" he would no longer find in the place where he had once been a prince of popularity. Much of the press had taken to writing stories that barely concealed contempt and that, coupled with calls that went unreturned by those he had considered his pals, added up to heartbreak for a man whose heart many thought was unbreakable. It was not. It was one of the most fragile hearts I have ever known.

Tim was a complicated maze of emotions and motives. For those who knew only his celebrity persona, it's hard to comprehend the childlike vulnerability that lay beneath. Anyone who had ever dealt with him had encountered his unpredictability and impetuosity, but his fragile, sensitive heart was something he kept hidden away among his other deep, dark secrets.

One of the saddest memories of my life is of Tim that weekend, during our conversation about his detractors and attackers, walking across the living room of his home in Lake Norman to the window. Silently, he looked out into the dark, empty night; then, after a long moment of reflection, he asked quietly, "*Why* do they have to kick a man when he's down?"

Jerry Potter from *USA Today* was in Charlotte that weekend, and he approached me with a suggestion. "Why don't you see if Tim will talk to me? The only way to calm these waters is for him to come out and tell his story. I like Tim, and I'd like to help him."

Jerry is a fair, ethical man who never exploits, never compromises but brings heart and perfect accuracy to diligent reporting. From some reporters, this would have been a self-serving offer, designed to enhance their careers; but from Jerry, I knew it was a selfless act of humanity. Surprisingly, Tim agreed, and both men arranged to fly to my home in Indianapolis for a dinner meeting that would, it was hoped, set the record straight.

It did not. Tim had stuck to his story for so long—the story that he was clean of drugs and basically healthy and that nothing out of the ordinary was awry in his life—that he believed it as fervently as he wished for others to believe it. Between bites of a thick steak poised precariously on the end of a tiny cocktail fork, Tim told his story convincingly while Jerry frantically scribbled notes and I listened quietly. After several hours, Jerry asked the most important question.

"All I need to clear all this up are your medical records. Would you arrange for me to see them?"

The request didn't anger Tim. He merely shook his head and replied evenly, "No. Why should I have to show my medical records? Would you want to show yours? To give up your privacy? It's a personal invasion, and I shouldn't have to do that."

Without records to verify Tim's account, Jerry told me the next day, there was no story. It died, and so did Tim's media attention, until three months later in Daytona. Then, it resurrected itself with a vengeance, as the press wrote of little else than the soap opera surrounding Tim's two drug tests, his refusal to release his medical records, his ban from NASCAR and then his reinstatement, Barry Slotnick and the lawsuit. Later, after Tim's death, we learned that while he did have abnormally high amounts of over-the-counter drugs in his system, he was completely clean of any medications, including AZT, at the time the only treatment for AIDS. Although it subjected him to tremendous pain, Tim had eliminated AZT for several weeks leading up to the drug test at Daytona so that there would be no traces of it in his system. That was why he had been adamant about "nothing" being in his system.

After that February in 1988, Tim was seldom seen or heard from by most people, although I continued to hear from him on a sporadic basis. When he did call, he no longer talked of grand dreams or high hopes, and since he rarely ventured out, there was little adventure for him to share. He was deeply embittered and did not wish to discuss my life in racing or the people we both knew. There was, it seemed, very little for two old friends to share. The last time I heard from him was five weeks before his death in 1989, when he asked Evelyn to call three special friends—Dr. Jerry Punch; an old friend in Martinsville, Virginia; and me. He wanted to wish us a Happy Fourth of July, he said. In June, he had reentered Good Samaritan Hospital in Fort Lauderdale, where he was to remain until his death in August. Those calls to the three of us were probably close to his last conscious acts as he wearily waited, drifting in and out of consciousness, for the final curtain to fall.

Of all the racing friends I've lost, it is the loss of Tim Richmond that still ravages my soul and pierces my heart with a pain as fresh today as the day he died.

Tim was a handsome, personable, famous bachelor living the kind of life bachelors lived in those days, right or wrong. It was his misfortune to contract a disease at a time when no one knew such a deadly ailment even existed. His doctor once said that it wasn't known when Tim contracted HIV, but it could have been in the late 1970s. The first known cases of AIDS were documented in 1981 and until Rock Hudson died of the disease in 1985, most Americans had never heard of it. So it wasn't as if Tim knew and deliberately played Russian roulette with his life. I have heard and read that some women believe he knew he was sick and knowingly endangered their lives. I can only say this—I was close to Tim in the last three years of his life, when it is documented that he did know, and I saw only chaste behavior from him. I used to joke to my friends that I was probably the only woman in the world that Tim

Richmond never made a pass at and "quite frankly, it hurts my feelings!" During that time, with the exception of his on-again, off-again girlfriend in Fort Lauderdale, I never heard him mention a woman or express any interest in one. I think he accepted that this part of his life was over.

I have finally realized why Tim's death continues to cause me more torturous sadness than the deaths of other friends. It's simple. The others died as heroes. Their tragic accidents have attached additional honor and glory to their names and will serve to perpetuate their legacy. There was no shame in the way that Alan, Davey, and Dale died. Tim, however, died in self-imposed seclusion, hidden away even from those of us who wanted to hug him one last time and say, "I love you no matter what."

The others died idolized by many. Tim died ignored by more. But here's the biggest reason that Tim's death pricks so painfully at my tender, wounded heart and keeps complete healing at bay— Alan, Davey, and Dale died at gloriously happy, successful times in their lives. They were content both personally and professionally. So much was so right for each of them that up until the moment when tragedy snatched them away, they were blissful and pleased with their accomplishments and their lives. On the contrary, the last two years of Tim's life were mostly misery, heartache, and raw loneliness.

It is one thing to die suddenly, leaving a legacy of historical glory behind. It is quite another to die slowly, tormented each waking moment by what might have been, what *should* have been. Given a choice between these men, which would you pick? Lives of grandiose glory, triumph, joy, and adoration until the end? Or the man whose last two years were filled with regret, ridicule, innuendo, loneliness, and pain? Tim, who retreated into hollow solitude, was forced to watch as death crept slowly toward him, burdened with the knowledge that he couldn't outrun its crawl. That torture scars the heart and mars an otherwise stellar existence. The others, however, never saw death coming. There surely must be a certain blessed mercy about that.

Who would choose Tim's life, knowing that the bargain would also include those last two years and death from a disease not understood or accepted by society, a disease that frightened others and caused them to shun him and treat him as an outcast? I also wonder which choice his harshest critics would make.

Once I realized that Tim was dying, I did something very selfish and unusual for me. I launched a campaign for his soul's salvation. I loved Tim so dearly that I wanted the assurance of knowing we'd meet again in heaven one day. It wasn't easy. Nothing was easy with Tim. He resisted and asked the hard questions. "If God is so good, why do bad things happen to people?" "Why do people suffer needlessly?" "Why are some people blessed and some people cursed?" "Why do some die young?"

Feebly, I tried my best to answer. I wasn't very good. But I knew that Tim wanted to believe, wanted to accept Jesus Christ as his Lord and Savior. Back when I lived in Indy, I had gone to a Bible study group every Tuesday night. Without fail, within thirty minutes of my returning home every week, Tim would call.

"Okay," he would say the moment I answered the phone, skipping the preamble. "Tell me what you learned in school tonight." For the next hour or so, he would pick every morsel of information from me. First, I would read the evening's scripture to him, give a brief synopsis, and then try to answer his endless questions. When I couldn't answer, he would say, "You need to study more." He knew, but I did not, that his date with eternity was drawing near. A couple of times in that last year, I prayed with him over the phone. But he never made any promises other than, "I just don't know. But I'll think about it."

When I talked to Evelyn a couple of weeks after Tim's death, I quivered with dread at the question that I needed to ask more than I wanted to ask it. It wasn't the question that scared me. It was the uncertainty of what the answer would be. Our conversation was drenched in tears. Finally, I forced the question, praying silently that the answer was one that would assure me of seeing my dear, irascible friend again.

"Evelyn," I began softly. "Did Tim make peace with God before he died?"

Her sobbing stopped. Tenderly and quietly, she replied, "Yes, he did. He told me about his conversations with you and your prayers. It worked, so you don't have to worry, because Tim's in heaven."

As Tim's time dwindled, it forced an important realization upon me—we should never hesitate to tell people how much they mean to us or what impact they've made on our lives. Once they're gone, we can't spin back the hands of time and make that correction. With Tim, I began to say "I love you" at the conclusion of every meeting or conversation, never knowing if these words would be the last shared between us. I used to share those words only romantically, never with close friends or family. Then I added my parents to the list, and gradually "I love you" became a regular part of my conversations with a wide circle of people who have enhanced my life. My best friends, male and female, always hear those words before I hang up, and often they find the words at the end of a message on their answering machines. This was one of Tim's most important contributions to my life. He would always return the sentiment—and a couple of times he offered it first.

"I love you, too," he responded one afternoon, but since that particular conversation had included a bit of a salvation sermon from me, he couldn't resist adding, "Even if you are a pain in the ass."

It is hard to say whether I learned more from Tim Richmond's living or from his dying. Tim's life continues to remind me almost daily that we have a choice between two powers in our lives—self-elevation and self-destruction. I believe that Tim began his self-destruction in the early days when his health peril was first discovered, hastening his downward spiral as evidenced by his behavior in Watkins Glen and Michigan. Had he been able to control or conquer his rage and desperation, perhaps he could have lengthened his life, as Magic Johnson has. I know that he could have had a stronger, better quality of life in those last two years. He certainly could have been surrounded by more of his loyal friends had he prevailed over his pride and told the truth to those of us who loved him, rather than hiding away in secret, made ashamed of his sickness by a heartless society.

As I watched while many deserted Tim during his time of desperation, I was forced to accept the cruelty of those who know how to befriend only during times of prosperity and joy. It is something I wish I didn't know. I am always saddened when I see people, particularly those who profess to be Christians, who criticize rather than console, who refuse to extend a hand of love because their judgments are so righteous and so harsh. How can others learn love and compassion if we do not teach it? How can we expect to receive kindness and charity if we do not offer it when others are hurting and forsaken?

And, most of all, how can we expect to have loyal friends who love us until the bitter end, if we stop loving others somewhere in the middle?

From Tim, I learned that sometimes the way you die is more important than how you lived. A heroic death will erase a multitude of sins and mistakes while a less noble death will only accentuate them. There are those who will argue that Tim's living and dying are inexplicably linked. I won't dispute that. But I will argue that there is good in the soul of every man and every life has a purpose and reason for being. That was as true about Tim Richmond as it is about anyone else. I saw a lot of his good and some of his bad, but I *never* saw a reason to quit being his friend somewhere in the middle.

NASCAR GETS HOT WHEN

TOM CRUISE MAKES IT COOL

The day Tim died, I spent the afternoon with Tom Cruise. I have thought often how painfully ironic it was that while Cruise was researching Tim's life and livelihood for his next movie, *Days of Thunder*, Tim's life was ending.

As a publicist on the Winston Cup circuit, I constantly rubbed elbows with superstars and was close friends with some of racing's most famous folks. But that day—August 13, 1989—brings forth conflicting emotions. My life was filled with joy, fun, deep friendships, and great adventure. But there was also a dark side that occasionally choked out the happiness and replaced it with lingering sorrow. I love remembering those days of frivolity. But it hurts to recall the dear friends who have crossed the finish line of life. Tim Richmond was the first. Sadly, he was far from the last.

That summer afternoon in Watkins Glen, New York, was fragrant and sweet. It was one of those fabulous days that reward us for enduring the bad ones that burden our spirits from time to time. Even now I can inhale deeply and smell that day's sweet air, free of the damp humidity that had plagued us that summer, as it does every year in the South. It's a funny thing about days like that, though. I remember clearly the joy and happiness but I don't feel the joy the way I still feel the sorrow. The brightness has dimmed considerably, and the darkness has deepened. I no longer laugh at the happy remembrances of that day, but I do still cry at the sadness it wrought.

The Hollywood superstar, with director Tony Scott in tow, was standing in the pits of Darrell Waltrip, who was sponsored by Tide. They were intently watching what little bit of a road course race can be viewed from any one spot in the jumbled maze of twists and turns. Cruise stood with his arms folded across his chest and his handsome face framed by trendy black wraparound sunglasses. He leaned over to me, standing to his right, and shouted a question above the whirl of shifting transmissions and roaring engines. After answering, I retreated to the nearby towering toolbox, painted to look exactly like a box of soap powder, and climbed up to sit beside Stevie Waltrip, who was scoring her husband's laps as usual.

My smile was a mixture of gloating and teasing. "I guess you noticed Tom Cruise asking *me* a question."

She grinned back. Stevie was hard to impress, but even she was a bit taken by the glamour that came with Cruise and Scott, the creative duo who had given the world the spectacular movie hit *Top Gun*. We were all tickled pink to have those big stars in our little orbit.

"I saw that. What did he ask?"

"He said, 'Ma'am, can you tell me what time it is, please?' " I smiled broadly.

"Wellll." She feigned a look of astonished admiration. "What did you say?"

"I said, 'It's ten till three.' "

We both threw back our heads and laughed delightedly as

though we had not a care in the world. But while my afternoon in upstate New York was saturated with silliness and glee, Tim's family was smothered in heart-wrenching sorrow in South Florida, where, hours earlier, unknown to us, the last droplets of his once full life had ebbed away.

Had Tim known that *he* was to be the primary inspiration for the movie's renegade driver Cole Trickle that Cruise would develop and play on the big screen, he would have loved it. The only thing he would have loved better than boasting that Tom Cruise was playing him in a movie would have been to brag, "I'm starring as *me* in the movie. It's the role I was born to play." A lopsided grin, a spontaneous snigger, and a cocky tilt of the head would have accented that boast.

Tim had once told a group of reporters, "I'd give up my front-row seat in hell" for the opportunity to star in a big Hollywood movie. Naturally, that quote made its way into print, as did most of Tim's colorful remarks. Perhaps it was this comment that gave him the nickname "Hollywood." While most NASCAR drivers brought country music stars like Brooks and Dunn to the races, Tim brought the likes of Bruce Springsteen and Huey Lewis. Undoubtedly it was Tim's brash yet alluring arrogance, his flair for life in the fast lane, and his enormous raw talent that inspired Cruise. After all, in a big Hollywood production, there is no room for characters who are boring. Only the brightest, most outrageous, most irrepressible will do. That was certainly Tim Richmond. And, as it turned out, it was also Cole Trickle.

Like the fictional Trickle, Tim had roared into the NASCAR world after strutting his stuff in Indy Car racing. In 1980, in his debut performance at the Indy 500, he had astounded veterans by turning the fastest lap in practice during the two-week preparation. He posted the fifth-fastest qualifying time overall, although a heavy crash had caused him to miss the first round of qualifying. In the race, he chalked up a ninth-place finish to capture the prestigious Indy 500 Rookie of the Year title. And, of course, Tim in his typical fashion left his special stamp on the event in a way that only he could do. When he ran out of gas on the last lap, he flagged down the 500 winner Johnny Rutherford on his victory lap, hopped onto the wing of Rutherford's car, and rode with the winner into Victory Lane to create a perfect press-making moment. In the Indy museum at the speedway hangs a wonderful painting that immortalizes this moment of racing history. It is appropriately titled "The Rookie and the Champ."

Several months before the Watkins Glen race of 1989, we had been racing at the tiny North Wilkesboro Speedway. I was in charge of public relations for a sports marketing company co-owned by my dear friend Carolyn Rudd. Two of the accounts we handled were Tide and Folgers, which, coincidentally, were both primary sponsors for teams owned by Charlotte businessman Rick Hendrick. On the morning of the race, I was on the Folgers transporter; at the back of the truck, there was always a pot of hot coffee brewing—Folgers, of course. I poured a cup of coffee and began to make a sandwich. Earlier, a couple of guys had followed Hendrick executive Jimmy Johnson onto the truck, and although I had smiled and said hello, I paid no attention to them, since sponsor reps and potential sponsors were always around. Somewhere in the midst of the sandwich making, I noticed a small group of women gathering at the back of the truck. Gradually, the group grew larger and larger until it numbered twenty-five or thirty. The women stood about 15 or 20 feet back, but they were craning their necks, staring at the truck, and whispering among themselves. I paused in my sandwich making and turned with a mayonnaise smeared knife suspended in midair to Jimmy, who was standing directly behind me.

"What's goin' on out there? Look at all those women!"

Jimmy grinned and shrugged. "They're here to see Tom."

I furrowed my brow. "Tom? Tom who?"

"Tom Cruise." His tone was as nonchalant as if he had said "Tom Smith."

With those two words, he had my full, enthusiastic attention. My mouth dropped open and my eyes widened. I grinned stupidly, a mirror image of the women gawking at the back of the transporter.

"Tom Cruise? He's *here*?" My mouth stretched into a wide smile. "Where?"

I felt a tap on my shoulder, which irritated me, since I was so close to sniffing out where the handsome matinee star was hidden. I did not have the time to be interrupted, especially if it meant having to work *before* I found Tom Cruise. I gripped the mayonnaise-laden knife tighter, fully prepared to use it if I needed it to free myself from any situation that would detain me. Irritated, I turned around, and one of the strangers to whom I had spoken earlier held up his hand and wiggled his fingers in a gesture of hello. I looked blankly at the man, who had barely any hair on his head, because it was cut so microscopically close that it was all but shaved. Then he grinned and a wave of nausea rippled through my stomach—because I realized that Tom Cruise had just heard my excited girlish babble.

My shoulders slumped and I threw my head back in theatrical anguish. "Why do I always have to be soooo *stupid*?" I wailed.

Tom Cruise apparently had never met a stupid woman, because he threw back his head and laughed. It was not a polite laugh either. It was a side-splitting, uproarious, enormously entertained laugh, a howling gale that stretched on for several moments. Finally, I frowned and commented dryly, "You don't know me well enough to laugh at me *that* hard." I stopped and eyed him with a strong, appraising gaze. I put my hands on my hips and impolitely asked, "*Where* is all your hair?" I figured I could be that impertinent, since he had gotten such a belly laugh at my expense.

"It's cut like this for a movie I'm filming now." That movie, I later learned, was *Born on the Fourth of July*. Several months later, when I saw the movie, his performance blew me away. It was in *that* movie that Cruise truly portrayed Tim Richmond, a man who, after a hard break, rebels against himself, life, and those who loved him. The movie was sad, and, coupled with the despair of losing Tim a few months earlier, it was crushing. For more than a week, I was heavyhearted and despondent. When I next saw Cruise in Daytona for the 500, a few weeks later, I had to tell him how profoundly his performance had moved me.

"That was the most incredible job of acting I have ever seen," I gushed, in complete sincerity. "If you don't win an Academy Award for that, there is no justice."

By that time, Cruise was a regular visitor to the racing tour as he did research for the new movie and then began filming. For NASCAR, it was akin to winning a national lottery—a major motion picture about stock car racing featuring Hollywood's hottest star.

While the sport had been growing steadily, owing to consistent television coverage and more corporate involvement, the biggest payoff came when Cruise put Winston Cup racing and its people in movie theaters across the nation. With his enthusiastic stamp of approval and the apparent blessing of Hollywood, the sport seeped deeper into the nation's pop culture. It took one large leap closer to today's superstar status.

The ending of *Days of Thunder* was Hollywood-happy for Cole Trickle. But real life for Tim Richmond was something else. In the movie, Cole got the girl, a doctor in Florida. In reality, Tim left the girl, a doctor in Florida, behind to mourn him. It was as if Hollywood took only the beauty and excitement of his life and left the sadness and tragedy on the cutting-room floor. Real life, however, is not that simple or easy. More often than not, it is from the bad and the sad that we learn our most priceless lessons, just as I did on August 13, 1989.

DAYTONA DREAMS COME TRUE

Darrell Waltrip's heart dropped like a rock, and a wave of nausea crashed through his stomach. His voice, when he spoke a moment later, was choking with emotion and trembling with the kind of disappointment that no one else could really understand. He pressed the button on the radio wired into his race helmet, bracing himself slightly to deliver the news. With less than three laps to go in the race and close to tears, he reported in a shrill voice from the back stretch of the speedway, "I'm out of gas. I'm coming in."

Darrell Waltrip, it appeared, had just lost the Daytona 500 for the seventeenth time.

A month earlier, in January 1989, we had been in Daytona for a Chevrolet preseason test session that had brought in, among others, the Hendrick race teams including Waltrip and his teammate

Kenny Schrader, and Richard Childress Racing with Dale Earnhardt. None of the three drivers had ever won the Daytona 500, despite the fact that all were high-caliber drivers with state-of-the-art technology and lucrative sponsorships, and Earnhardt and Waltrip were each three-time Winston Cup champions. The three days of tests in Daytona were crucial and not taken lightly. Each driver was there to test new racecars and, he hoped, find that little extra oomph that would guide his car into the most coveted of the sport's Winner's Circles. On our second morning there, *USA Today* had run a story that proclaimed Earnhardt the Driver of the Decade, a story which was met by a frown from Waltrip.

"Did you see this?" Darrell asked when I stopped by his garage space to find him leaning against his car and reading the story. It was my first year as the publicist for Tide and Folgers, primary sponsors for, respectively, Darrell and Kenny Schrader. Darrell and his wife Stevie had been my friends long before we found ourselves in a professional relationship. Perhaps because of this bond, DW was willing to be more candid, more sharing of his heart's desire. Shaking his head, he handed the sports section to me.

"I've won three championships, too. All in this decade. And look at all the races I've won during the 1980s."

"And you were the first driver to win $10 million in prize money," I chirped in, remembering the story from my days at *USA Today* when it was significant enough to warrant space in the paper's hallowed pages.

"Right. Now, why am I not the Driver of the Decade?"

Darrell is articulate and analytical and can always present a reasonable, smart argument, which he can amply dress in unforgettable witticisms. He paused quietly to look toward the front straightaway of Daytona International Speedway with a dreamy, faraway expression as he surveyed the real estate he longed to conquer, two and a half miles of asphalt over which he, like every other NASCAR driver, wanted to reign. That day, though, would be the day that counted most—at the end of a grueling 500-mile race on a Sunday in February. Darrell had scored many victories at Daytona International Speedway, but it had always been in the "lesser" races such as July's Firecracker 400, Busch Grand National Races, and IROC races, events in which the best from each motorsports arena compete against each other in identically prepared cars. He knew how to win at Daytona. He just hadn't won the one that mattered most.

"The only thing I haven't done is win the Daytona 500," he said softly. "But Dale hasn't either." He shook his handsome head as if to throw that last thought from his mind. It didn't matter that Dale hadn't won. All that mattered was that he hadn't. "Dadgum it. It's the one thing I've worked for all of my career. The only thing I've dreamed of since I was a little boy."

My heart was bathed in wrenching emotion and I didn't know what to say. I could only look sympathetic and twist my mouth into a tight, sad line. Darrell turned away from the straightaway, folded his arms, and leaned against his racecar. His voice was still quiet and reflective.

"I'm grateful for the success and the great racing career I've had. But unless I win the Daytona 500, it won't be complete. Something will always be missing in my heart and in my career."

I imagined DW as a child, sitting on the front porch of the family's home in Owensboro, Kentucky, waiting for his dad, Leroy, to come home from his job as a Pepsi route man. I began to realize that the dreams of a child's heart are the most important. Those who follow their juvenile dreams are the happiest adults—for they are doing what they were meant to do from the beginning.

I was still thinking about Darrell's dream when we arrived back in Daytona in February for the ten days of activity referred to as SpeedWeeks. From what I had seen at the Chevy test sessions, I had no reason to believe that his dream would become a reality that year. His testing had been good but not great. We didn't know it then, but 1989 would turn out to be one of the greatest years of his formidable career.

From the test session and the early practice times, I thought that I had a very strong chance of going to Winner's Circle with my buddy Kenny Schrader. He was strong, fast, and determined, so no one was surprised when he captured his second consecutive pole for the Daytona 500 eight days before the event. In Daytona, Pole Day is on Saturday, one full week before the big event, and unlike any other race, only the front row is locked in for the 500. The positions for the rest of the starting field are determined by the Twin 125 qualifying races on Thursday, two days before the big race. They line up for those two races on the basis of their qualifying speed on Pole Day with the front-row starters, each leading a 125-miler from the pole position. (This is completely up to the driver, because the front-row qualifiers do not have to run the qualifying races—their positions are secured. But I've never known a racer to miss out on a race, rules or not.)

While no one was surprised by Kenny's run, many were delighted that Darrell's Chevy had that tiny bit extra to push him into the number 2 spot and make him a guaranteed front-row starter for the Daytona 500. Kenny illustrated his speed dominance with a pole-grabbing speed of 196.997 mph, more than a full mile an hour faster than Darrell's 195.916. The third-fastest was Bill Elliott at 195.737 mph, followed by Dale Earnhardt at 195.529 mph. They were only slight ticks of the clock slower than Darrell's speed, while no one was anywhere close to Kenny.

Of the bystanders, I was probably the most delighted. With Kenny and Darrell lining up on the front row, I had the unparalleled pleasure of being the publicist for the two fastest cars in the starting field of the Daytona 500. Since practically every major newspaper and electronic medium covers the Daytona race, it meant eight days of incredible press opportunities. Rather than begging reporters to interview my drivers, I was in the enviable position of scheduling interviews for the reporters begging *me* to interview my drivers. It was the best week of my entire public relations career, sweetened by Kenny's red-hot streak and incredible good fortune. For the Busch Clash (now called the Bud Shootout), a race for pole sitters from the previous season, Kenny drew the pole position in the event's lottery. Then he won the race, following this with a victory in one of the Twin 125s in which he started from the pole. To add to the momentum, Kenny was rocket-fast in practice all week. He was indisputably sitting in the catbird seat.

For Darrell, however, the week was merely ordinary, bordering on mundane, with only one hitch. On Wednesday, I stopped by the Waltrips' motor coach to find Stevie frantically pulling cushions from sofas and plunging her hands down into the crevices of the chairs. "What are you doing?" I asked, taking a soft drink from the fridge.

She shook her head with despair and explained that she was looking for Darrell's championship ring from the 1985 season. He had lost it the day before and was heartsick over its disappearance. He couldn't find it anywhere. For the next few days, the Waltrips vigilantly hunted for the ring, but by Sunday morning they had resigned themselves to the notion that it was gone forever.

Race day was severely overcast, with threatening skies and a temperature that had turned from perfectly pleasant to chilly. I shepherded Darrell to a couple of pre-race interviews and a small meet-and-greet with some Procter and Gamble executives; then he and I headed to the chapel service where we were to meet Stevie and Jessica. En route to the chapel, Darrell, who loves music, had hummed happily.

"This is going to be a good day," he predicted as he squeezed my elbow and pushed me through the crowd gathering in the garage. My puzzled look was addressed with a nod of reassurance. "The numbers are lining up."

"What numbers?" Before he answered, I knew that the ever-active mind of Darrell Waltrip had developed a theory that no one else would have conceived.

"The number seventeen. Look—my car number is seventeen; Jessica was seventeen months old on the seventeenth, two days ago; and this is my seventeenth Daytona 500. It's going to be hard to beat ol' DW today." He grinned confidently, and I shook my head in amusement. Trust me when I say that only Darrell Waltrip would have thought of all that.

Stevie and I were settling down for the race atop the 6-foot-high toolbox when she began to dig in her sacklike purse for her calculator, which she needed to calculate fuel mileage as she scored Darrell's car from the pits. I was in the middle of telling a story when Stevie, with her hand deep in her purse, suddenly froze. Her eyes widened, and it was evident that she was not hearing me.

"Are you listening to me?" I demanded. Her frozen expression melted into a wide smile and she pulled her hand from her purse.

"Look!" she screamed. In her fingers was the gold championship ring, the ring that had been given up for lost. For a brief moment, we stared at first the ring and then at each other. Chills ran over my body.

"Oh, my gosh. This is an omen!" I blurted out in complete seriousness.

"I've got to tell Darrell," she exclaimed excitedly. We both scrambled down from the toolbox just as we heard the command, "Gentlemen, start your engines."

"Jeff!" Stevie yelled at the crew chief Jeff Hammond as she ran over to tell him what had happened and to instruct him to radio Darrell with the good news. Both Stevie and I had radio headsets, but we could use them only to listen, not to communicate. The enormous thundering of forty-two cars firing up 294,000 of combined horsepower was deafening as Jeff relayed the message. Darrell responded with an emotional, "Man, are you serious?" As the cars began to roll off pit row, Stevie and I stood close to the pit wall and she waved the ring in the air. Darrell slowed as he came by us. He shook his head and threw up his hand as he eased onto the track of the Daytona International Speedway for what would be one of the biggest days of his life.

"I'm serious," I reiterated as we settled back into our race positions and pulled our coats around us for protection against the chill. "This is an omen. Just wait and see." Stevie, who is spiritual rather than superstitious, smiled indulgently.

Halfway through the race, it was evident that unless Kenny crashed, broke, or fell out of the race, he was going to win the Daytona 500. Jeff Hammond had an idea with about forty laps remaining.

"Stevie, if this race stays under green, is there any chance that we can go the distance without pitting?" he asked. This would be irrelevant if a caution flag came out because the entire field, without question, would pit for fuel and fresh tires. But should the race finish up without a caution, cars would dash in for a splash of fuel and out again. Jeff Hammond wondered if Darrell could stretch his mileage and not require that last bit of fuel, which would allow him to avoid losing several precious seconds in the pits.

Stevie Waltrip, who is one of the most careful thinkers I have ever met, grabbed her calculator and quickly ran the numbers. "Yeah, we can do it if he's careful," she replied brightly and lightly.

"Are you sure?" a serious Jeff, with tightly knitted eyebrows, asked.

She grinned broadly. "Yeah! Go for it!"

"Go for it?" I mouthed quietly, shaking my head in wonderment. I had never seen Stevie so casual and relaxed. It was as if she were talking about ordering a dessert after dinner rather than her husband's most cherished dream. Puzzled, I shook my head as Jeff radioed Darrell.

"Now, listen here, buddy," he began. "Schrader's fast, so our best chance to win this is to try and go the distance on gas. I want you to drop back and draft. Lay off the gas and do everything you can to conserve fuel. Okay?"

"Whatta Stevie say?" asked a concerned Darrell, who knew he would have to stretch his fuel supply by an almost impossible seven laps.

"She said to go for it," Jeff replied. I'm surprised that Darrell, knowing how conservative and cautious Stevie is, didn't wreck right then and there. But he didn't. Instead, he sighed heavily and said thoughtfully, "Okay."

Obediently, Darrell dropped behind a line of cars and took advantage of an aerodynamic tunnel they created by using their cars and fuel to part the wind resistance. Darrell pulled up on the bumper of another car and let it pull him through the wind tunnel, thus using less of his own fuel. The drama played out when Kenny and the other front cars dipped down on pit road, took a few gallons of fuel, and then hit the track again. With five laps to go, Darrell, with his heart in his throat, was leading the race, and Stevie and I were clinging nervously to each other.

"Pray!" a tearful Stevie frantically urged me. "Pray!" And I did. Later, my pragmatic brother-in-law asked cynically, "Do you really think that God *cares* who wins the Daytona 500?"

I glared at him. "Yes, I do," I replied firmly. "I think that if it's important to us, it's important to him." And certainly, nothing was much more important to Darrell Waltrip than winning the Daytona 500. I have watched the tape of that race and when I see Stevie's and my anxious faces, and how we are nervously clutching hands, I relive fifteen minutes of the most incredible emotion.

God gave us a scare, though, for the car began to spit and sputter with three laps to go and Darrell began to scream that he was out of gas and was coming in to pit.

"Don't you dare come in!" Jeff screamed. "Jiggle it, move it up and down, and get some fuel pickup. But don't come into these pits. This is our only chance to win."

Wordlessly, Darrell slung the car from high to low on the steep embankment, and miraculously the car no longer sputtered. It hummed as it came by us to take the white flag and head for the last lap. It takes only about 55 seconds to travel the length of the Daytona International Speedway under race conditions, but this was the longest 55 seconds that ever ticked through my life. Darrell finally shot over the finish line, and I was so emotional that I still tear up when I watch the tape of that race and see all of us, crying, embracing, and jumping up and down with exuberant glee. It was one of the single greatest moments of my life. Not to mention that my other car, Kenny Schrader, finished second, so my cars, which had started the great race one and two, finished one and two—only in reverse order.

From Darrell Waltrip and that victory in the Daytona 500, I learned the greatest lesson of all. I learned that you don't always have to be the *very best* to win. You don't have to be the brightest, the smartest, the most talented to prevail. You don't even have to be the *fastest* to win the Daytona 500. Sometimes to win, all you have to be is willing to take a risk, a chance, a bold gamble. Sometimes you just have to step out of the box of comfort and security that we love so and just "go for it!" I always remember this when I take on something grand, something that others consider unattainable. I only have to be willing to take the chance and not be intimidated by the thought of failure.

I've failed more times than I have ever succeeded, but you can't have one without the other. It takes only one success to wipe out a thousand failures. Out of twenty-eight tries, Darrell Waltrip won only one Daytona 500. Yet no one talks about the ones he lost. People talk instead about the one he won and how he won it with such daring bravado. That one Daytona 500 wiped out the memory of the others.

That day, it didn't appear that DW was going to win, but he proved something very important—that victory or success, even when it doesn't seem probable, is *always* possible.

FAN POWER

Most NASCAR fans are like my brother-in-law, Rodney. They pick a driver to root for, and they stick with him through thick and thin. That's the way Rodney always was about Darrell Waltrip. He pulled for Darrell during the glory years and then refused to abandon him when Darrell went eight years without a win.

A couple of years ago, we were in Philadelphia for a convention which he and my sister were attending and at which I was speaking. We met in the lobby for dinner, and Rodney said, "Okay. Now, we've got to be back here by eight because I've got to watch the Bristol race. Darrell can't win without me to cheer him on."

I started laughing and said, "God bless you, Rodney, for your loyalty. Most people would have long ago abandoned hope, but you just keep hangin' in there."

He looked me straight in the eye and said very seriously, "But

I'm an optimist. I believe that we're gonna win again one day." (They didn't.)

When I briefly tried marriage, Darrell's wife Stevie and daughter Jessica were both in my wedding. Since Rodney was an usher, he began early to lobby to be the one who escorted Stevie up the aisle.

"I want to walk with Darrell's wife," he repeatedly insisted. We heard it so much that finally, my sister, Louise, who was directing the wedding said, "Rodney! If you will just shut up, I *promise* you can walk up the aisle with Stevie." He did, and it was a highlight of his life. That and the fact that Darrell called him once from Bristol to tell him how much he appreciated his support. But when Darrell handed me the phone, Rodney thought I was playing a joke on him. When they finally met in person, Darrell managed to assure Rodney that it had been, in fact, the real Darrell Waltrip on the phone.

One of my all-time favorite stories concerns Rodney during the Firecracker 400 in Daytona one summer. He and Louise and their children, Rod and Nicole, watched the race from the stands and then congregated in a designated area to meet me following the event. As they were waiting, Rodney, who was wearing a Darrell Waltrip hat, sat down on a curb. Four guys, each wearing a Dale Earnhardt shirt, were leaving the track when they spotted my brother-in-law. Now, you must understand that Earnhardt and Waltrip were fierce rivals in those days, and that this sometimes caused, shall we say, disagreements between their fans. That day, the four Earnhardt fans were paired off, with each pair carrying a large cooler between them. Judging from their slight stagger, I can only surmise what was in those two coolers. Just as I arrived, I heard one of the men say, "Look, guys! A Waltrip fan!"

The four drew to a stop and recoiled as if the guy had, instead, said, "Look, guys! A rattlesnake!"

The guy then looked at his comrades and said, "Let's heckle him!" They each nodded and set down their coolers. I froze and held my breath, uneasy about what was about to happen. After all, there were four of them and only one Rodney, and the rest of us were women and children, so we couldn't be much help. My brother-in-law is exceptionally well-tempered. So he just looked at them and grinned and remained seated on the curb while they formed a circle around him. I tensed up tighter, fearing some kind of ambush. They then each held out an arm with a finger pointed at Rodney and began to chant, "Heckle, heckle. Heckle, heckle. Heckle, heckle."

The rest of us fell over in laughter while the serious quartet continued their mission. When they finished, they solemnly picked up their coolers and walked away. It's one of those stories that is so priceless that we laugh as hard today as we did when it happened. Even Earnhardt and Waltrip got a big kick out of it. Earnhardt, as you might imagine, got the biggest laugh.

Stock car fans are like that—loyal through and through—and they use the word "we" a lot. "We won." "We're gonna blister their butts today." "We've had some tough breaks lately, but we're comin' back." "We're fast enough to get the pole."

But in the short track amateur ranks, it tends to be "we won" if their favorite driver triumphs but "*he* lost" if their driver fails. Trust me. I've seen plenty of that, since I was married to a short track racer.

I love NASCAR fans. One of my favorite treats is to visit a racetrack and just watch 'em. They're loaded down with hats, T-shirts, and banners that extol their favorite drivers. They get into shouting matches in the stands with fans of other drivers. My all-time favorite story of an obsessive fan involved a man who lived close to the track in Darlington, South Carolina. He resided in a small mobile home that he painted just like Dale Earnhardt's car when he was driving for Wrangler. Honest to God, this man had a big number 3 on his home, and it was painted in bright yellow with a blue stripe. And he *lived* in it. Someone brought Earnhardt and Childress a photo of the trailer, and they called me over to see it.

"I want to show you a picture of my new home," Childress said with a grin as he handed it to me. When I saw it, I started laughing.

"I know! I saw this when I was driving to the track from the airport the other day. Have you not seen it in person?"

They both chuckled. "No, but we've got to," Earnhardt replied, completely tickled with the tribute. "Now, *that's* a real fan for ya!"

Research companies and major corporations have spent lots of money to document the loyalty of NASCAR fans and how they spend money with the companies that are sponsors of the sport and drivers. Executives from one big company told me that they spent marketing money in every major sport, but they had discovered that the NASCAR fans gave them the best return on investment. I personally know of one such success story, since I worked as a publicist for the brand.

In the mid-1980s, Procter and Gamble, always innovative in terms of marketing, turned an eye toward NASCAR. Even back then, the female audience was substantial—about 42 percent. Yet the sport continued to be dominated by traditional automotive products and male-oriented products like beer and cigarettes. P&G, however, believed there was a substantial target market to be captured: the women who were the primary consumers of their products. It probably wasn't hard for the Cincinnati-based company to select which of its products to try first.

Folgers coffee, founded by the Folgers on the West Coast, was acquired by P&G in the 1960s. While the coffee sold well west of the Mississippi, the southern market had been a challenge to penetrate because of the immense popularity of Maxwell House coffee, a special blend developed at the famous Maxwell House in Nashville, Tennessee. Sometime around the turn of the century, as the legend goes, Teddy Roosevelt visited the Maxwell House, and when a waiter asked if he would like more coffee, Roosevelt is said to have replied, "I sure do. That coffee is good to the last drop!" Miraculously, in the ever-changing world of advertising, that slogan has withstood the test of time for a hundred years. Since Southerners are renowned for their loyalty and traditions, particularly those passed from mother to daughter, Maxwell House coffee was king of the Southern marketplace. When a Southern daughter leaves her mother's home and sets up housekeeping, she usually chooses to use the same household products as her mother. Since stock car racing was the sport of choice in the South, it made a lot of sense for Procter and Gamble to make Folgers a primary sponsor of a car, thereby introducing it to a strong audience of female fans.

I was new to the sport when Folgers made its debut in a few races at the end of 1984 and then announced that it would join the circuit full time in 1985, but I knew that the P&G sponsorship was a big deal. In retrospect, it was most fitting because the Folgers sponsorship marked the beginning of a new era in which NASCAR would no longer be considered as playing to a strictly male audience. Once the door was opened by the austere P&G, more products aimed at women began to join the ranks. As for P&G, they were so pleased with the results that Folgers would soon be joined by Procter and Gamble's Crisco and the respected eldest product, Tide.

Once during SpeedWeeks in Daytona, when I was working with both Tide and Folgers (I was also the sport's first publicist for the Crisco brands), I decided to do an informal survey, thinking I might dig up a good press release or newspaper story. I wandered through the crowds and stopped women who were wearing Tide and Folgers apparel and asked, "Do you use these brands?" Down to the last person, the general answer was "Yes. I want to support the companies that sponsor my team and my sport."

I know the feeling. I switched from Maxwell House to Folgers even before I did the brand's team publicity. Then and now, I try to purchase brands that put marketing dollars into the sport. I recently bought my first European-made car, the first non-American car of my life. No one will ever believe how excruciatingly hard that was for me. For years, I would test-drive the cars, but I could never make myself buy one because of my tremendous loyalty to the American auto industry. My daddy, first of all, was loyal to American products, but when I moved into NASCAR racing, I made my own choice, based on gratitude. I have always been appreciative of the wonderful career I had, thanks, in part, to Detroit's automakers.

I love this kind of loyalty, and I am inspired by it. My family's philosophy has always been to stay loyal to the people and companies that have always been there for us. Daddy never forgot the bank that gave him his first loan when no other would. For the rest of his life, despite the fact he could have gotten higher deposit rates elsewhere, he refused to bank anywhere else. This kind of admirable loyalty was further ingrained in me during the years that I spent in Winston Cup racing. In a world that can often be wishy-washy, loyalty is one of the greatest gifts we can offer. It's a true treasure of friendship, a true measure of goodness and sincerity. In NASCAR racing, you'll find a host of people—drivers, teams, and fans—who abide by their word and practice loyalty of the most steadfast kind.

Junie Donlavey, a Virginia gentleman with the most beautiful Southern lilt, has always run a low-budget race team, the kind that can't compete with the top-dollar teams. However, his team was the perfect entrée into the sport for young, upcoming stars like Kenny Schrader. He gave a start to many young men, and he has always been a man of integrity and kindness. When Mr. Donlavey dies, there's not a church in Virginia that will be big enough to hold all his grateful, admiring friends. All the people he has helped will be forever loyal.

In the spring of 2000, Dale Earnhardt delightfully reminded me of his loyalty and how he had not forgotten who made him a star. In NASCAR, there is a program that pays "appearance money." It's called Winner's Circle. The program has a dozen slots that are filled by the first twelve different race winners each season. These drivers are guaranteed a certain amount of money just to show up and qualify for a race. In return, the promoters of Winston Cup events are allowed to use these drivers and their images to advertise races. That guaranteed money is quite a help to the teams, so it's a big deal to be on the Winner's Circle program. Each driver on the program must make two or three Winner's Circle appearances during the season. In other words, a driver gives a track one full day of his time. Normally, he goes to the track a day early and does media presentations for the upcoming race, such as press conferences and individual interviews.

That spring, one of Earnhardt's appearances assigned by NASCAR was the race in May at Talladega Superspeedway, where Troi Hayes, one of the finest marketing wizards I've ever known, is the director of marketing. Troi came up with an absolutely sensational promotion. He decided to team Earnhardt with an Alabama state trooper. Together, they would spend the day patrolling the interstate and would pull over law-abiding citizens. The plan was for Earnhardt to hop out of the patrol car and give the law-abider a set of tickets to the big Sunday race. Great, huh? Well, Earnhardt thought so, too, but he was crafty enough to ask who manufactured the patrol cars—Ford or General Motors. Turns out that every patrol car in the state of Alabama is a Ford. So when Earnhardt, a devoted Chevy driver who had also had a fifteen-year sponsor relationship with GM's Goodwrench, discovered that the promotion required him to ride in a Ford, he said, "No go. I ain't ridin' in no Ford. Get me a Chevrolet and I'll do it; otherwise, it's off."

I roared with appreciation of his loyalty when Troi told me the complete story. Earnhardt was such a huge star that he could have done whatever he doggone pleased, yet he remained loyal to the company that had stuck by him in the lean years. It was quite a challenge for poor Troi, but he scrambled and managed to get a special Chevrolet shipped to Birmingham and then painted and equipped like the Ford patrol cars. The day that Earnhardt spent several hours "ticketing" good citizens, the promotion turned out to be a media magnet. The story was carried on almost every major news outlet in America, and rightly so.

I learned a lot, too, about the loyalty of NASCAR fans like my friend Jack Friedman. He's the kind of fan who has an entire room devoted to his NASCAR collection. When he married, his favorite wedding present came from me—a limited-edition drawing of the famous turn-one tussle between Earnhardt, Elliott, and Geoff Bodine in the 1987 Winston. While working on this book, I took Jack to a race, complete with garage credentials and personal introductions to many of his heroes. It was, without a doubt, one of the greatest days of his life. While I introduced him into the heart of his beloved sport, he introduced me into the mind of a rabid NASCAR fan. It was quite an eye-opening experience. Did you know that a true fan, just like all the drivers, always carries a Sharpie, the wide-tipped black ink marker that will write on anything from hats to plastic cups to glossy photos? I discovered this while Jack and I were sitting around in lawn chairs and shooting the breeze with Richard Petty. A fan approached Petty to autograph a glossy poster and handed a regular ink pen to the King.

Richard shook his head and said, "Naw, that won't do. I need a Sharpie." Before Richard could pull out the Sharpie that he invariably had in his pocket—I have yet to see a driver or NASCAR star without one—Jack beat him to the draw and handed over his Sharpie. I thought nothing more of it until we were leaving Richard's motor coach and Jack turned to me and shook his head.

"I can't believe that guy didn't bring a Sharpie with him." There was a strong sound of disgust in Jack's voice, and he rolled his eyes. "Every true NASCAR fan knows that if there's a chance you might see a driver to get an autograph, you *have* to have a Sharpie. I can't believe he didn't know that."

Me neither.

THE TIES THAT BIND

AND SOMETIMES CHOKE

(THE OPPOSITION)

It was a family feud, done NASCAR-style. That is, a family combined its considerable heft and bloodlines against an unfortunate soul who thought he was taking on just one guy.

It is, undoubtedly, one of the most famous scenes in the television history of stock car racing. There on the back straightaway of the Daytona International Speedway, the CBS cameras zoomed in on two brothers and a longtime nemesis slinging fists and behaving as if they were in a dispute at a Saturday night short-track race rather than the sport's most famous event, the Daytona 500. It was 1979, and the race was being televised live for the first time in NASCAR history—flag-to-flag coverage on a major network. Until that point, the race had been shown only in excerpts, usually delayed. This year's Daytona 500 signified that William Paley and the other bigwigs at CBS no longer viewed stock car racing as simply a Southern sport with redneck roots. The "Tiffany Network," known for its high-class highbrow programming, had cleverly entered the arena of racing coverage.

To make a 500-mile story short, Cale Yarborough and Donnie Allison had been trading paint all day, and as the laps wound down, the trading got more intense. Allison was leading on the final lap with a tenacious Yarborough hot on his rear bumper. The hitting got rougher on the back straightaway, and just before the two entered turn three, they wrecked each other, crashing to the apron of the track. A surprised Richard Petty, who was running a distant third, cruised on by and took the checkered flag for his sixth Daytona 500. But Petty's win wasn't the big story. That story was what was happening on the back straightaway, where Yarborough, a former Golden Gloves boxer, and Allison had climbed out of their racecars and were hotly disagreeing. When Donnie's brother, Bobby, saw the shuffle, he pulled down on the apron, parked his car, and joined the brawl.

For the millions watching the race, that bit of color would be remembered long after folks had forgotten who won. For Paley and the CBS people, there had to be no doubt that they had made the right decision when they got one look at the ratings and saw that fight being rebroadcast repeatedly on competing networks.

But remember that I didn't step into NASCAR until the middle 1980s, so I was completely naive about what had gone before. I didn't know the story until Donnie and Bobby regaled me with their version of the infamous fight. Bobby had pulled one of his pranks on me while we were in Charlotte, and I was giving him down the road for it. This only delighted him more, and Donnie chuckled at his brother's cleverness.

I turned to Donnie and said, "It would help if you wouldn't encourage him! He's bad enough as it is."

Donnie he-he'd in that famous Allison way and retorted, "I have to stick up for him 'cause he's my brother."

"Are you two always partners in everything?" I asked sarcastically.

Both nodded vigorously. "Sure are," Bobby said.

"Like that time me and ol' Cale got into it in Daytona," Donnie began. "Bobby just parked his car and joined the fight!"

With the delighted glee of children, they proudly told the story to a new audience. I was astounded and turned to Bobby.

"You got out of the racecar and starting fighting Cale?" I exclaimed.

He nodded happily.

"Why?"

Bobby grinned broadly. "I had to!" He replied with that Allison twinkle in his eyes. He spread out his hands, palms up. "He was hittin' my brother!"

I started laughing at the wonderful boyishness of those two, telling the story as if one of them had rescued the other from a playground tussle. To tell you the truth, I think they're prouder of that moment than of any race or championship they ever won. But for what it's worth, there is some dispute about whether Cale and Donnie ever exchanged blows. Cale once said in an interview that he and Donnie were merely fussing until Bobby came along and started fistfighting. Richard Petty said that from what he could see, it looked like it was mostly Bobby's fight.

"I stopped to see if Donnie needed a ride," Bobby explained to me recently. "Cale came running over and hit me while I was still sitting in the car!" Bobby may have lost some of his memory from that Pocono wreck in 1988, but he still remembers that day quite clearly. *Every* detail.

Nonetheless, Bobby's brother had just lost the Daytona 500, so there was family honor to protect. I have never seen a family so intensely loyal as the Allisons. Whenever you took on one, you took on all of them. The thing that always intrigued me was that no matter which side an Allison was on and regardless of whether he was right or wrong, all the others were on that same side.

The Allisons extended an honorary family membership to the wonderful and enormously well-liked Neil Bonnett. He was part of the Hueytown Gang, and the Allisons would fight for Neil as quickly as they'd fight for each other. When Neil was injured in

1986 and couldn't drive for a few races, he convinced his veteran car owner, Junior Johnson, to put the young Davey Allison in his car at Talladega. Neil told me that Bobby and his family had done so much to help him that he wanted to return the favor. Six months after Davey died, Neil was killed in an accident in Daytona (in the same spot where his best buddy, Dale Earnhardt, would later die). I know that this was another brutal heartache for Bobby, who lost both of his sons within eleven months of each other, and then one of the best friends he ever had.

NASCAR is a family sport in every sense of the word. It was built by a family and is sustained by family racers and supported by the families who watch together and often square off against each other as fans of different drivers. In no other sport will you find so many families. In the NFL, the rare occasion when two brothers wind up in the league and meet in a playoff game on opposite teams makes a great media story. But this is so common in NASCAR that it isn't a story at all. There are many families in the sport, and I've worked with many of them—the Elliotts, Rudds, Bodines, Waltrips, Earnhardts, Allisons, Pettys, Parrotts, Pembertons, Woods, Parsons, Jarretts, Wallaces, and Burtons.

One major factor that makes stock car racing so enormously popular is its unique and overwhelming appeal to women, an appeal that isn't found to the same extent in other sports. An interviewer recently asked me why I thought there were so many female NASCAR fans, and I replied, "Because women drive cars that look similar to the ones that are raced. They understand trying to pass a car on the interstate or being cut off by someone else. It's harder to understand football on a similar emotional level. Women connect with the sport in an emotional way. These drivers and their families are like family to the female fans, and that makes a big difference."

There are a lot of families in the sport because once one family member gets in, he or she can introduce the others and share valuable connections. Darrell Waltrip once told me, "People are always asking me how to get into the sport to work. It's a funny thing about (Winston Cup) racing. It's hard to get into the inner sanctum, but once you get in, it's just as hard to get out."

I've thought about that statement a lot. The sport is such a tight circle that people have to really work hard and make strong connections to get in, but once there they seldom escape. It's a self-sufficient world that continues to offer its people endless opportunities. Consider, for instance, drivers who break into the big time but never win or make a great showing. Still, they continue to move from team to team in the sport and always have a great ride. That would probably never happen in the corporate world.

Adam Petty was a fourth-generation driver, the only fourth generation in any professional sport. Tragically, this handsome, personable young man was killed in a practice crash in New Hampshire in May 2000. I will always remember one Sunday afternoon in Charlotte when Adam was four and I had joined the Pettys and my friends the Parkses, for a picnic before the race. We were talking about the race and how everyone had qualified. Someone said, "Richard ought to have a good chance today because the car ran so good in practice yesterday afternoon."

Little Adam had started to take a bite from his sandwich but stopped and practically screamed, "Well, I want BILL ELLIOTT to win! That's who I'm pulling for!"

His grandmother, Lynda, looked as if she had been slapped. She rushed over to Adam, grabbed him by the arms, looked straight into his eyes, and said very seriously, "Adam, your granddaddy and your daddy are both out there racing, and we don't pull for anyone else but them. Do you understand?"

Adam didn't blink. Defiantly, he looked at his grandmother, straightened his shoulders, and replied very earnestly, "I know they're racin'. But I want *Bill Elliott* to win."

I don't know what Lynda said after that, because I was chuckling so hard that I had to walk away before *I* got a scolding.

The phone shrilled in my hotel room in Charlotte early one October morning. When I answered it, Carolyn Rudd dispensed with any formalities and urgently demanded, "Have you seen the paper this morning?"

I knew immediately that something was terribly wrong, for very few things fluster Carolyn. I assumed it had to do with one of our clients, Tide or Folgers, or one of our drivers, Mark Martin or Darrell Waltrip. Carolyn was president of the sport's top marketing company, SMG, and she subcontracted her public relations to me.

"No," I answered. "I'm getting ready to go to the track."

"Well, get it and call me right back."

My heart paused for a second. "Is anyone dead?" I asked nervously.

"Not yet," she replied tersely. "Get it and call me back."

I hung up the phone, certain that some kind of public relations disaster awaited me outside the hotel room. It didn't take long to decipher, either. The moment I saw the bold headline of the *Charlotte Observer* that lay outside my door, I knew why Carolyn was so upset. I heaved a heavy sigh. I quickly perused the story and then picked up the phone to call Carolyn and determine our plan of action.

A few days earlier, our little world had been shaken severely by the highway death of Rob Moroso, who had been a sensation on the Grand National circuit and was the favorite to win Winston Cup Rookie of the Year title for 1990 (which he did posthumously). Moroso was also the prince of the Moroso kingdom, which was centered around a performance auto parts company that specialized in parts for racecars. Rob appeared to have everything that a young man could desire—looks, money, superb racing talent, a meteoric rise to fame, a beautiful girlfriend, and a devoted father determined to give his son the very best. All that promise came to a horrible end when Rob, his blood saturated with alcohol (0.22 percent, more than twice the 0.10 percent legal level), left a tavern in Charlotte with his girlfriend and crashed into another car almost immediately. Rob and the female driver of the other car died, and Rob's girlfriend and the passenger in the other car were critically injured. The day before Carolyn's urgent phone call, Rob had been eulogized in a memorial service at Charlotte Motor Speedway. The face of Rob's father, Dick Moroso, was deeply etched with devastation. Bravely, though, he had stood by the door to accept embraces and condolences from Rob's other family—the racing community. As I left the service, my eye caught the front page of *USA Today* in its box located at the front entrance of the speedway. I stopped to buy the paper, which announced a tragic death in a European royal family.

"Ronda?" I heard someone behind me ask softly. I turned to see my dear old friend Alan Kulwicki.

"Hi, Alan," I said, leaning over to hug him. "It's a sad day, isn't it? I'll never forget the sadness on Dick Moroso's face. And did you see this?" I held up the newspaper. "Princess Caroline's husband was killed in a speedboat accident."

He took the newspaper, read the headline, and shook his head. "At least her husband died doing what he loved and he knew the risk, but Rob—" He broke off and again shook his head. It's an odd thing about racecar drivers. They accept that death can come at any moment in a race. They live with it and are completely undaunted by it. But death at an early age outside of a racecar is a thought that makes them shudder, a cruel hoax played by the unjust hands of fate. After coming perilously close to dying of pneumonia in 1986, Tim Richmond said to me, "If I go out in a racecar, that's fine. That's part of the deal. But dying from something like pneumonia is unacceptable."

According to that belief, both Tim and Alan died in unacceptable ways. Earnhardt, however, died within sight of the checkered flag at the Daytona 500. That was the sole thought that comforted me that day—he died as he would have chosen to die. If we had to lose the sport's anointed star, at least he died on the last lap, because if it had been the first lap, Dale Earnhardt would have been teed off that he didn't get to run the whole race.

Rob Moroso's death and the part that alcohol had played in it were extremely controversial. The media had done various stories on drinking and driving, but it was the *Observer*, with Charlotte playing host to the racing series that week, that had found a unique investigative angle. The *Observer*, after all, won a Pulitzer for its splendid journalistic investigation that tumbled Jim Bakker and his Charlotte-based PTL organization. The headline story on the morning that Carolyn called me was an investigation by an *Observer* reporter into Winston Cup drivers and their driving records from the Department of Motor Vehicles. In addition to speeding violations, the reporter was most interested in drivers who had been charged with DUI. To be honest, journalistically, it was a sound approach—except that there was little to uncover, since the drivers had been well behaved, apart, as you might expect, from speeding tickets. The story, however, fingered an innocent Ricky Rudd, Carolyn's brother, and said that he had a conviction for DUI.

As soon as I read it, my mouth dropped and I blinked hard. "Not Ricky," I mumbled to myself. I knew, without asking, that it wasn't true. Ricky is a teetotaler. He doesn't care for alcohol. I knew then that Carolyn was calling to ask for my help as a friend rather than professionally. I dialed her back.

"I am not believing this," I said when she answered.

"Me either!" she stormed. "You know Ricky. You know he doesn't drink. Bless his heart, he's so upset about this; but I told him not to worry—that we'd get it straightened out. Can you help?"

"Sure. I'll be glad to. What do you need?"

"I've already called an attorney, but what's the best way to handle it with the newspaper?"

"Call the editor on the story. He's responsible for making certain that facts are accurate and double-checked. I think it's a waste of time to call the reporter. Want me to call?"

"Yes, honey, if you would. Here are the facts they got wrong." No one can dive into an issue more deeply or more quickly than Carolyn. She then ticked off three major statements that were incorrect, that should have been double-checked, and that would have proved the story wrong. I was dumbstruck.

"You're kiddin' me!"

"No, I'm not." She was furious. No mother cub has ever more fiercely defended her babies than Carolyn. She always protects and defends Ricky, who is one of the sweetest, most amicable guys in racing. Carolyn never hesitates to fight for Ricky. In a very gentle, Southern kind of way, Carolyn can put the biggest brute back in his place.

I called the newspaper and asked to be put through to the story's editor. He was very nice but firm as he told me that he and the newspaper stood behind the story.

"But it isn't the same Ricky Rudd who races in Winston Cup. That Ricky Rudd doesn't even drink," I insisted.

"We stand behind the reporter," he replied. (By the way, this is the kind of editor that every reporter wants.)

"Would you still stand behind him if I told you that the age and state of residence of your Ricky Rudd are not the same as those of our Ricky Rudd?"

There was a pause. Then he said, "What are you talking about?" I explained that the Ricky in the story and the racing Ricky lived in different states and were several years apart in age. He still didn't seem convinced, until I lowered the boom that Carolyn had provided.

"And the Ricky Rudd in your story is black. Our Ricky is white. Now, if a layperson can find that out, why didn't your reporter?"

He was stunned and said that he would check into it further and call back.

"Just so you know," I said in concluding the conversation. "We want a full retraction on the front page, *above* the fold." That's the most important part of the newspaper, because it's the only area that can be viewed when the papers are in a rack or on a newsstand. It was only fair, too, since the original story had been awarded that prime space. Upon further investigation, the newspaper editors discovered the error and called to express sincere regrets and assurances that the wrong would be made right.

The next day, the newspaper ran a retraction on the front page with a heartfelt apology and a headline above the fold that said, "Observer Incorrectly Reported Ricky Rudd Has DWI Conviction." As Ricky sadly noted, "There'll be people who saw the first story but never see the second with the apology so they'll always think the story was true." The irony is that Ricky has always been staunchly opposed to drinking and driving, so much so that he had donated many hours to taping public service announcements for radio and television against it.

Ricky's saga was a powerful reminder to me how a piece of incorrect gossip and a poorly checked story can injure innocent lives, how we should treat another person's reputation as gently as if it were our own. But I also discovered that the power of the press is nothing compared with the power of family and love. Long after a race ends and the fans leave the stands, your family will still be there.

For humor and delicious wit, you'd have to look far to find a family funnier than the Waltrips. Of course, if you watch racing on a regular basis, you know about the incredibly quick-witted Darrell, but the rest of the family is like that, too, including his sister Carolyn and his brother Michael. If you had known their dad, Leroy, you'd understand exactly where the sense of humor originated. I don't remember how it began, but I started calling Leroy "old goat." "Well, hey there, you old goat." He would always laugh delightedly and tossed back some sharp comment. Leroy could take it as well as give it, and this is the mark of the finest funnyman.

One of my favorite family stories involves Michael, who was doing an early morning radio show in Atlanta. He asked the disc jockey if he could mention his sponsor. Obviously, with all the money that the sponsors spend, the drivers and teams are under significant pressure to plug them at every opportunity.

"Tell you what," the deejay replied. "If you'll call a famous person right now and get him on the phone, I'll let you mention your sponsor."

So, of course, Michael picked up the phone and called his brother, Darrell, in Franklin, Tennessee, where, owing to the one-hour time difference, he was still asleep. On the air Michael explained the situation to him.

"He said he'd let me mention my sponsor if I'd call someone famous. So, I was wondering—do you have Bill Elliott's phone number?"

WINNERS, LOSERS, AND
FRIENDS GONE FOREVER

Just as racecars can reshuffle on a restart, my priorities quickly reshuffled on November 18, 1990, in Hampton, Georgia, a small rural town on the south side of Atlanta.

When I watch a video replay of the event, it happens quickly on my television screen. But while it was actually happening, it seemed creepingly slow, almost static. Life-changing moments of crystallization are like that—they stand perfectly still, producing photographic images that burn deeply into one's mind, heart, and soul. This was my experience on that ill-fated day, and today I can still see it all as clearly as I saw it that afternoon.

When I awoke that morning, I believed that nothing was more important than who would reign as Winston Cup champion when the day drew to a close. We were entering the final race of the season, a heated race for the championship with only six points separating Dale Earnhardt and Mark Martin. We—Mark; the team owned by Jack Roush; the primary sponsor, Folgers; and me as the publicist—had captured the points lead in Sonoma in June and had led steadily until the previous race in Phoenix when Earnhardt squeaked past us by the slender six points. Everything that we had worked for since February came down to Mark finishing at least one and probably two positions in front of Earnhardt, who was hungry for another championship. He was on a two-year dry spell in which his run of championships had been invaded by Bill Elliott in 1988 and Rusty Wallace in 1989. Mark and everyone around him were racked with anxiety. Indisputably, the Folgers car and driver had been the best for most of the season, but now we faced the possibility that best might become second best.

It also did not help that in the two weeks since Phoenix, the February race in Richmond had preyed on our weary minds. Mark won soundly, but post-race inspectors discovered that a spacer between the carburetor and intake manifold was half an inch taller than the two-inch NASCAR allowance. It probably did not add any horsepower to the engine, but even if it had it wouldn't have mattered, since a short track like Richmond is won more on handling and strategy than on speed. Mark was allowed to keep his win, but the team was slapped with what was at that time the largest fine in NASCAR history, $40,000, and penalized 46 of the 185 Winston Cup points that his win had earned. The Roush team didn't mind taking home only $19,150 of the $59,150 first-place money so much as losing the Winston Cup points. Since the Richmond race, those 46 points had haunted everyone connected to the team. Had they not been taken, Mark would have been entering the Atlanta race with a 40-point lead rather than a 6-point deficit.

Of course, the media had been kind and did not bother us with any questions over those points. (And if you believe that, I have some beautiful oceanfront property in the North Georgia mountains that I would love to sell.) For two weeks, Mark and I had been pulled hither and yon by the press. To complicate the matter, we were battling with Earnhardt, a man whom the team manager Steve Hmiel called "the toughest cat in the alley." He was just plain tough and had won three previous championships. That made him calm in the center of the storm, while we shook so badly that you could hear the jittering sound of our teeth and bones. To make matters even worse with the media, when we got to Atlanta, Roush had made a somewhat controversial call to buy a car from Ford teammate Davey Allison. The press spent the week second-guessing that call and digging up quotes from every so-called expert in the garage. As a result, it was a media circus in Atlanta. We had to rope off the area around the Folgers car in the garage so the crew could work on it. Mark, his eyes heavy and with puffy bags beneath them, was tired and stressed, so he asked me to keep the media and others away as much as possible. Since I was fiercely loyal to my drivers, I was happy to do so, especially when there was so much at stake.

By Saturday afternoon, I was worn out. I plopped down on the sofa in Darrell and Stevie Waltrip's motor home, where I planned to spend the night, since they had a hotel suite. The Waltrips were still there and listened sympathetically as I moaned and rubbed my eyes, blurred with weariness. "I have spent the entire day telling people why they can't talk to Mark," I whimpered. "I've had to be so mean that I feel like a witch."

Young Jessica Waltrip, who was three, overheard the comment, though we didn't realize that until the next day. As her sitter watched the pre-race activities on television, the cameras followed Mark and me as we walked to his car on pit road. Jessica looked up from playing and saw us.

"Look!" she exclaimed, pointing to the television screen. "There's Martin Martin and the wicked witch!"

Out of the mouths of babes.

Earlier that morning, I had been walking through the garage when I heard a low "Ron*da!*" I turned to see the grinning face of Mike Rich, the rear tire changer for Bill Elliott. Mike, age thirty-two, was a handsome man with blond hair the color of cornsilk that was cut in a short, stylish shag. A short strawberry-blond beard, a couple of shades darker than his hair, covered his face. Since Mike had a full-time job back home in Blairsville, Georgia, he was part of the crew that comes to the track only on Sunday. As the rear tire changer, Mike was good, quick, and dependable and never complained. He was extremely likable and often reminded me of an adorable, cuddly teddy bear. If he liked you, he talked to you. Otherwise, he wasted no words.

"What's up?" he asked as he pulled up beside me. I put my arm around his shoulders and we walked along, talking about the hassle of contending for a championship when you're behind by six points and you're chasing an intimidating giant named Dale Earnhardt.

I sighed wearily. "I'll be so happy when this day is over."

"Win or lose?" he asked with a lopsided grin.

"Winning would definitely be better," I replied with a wink.

He laughed. "I hear ya! Well, good luck." He patted my shoulder and walked off to the pits.

From the moment the green flag fell, it was evident that Bill's car was the one to beat and that the second race was between Earnhardt and Martin for position only. It was also clear that Earnhardt's car was stronger than Mark's. In Mark's pits, we were hoping against hope when a caution came out on lap 300 of the 328-lap race. Our pits were situated between Elliott's, on our left, and Earnhardt's, on our right. As the leader, Bill was first in the pits several seconds before Mark arrived. Bill's guys jumped the wall and went to work. Suddenly, I heard tires screeching and looked up just in time to see Ricky Rudd's car careening down pit road—and then suddenly, violently, it whipped around 180 degrees. With the nose of Ricky's car pointing in the opposite direction from the other cars, the rear half of his car slammed into Bill's with a thunderous bang. I froze in horror and I don't think I breathed for the next several seconds. I heard a sickening thump as Mike Rich's body smashed against Bill's car, then I saw his head snap back against Ricky's car. The squeezing of his body between the two cars produced a viselike effect, causing his radio headset to fly from his head and straight up about fifteen or twenty feet. I focused on the headset, refusing to look again at Mike, and watched it as it fell back toward earth and landed somewhere in the traffic on pit road. There was instant mayhem in the pits as emergency crews, team members, and, yes, the television cameras crowded in. As tears filled my eyes and a sick feeling spread through my body, I watched the grisly scene as they lifted my battered friend and gingerly placed him on a stretcher. I could see that he was still alive and I began to pray.

Scenes of Riverside, California, from two years earlier popped into my mind. That day, I was in the press box about fifty yards away from Bill's pit when a car on pit road knocked another car into Bill's, which knocked Bill's car off the jack and onto the guys who were working. Dan Elliott and three others were injured, including the rear tire changer Chuck Hill, one of my very favorites of the crew from Dawsonville.

After that tragic pit stop, Chuck lay in a hospital two thousand miles from home and family as he fought for his life. It was touch and go and then many long months of recovery, but Chuck did live through that accident. I knew, though, as Mike was carried away, that he would not be as lucky as Chuck. I shook my head, rebelling against the horrific thought. I couldn't believe this was happening again. Not to the Elliotts. Not to another friend of mine.

That was the moment of crystallization, the moment when my priorities shifted and reshuffled.

Twenty-seven laps later, the race ended and I alone was waiting for Mark as he pulled into the garage where the Folgers truck happened to be parked next to Bill's truck. Mark pulled to a stop and solemnly crawled out of the car. He had finished three positions behind Earnhardt. Wordlessly, we looked at each other and silently, slowly shook our heads. Something much more important than a championship had just been lost.

After a long silence, Mark asked quietly, "What's a championship? What does it matter when you see something like that?"

"You're right," I agreed. "What does it matter when a life is lost?"

Bill pulled in behind his truck and was met by Dan, who had also been slightly injured while changing the front tires and whose bandaged arm was in a sling. Poor Dan. He had been injured twice in two years on pit road. Shortly before the accident in Riverside, he had moved forward to become front tire changer, because changing the rear tires is the most dangerous job in the pit. After the disaster in Atlanta, Dan would go over the wall to change tires only four more times, and then only to prove to himself that he still had the nerve after two horribly close calls. Once that was done, he walked away and never looked back.

"It's bad, Bill," Dan said, his voice quivering. "It's really bad." Bill hurried off with an anxious stomp and Dan turned his soulful, sad eyes to me. Wordlessly, we shared a moment of quiet sadness, reunited once again by common grief.

I was as sad for Ricky Rudd as I was for Mike. It was an accident. Ricky's back wheels had locked up when he came down pit road. It could not have been avoided, but I knew he was devastated. Mark and I met with the press, and as we finished up, Carolyn Rudd grabbed me by the arm.

"Will you do me a favor?" she asked and when I nodded, she continued, "I know your car is parked here in the garage. Will you take Linda and Ricky to the airport so that he doesn't have to go through a crowd to get to another car?" Ricky and his wife Linda were both pale and shaken as they climbed in my SUV. Anxiously, Ricky looked out the window and tapped his foot nervously as we threaded our way to the small private airport a couple of miles away.

"I hope he's gonna be okay," he said, almost to himself. "They told me that he was fine and that he'd be okay." His tone was wistful.

"Maybe he will be," I said quietly, knowing from what I saw that he wouldn't.

Mike Rich died a couple of hours after the accident, and with him died a lot of false pretenses and adoration of worldly honors. Some of them belonged to me. We lost the Winston Cup championship by 26 points to Dale Earnhardt, who finished third in the race while Mark finished sixth. No one, not even the press, mentioned what had happened in Richmond or the 46-point penalty that, had those points not been taken, would have allowed Mark to win the championship by a margin of 20 points. Somehow, it didn't seem important any more.

PLAYING SECOND FIDDLE

TO A RACECAR

As Richard Petty approached his fiftieth year on earth, his wife, Lynda, began to inquire ever so gently, yet ever so insistently, as to when he planned to retire. Without fail, Richard always shot back with an honest, completely practical reply, "When it quits being fun."

Sounds like every racecar driver I've ever known.

When Richard's car barrel-rolled seven times down the front straightaway at Daytona International Speedway in the 1988 Daytona 500, it didn't look like a lot of fun to me. It looked horrifying—the car completely disintegrated, with large pieces of sheet metal ripping and flying away from the chassis with each heart-stopping tumble. To the King's fans, it was scary. To those of us who know him, it was chilling. But to Lynda and her three daughters, it was pure terror.

An unconscious Petty was pulled from the wreckage and transported to the infield care center. When he awakened, the first person he saw was his distraught wife, her face streaked with tears, mascara, and makeup. She spoke through tightly gritted teeth. "Well, Richard. Are we *still* having *fun*?"

Unfazed by the near tragedy or Lynda's anger, he was back in the racecar the next week in Richmond, where he was a top contender all day. Again, it sounds like every racecar driver I've ever known. I was married to a man like that—a man who almost lost his life when, while he was leading a big season-ending race, the steering rod broke, he crashed, another car hit his in the vicinity of the gas cell, and fire erupted. To escape, he had to first pull the pin from the steering wheel and take it off (a driver cannot get out of a car until the steering wheel is removed because of the tightness of the compartment), unsnap his safety harness, and crawl through the window. In those precious seconds before his burning body could be extinguished, eighty percent of his upper body received third-degree burns. The fire was so hot that the mouthpiece of his radio, which the driver always wears against his mouth so that he can transmit clearly over the roar of the engines, was melted and fused to his mouth. When he arrived at the hospital emergency room, the doctor had to use a scalpel to cut it away from his lips. Later, the doctor would say that the melted mouthpiece had, in all likelihood, saved his life because it kept his lungs healthy rather than subjecting them to damage from the fire. Still, that night in the emergency room, when the doctor reviewed the horrible injuries on the body convulsing in hard jerks from pain and morphine, he said softly, "Son, if you need to make things right with God, do it now because you're not going to make it through the night."

Yet he lived. After a month in the hospital and another month of recovery, he went back to race again. Yes, he did. He absolutely did. With wounds that still oozed and needed new bandaging in between practice and the race and with a doctor standing by, he raced again. And he won. The crowds went wild with approval for the handsome blond star who managed to triumph over disaster.

That was his worst accident, but it wasn't his last. One weekend when I was away with the Winston Cup Series, he was running NASCAR's Winston Racing Series when he crashed and was knocked unconscious. His brother, a huge, muscular sort, was so frightened that he refused to wait for the emergency crew to cut him free. He jumped up on the hood of the car and hit the windshield with a massive elbow that knocked the rivets loose and sprang the windshield open. He then grabbed the roof of the car and tore it loose so the paramedics could reach his brother immediately. I am told that the stunt was so spectacular that it silenced the spectators, who stood and watched with stunned amazement.

"Honest to God," my friend Debbie Lunsford told me, "if I hadn't seen it with my own eyes, I wouldn't have believed it. It was like something the Incredible Hulk would do."

When I heard the story, I wasn't surprised at the fear that had driven his brother to such a Herculean performance. When you come so close to losing a loved one in a tragic accident that happens right before your eyes, you're never the same again. You never manage to escape the prison of fear. Then when an accident, major or minor, occurs, time is suspended until you hear someone say over the radio, "He's moving. He's talking. He's fine." When my husband's brother did not hear a voice of reassurance over the radio, the fear pumped up his adrenaline so high that he was literally able to rip a racecar apart.

For several years following his death-defying crash, my husband remained under the care of a plastic surgeon, who worked diligently to repair the extensive damage. A long scar ran down the left side of his face and under his chin, and there were massive burn scars on his arms, back, and sides. Every couple of months, he would visit the surgeon for painful injections deep into the facial scar, injections that slowly but gradually reduced its size and severity. The shots hurt so badly that he would grasp my hand, squeezing it so tightly that I was certain my bones were close to cracking. It broke my heart to see him in such incredible pain, and I always thought of Lynda Petty. Like her, I wanted to ask, "Are we *still* having *fun*?"

I have to stop here and say something about NASCAR, especially since the organization has taken so much flak from time to time. About five years after my husband's fiery accident, he was still receiving treatment when a couple of the plastic surgeon's bills were returned to us from NASCAR's insurance company with an explanation that the time limit for treatment had expired. I called Jim Hunter, one of the organization's key executives, and explained that his scars were extensive and required a long time to heal before repair could be attempted. Without hesitation, he replied, "You send the bills to me and I'll see that they get paid, regardless of how long it takes." And he did.

So while my battered heart wanted to cry out, "Are we still having fun?"—I didn't. For to love a man is to accept his dreams, whether you understand them or not. If you strip him of his dreams, you've stripped him of his soul, and without that he cannot completely love you. I learned early in my life that to love a racer is to accept that, more often than not, in the race for his heart, you will come in second. I wasn't used to being second in a boyfriend's life when I started dating Dan Elliott, but he quickly taught me. I wish I had a dollar for every date he canceled or for all the times when, if I wanted to see him at all, I had to sit on a high stool next to him in the race shop and watch him as he worked on a transmission. One night, after he canceled yet another date, I stopped by to see my friends the Lunsfords. Before turning to the business of building and owning racetracks, Bud Lunsford had been one of the most famous short-track drivers in the nation, winning more than 1,200 races.

"Hey, there!" LaQuita greeted me as I shuffled into the kitchen and tossed my purse onto the counter. She was cooking dinner for the family, and as she stirred a pot simmering on the stove, she turned to me with a quizzical expression. "I thought you and Dan had a date tonight."

I sighed heavily and crossed my arms as I leaned against the doorframe. "We did." I frowned with a mixture of disgust and disappointment. Then I spoke in a childish, sarcastic voice. "But the racecar's not ready for Michigan and they have to leave with it tomorrow night, so he had to work."

This woman, who was married to a racecar that owned a man, swirled around to face me. She planted her hands on her hips and eyed me for a moment with the kind of motherly look that you get just before you get a lecture. She wagged her finger at me. "Let me tell you something, young lady. I've played second fiddle to a racecar for twenty-five years—and I'd much rather play second fiddle to a racecar than to another woman!" Her voice was so firm, and her words were so wise and strong, that I immediately straightened up and took notice. When she saw that she had gotten my attention, she continued, "When he's with the racecar, you always know where you'll find him. If you want to speak to Dan right now, walk to the phone and dial the shop and you'll hear his voice. As long as he's with that racecar, you don't have to worry about another woman."

I was young but smart enough to know that I was hearing wise words. They changed my entire thinking. From that moment forward, I realized that if I was going to love a racer, then I was willingly choosing to come in second to a metal monster. Also contributing to my education at the same time were Martha Elliott, Bill's first wife; and Sheila Elliott, who is married to Ernie, the oldest brother. More than once, they both got a good chuckle over my unrealistic expectations of romance with an Elliott brother. I thought that the least Dan could do was to treat me to dinner or a movie once a week. One Sunday afternoon during a nonrace weekend, after church and lunch, the guys had gone to the race shop to work and Martha and I were taking a stroll along the winding, country road that connected the various Elliott homes and race shop buildings.

"Martha, don't you ever get tired of not having a complete day without the presence of a racecar?" I asked as I reached down and plucked a dandelion. As I blew it into the wind, she answered with complete honesty.

"There's no choice. If you're goin' to choose to be part of this family, you choose to take second place." She tossed her head back and laughed. "That is, if you're lucky, you'll be as high as second place! This is what makes Bill happy, so I just accept it. I can tell you that if he had to choose between me and that racecar, he wouldn't think long! He may be able to live without me, but he can't live without that racecar." Strong words coming from a woman who had supported her husband and his dreams in the early years with a job in a sewing plant that paid her $6,000 a year.

"Honey, just because he pays more attention to the racecar than he pays to you, don't mean he don't love you," Dan's mother, Mildred, reassured me. "It just means he thinks *more* of the racecar than he thinks of you." I had already figured that out.

Being a woman who chooses a life or love in racing is not for the faint of heart. It is for women who are stoic, strong-willed, invincible, and bendable but not breakable. It is an emotionally draining sport that will rob you of peace of mind and sometimes, for a brief moment, your sanity.

Once, when I was dating Dan, we were in Charlotte for a race. Since Dan worked on the pit crew, I was watching the race with Lynda Petty, Kyle's wife Pattie, other members of the Petty family, and our friend Randy Parks. Suddenly there was a huge commotion, and we all turned to see several cars colliding as they came out of the fourth turn, then crashing and spinning down the front straight. When Lynda saw that both her husband and her son were involved, she grabbed her head with her hands, started screaming, and ran to the chain-link fence that was the only thing separating her from the crashed car, about fifteen yards away. She clung to the fence until both of her men had crawled from the wreckage; then, emotionally whipped, she turned and walked away, shaking her head. I was stunned because Lynda is one of the most unflappable women I have ever known. She's normally cool, confident, and always in charge. I couldn't believe what I'd seen. Wide-eyed, I asked Randy, "Is she always like this?"

Sympathetically, Randy shook her head and eyed her good friend with compassionate concern as she softly answered, "Well, when

Kyle started racing, that made it much harder on her. I think it would be very difficult to have both your husband and your son out there."

Lynda Petty has long been a guiding force in the Racing Wives Auxiliary, an organization that raises money to help injured drivers and their families, and is very concerned with safety measures at racetracks. She has given more than her heart and support to the sport. She has given the blood of men she loved.

Lynda's younger brother, Randy Owens, was killed in Talladega in the mid-1970s while working on Richard's crew. Richard was leading the race when Randy, who was leaning over an air tank, died instantly when the tank exploded in his face. When the news was radioed to Richard, he came in, parked the car, and took care of his family. Tragedy struck the family again when Kyle's son Adam was running an ASA race in Milwaukee. He came in for a pit stop, and his crew chief crawled under the car to make an adjustment. The only way a driver knows when to leave the pits is that the jack drops and the car hits the ground. As soon as he feels the tires hit the asphalt, he spins off. That day, the jack fell accidentally and when Adam felt it, he took off, running over and killing his beloved crew chief. In the spring of 2000, Adam himself, the sparkling scion of the famous family, was killed in a crash while practicing for a race in New Hampshire.

Lynda isn't the only woman who has suffered such great emotional losses, enduring pain for the men she loves. Judy Allison spent years helping to nurse her husband, Bobby, back to health after his disastrous crash in Pocono. Then her son, Clifford, was killed in a practice crash in Michigan, followed in less than a year by her oldest son, Davey, who died in a helicopter crash at Talladega. After Davey's death, I went to Birmingham. I dreaded seeing Judy and Davey's wife, Liz. I was already so devastated that, selfishly, I thought only of how much their tears would hurt me. To my surprise, I found two women, drenched in sorrow, but stoically withholding tears and treating each guest with graciousness and warmth. It was the men—particularly Bobby; his brother Donnie;

and Davey's favorite cousin, Tommy—whose tears were flowing unabashedly. The women retained their composure and were remarkably strong.

"Hey, Ronda," Liz said, smiling bravely while clutching my hands tightly in hers. "You've got to come and see our baby, Robbie. He is his daddy made over!" Her smile spread wider, and I was conscious that she, the bereaved widow, was trying to comfort me. "He's just like Davey. He's so funny because all he wants to wear is his diaper and cowboy boots! He's hilarious. Please promise me that you'll come to see us."

A few years earlier, I had been sitting on the back of Neil Bonnett's truck in Bristol, Tennessee, with Neil's wife, Susan. We were just killing time, having a girlfriend chat, when Susan began to talk about the pit bunnies that popped up around her husband from time to time. "One of them came around the corner a while ago and she apparently didn't know I was here but when she saw me, she twirled around and left." She shrugged as if it didn't matter at all.

"It's tough, isn't it?" I asked softly.

She looked out toward the pits and without turning her eyes back to me, she nodded. "There isn't much about this sport that *is* easy, if you're a wife."

The last few years of Neil's career were riddled with severe crashes, any one of which could have easily ended his career and his life. One crash in 1990 caused such a terrible head injury that Neil's memory was completely wiped away for quite some time. I ran into him in Darlington a few months after the crash and, jokingly, I said, "Hey, do you remember me?"

He grinned. "Of course I do. Lisa, how could I forget you?"

My joke had backfired, and I just stared dumbly at him, believing that he really didn't know who I was. After thoroughly enjoying my expression, he started laughing, and I realized that the joke was on me. After that accident, Susan wasn't keen on Neil's racing again, but he crawled back into the car. Then, after another horrific crash, Susan put her foot down—stomped it down firmly, in fact.

When I saw her in the family compound in Talladega, I put my arm around her shoulders and smiled.

"I heard you put the brakes on Neil's racing," I commented in a teasing tone.

Fire flashed in the eyes framed by wisps of beautiful red hair and she put her hands on her hips. "You're darn right I did! I told him I'd divorce him if he ever got into a racecar again. And I mean it!" I wish I had a dollar for every time I heard that threat from a wife, but Susan was completely serious. Her jaws were clenched with such stubbornness that one side pulsated in a spasm. I thought of all the trauma she had faced over the years and how difficult it must have been to raise her children, almost alone, as Neil followed the caravan of his dreams across the country. I put my arms around her and hugged her tightly.

"I'm sorry. I know this must be harder on you than on him."

She nodded emphatically. "It is. And I'm not going through this again." Her voice softened. "I can't. Every time he gets into a racecar, it makes me a nervous wreck. My stomach ties up in knots, and I get sick. Physically and emotionally, I can't take it again."

Neil tried his best to comply with his wife's demand. For three years, he stayed out of racecars and focused on his television career and his various businesses, including a Honda dealership he owned in Birmingham. But, in the end, the pull of a 700-horsepower engine and the adrenaline rush associated with putting the pedal to metal won out, and Neil Bonnett headed to the 1994 Daytona 500, against his wife's wishes. Within the first thirty minutes of practice on the first day of the event, Neil crashed between the third and fourth turns. He was pronounced dead on arrival at Halifax Memorial Hospital. Susan Bonnett had lost her adored husband, and Dale Earnhardt had lost his best friend. Earnhardt died in the very same spot on that track seven years later.

For women like Susan Bonnett, Lynda Petty, Pattie Petty, Judy Allison, Teresa Earnhardt, and Liz Allison, a large piece of their soul lies buried in a grave of death and dreams. They sacrificed so that the men they loved could die with *their* souls intact. It is a high price to pay for loving a man who loves risk. But the greatest risk taker is not the man who barrels toward victory at 200 mph, protected from eternity by only sheet metal, a helmet, and a seat belt. The greatest risk taker is the woman who loves him, whose heart has no protection at all. She lays it on the line every Sunday afternoon, waiting with bated breath until the finish line of another race is crossed. Then, when the checkered flag falls, she takes a deep breath, whispers a quiet prayer of thanks, and promises herself that she will enjoy the next few days of respite before she must endure the agony again.

Any kind of love comes with a cost. But I have found no higher price demanded than that of loving a racer. Love ends with tears, whether it's through a breakup or death. But for women who love racers, their entire lives are scattered with tears, fears, and heartaches. As hard as they try to be brave and fearless, it just isn't possible. The death of Dale Earnhardt, the man considered to be invincible and immortal when it came to a racecar, was the cruelest blow of all. It was evidence to all that if Earnhardt, the sport's superhero, could die in an accident, then no one was completely safe.

I realized when I dated Dan that his life was in as much danger as his brother's, perhaps even more so. Bill was protected by safety equipment and car but Dan, the pit road warrior, was protected by nothing. Time after time, I watched Dan leap over the pit wall. More than once, my heart stopped when a speeding 3,400-pound racecar missed hitting him by only an inch or so as it sped up pit road.

"Why do you do this?" I asked one day after witnessing a very close miss.

His blue eyes sparkled with excitement, and he grinned like a little boy. "It's the greatest adrenaline rush in the world. Wow! It's incredible!"

Later, NASCAR implemented a rule that slowed cars down on pit road. Any driver who went faster than 60 mph (shorter tracks have slower speeds on pit road), was penalized by being held for several seconds. Dan was devastated. "It just isn't as much fun any-more," he complained. I looked at him as if he were crazy. But don't ask me to explain that mentality. All I can say is that I learned these men all have the hearts of wild mustangs, hearts that cannot be tamed by any woman. Even Alan Kulwicki, as somber and quiet as he was, had a reckless heart that lured him into breakneck action on the racetrack.

As surely as women of the Wild West loved the renegade spirits of men like Jesse James and Wyatt Earp, there is something that draws modern-day women to racers. It isn't easy to explain, and it's much harder to live with. Still, the important lesson is that when you love a man, you must take him for what he is and you must accept his dreams. God forbid that you should ever ask him to walk away from them. Instead, be like Linda Rudd, a woman of gentle-ness and kindness, who is her husband Ricky's best friend and is there for him, week after week, scoring his laps and supporting him. When Ricky, a couple of years into his career, crashed spectac-ularly a few days before the Daytona 500, Linda later said his face was so beaten up that she didn't recognize him. The trauma of the accident had bruised his head so badly that his eyes were swollen shut. To compete in the 500, he insisted that she tape his eyes open so that he could see to race. She did and he did.

There is a story about Kenny Schrader that I think perfectly illustrates the mind of a true racer. In addition to his Winston Cup racing, Kenny owns a truck racing team. A few years ago, he was at a track with the team and was helping out. He was under the hood, working on something, when someone started the engine and Kenny's thumb got caught in the fan belt, which ripped it off. Some quick-thinking crew guy found the thumb and put it on ice, and they rushed Kenny to the emergency room. The doctor came in, surveyed the situation, and announced that he could definitely reattach the thumb. He then explained that once the thumb was reattached, they would sew it into the palm of his hand for a few weeks to enhance the skin graft. Kenny thought about it for a sec-ond and said, "Yeah, but that's the hand I drive with when I shift."

The doctor shrugged. "Well, that's the way we have to do it. So, you'll just have to miss a few races. I think it would probably take eight or nine weeks."

Kenny was incredulous. "For a thumb?" he asked in wide-eyed disbelief.

The doctor nodded, certain, I am sure, that there was no choice. After all, a left-handed thumb is a once-in-a-lifetime gift. But as well educated as he surely was, the doctor didn't know how a racer's mind works. It took no more than a second or two for Kenny to make his choice.

"Toss the thumb," he instructed as calmly as if he was talking about tossing out a pair of old socks. "Just bandage me up and get me outta here. I ain't got no time to be missin' no races."

So Kenny left the hospital without his thumb, and when the next race ended, Michael Waltrip pulled up beside him and gave him the thumbs-up. Kenny responded with a hand gesture of his own.

The moral of this story is—don't ever ask a racer to choose between you and a racecar. From personal experience, I can promise that you won't be happy with his answer.

THE VOICE WITHIN

When Dale Earnhardt's car hit the wall on that fatal day, I knew almost immediately that he was dead. When Richard Childress heard this later, he shook his head and looked at me in complete puzzlement. "How," he asked, "could you have known that? It didn't look that bad." The voice within—my intuition—told me.

I was in Washington, D.C., to do some library research and was sharing a room with my sister, who was there for a conference. I watched the pre-race show on Fox before going to the library and returned in time to see the last twenty-five laps. The pre-race show was filled with images of Earnhardt, the sport's megastar. There was footage of Earnhardt and his wife, Teresa. Earnhardt and Dale Jr. Earnhardt and his daughter, Taylor Nicole. Earnhardt alone. As I watched the show that day, I detected a subtle difference in the tough hero. He displayed a strong sentiment and tenderness; to me, it seemed unusual that he would expose this side of himself to the television cameras. I watched as he put his arm around Dale, Jr., and draped his other arm around Teresa's shoulders, pulling her tight to his side. He leaned over and whispered conspiratorially in Junior's ear, then stepped back and chuckled gloriously. When he turned to walk toward his car, Dad slapped his son on the back and smiled as if to say, "So long." That image hit me and filled me with foreboding. I shook it off and said aloud, "Stop being silly."

Then there was the kiss. Before he climbed into the car, Teresa reached up, took his face in her hands, and pulled him toward her. They kissed for what seemed like an eternity in television time. Again, that sinister feeling of foreboding. "*What* is going on?" I said to the television screen as if Earnhardt would answer me through the camera lens. I was alone in the hotel room and was talking to myself when I said fretfully, "Something's not right."

I came back to the hotel to watch the end of the race and from the first squiggle of the black Goodwrench car, I knew something was wrong. I had watched Earnhardt race for years and I had never seen him lose control of a car, even momentarily. My first thought was that he had blacked out—had a stroke, a heart attack, or an aneurysm. The impact didn't look capable of wreaking the devastation it would force upon the racing world and the nation. Yet I immediately began to pray for him.

"Dear God, please let him be all right." But instantly, my heart darkened and the voice within said, "It's too late. He's gone." I heard it as clearly as if someone had spoken. I watched the final fifteen minutes of the broadcast and nothing, other than Darrell Waltrip's concern, indicated that the wreck might have been serious, let alone fatal. After the race ended, my sister returned to the hotel room and was chatting, but I was preoccupied. Finally, in the middle of her story, I blurted out, "I think Dale Earnhardt got killed in Daytona a while ago."

"What!" she shrieked. "What happened? Why do you say that? Did they say he's dead?"

"No, they haven't said a word," I admitted. "But I've got a *bad* feeling about this. *Bad*. I'm sick about it."

Since we were in a hotel room, we didn't have access to the Fox Sports Network and I believed that, if my feeling was right, Fox would be the first to know. I called my nephew, Rod, back home in Georgia and asked him to turn on Fox Sports.

"I'm afraid that Earnhardt got killed," I explained, worriedly.

He casually waved away my concern. "I'll turn it on, but I'm sure he's fine," Rod protested. "I saw the wreck and there wasn't nothin' to it. Don't worry about it."

Validating my concern was the fact that Earnhardt's ambulance had headed straight to the hospital rather than to the infield care center. Here's a tip—if you're watching a NASCAR race and there's a wreck where the ambulance "loads and goes" straight to the hospital rather than the infield care center, there's an overwhelming probability that it's life-threatening.

Thirty minutes later, Rod called to say that he was leaving for a dinner engagement. "But they haven't said anything else about it, so stop worryin'. He's okay." I wish I had been the one who was wrong rather than my nephew.

I believe that everyone has the kind of intuition that warned me about the severity of Earnhardt's accident, but many people overlook the signals—such as Earnhardt's behavior in the pre-race show that seemed out of the ordinary to me. Intuition can be fine-tuned, but we have to listen closely to the voice within. A few episodes while I was on the Winston Cup circuit convinced me of the importance of not only hearing what my intuition says but following it.

The night skies over Florence, South Carolina, were somewhat threatening with a little lightning and light rain when I ran into Alan Kulwicki one Sunday night after a Darlington race. You could always count on seeing many of the Winston Cup folks who used private aircraft at the local, private airport. I was preparing to board a corporate plane that would take me home to Indianapolis. Alan, still struggling with his team, did not have a plane, but sometimes he caught a ride with another team. That night he was anxious, pacing nervously. It was apparent that he was distracted.

"What's wrong with you?" I finally asked.

"Oh, I don't really like flying in weather like this," he replied, trying to act casual about it.

I waved my hand and responded airily, "Oh, don't worry about it. It's fine. No big deal." That was in my youthful days when death seldom crossed my mind, and I never gave a second thought to a rough airplane ride.

Alan, however, shuddered. "I'm just not crazy about flying." Another tiny layer peeled away from the man who never ceased to surprise me. My mouth dropped open. "You're a daring racecar driver, yet flying bothers you?" I suppose I expected racecar drivers to be absolutely fearless, but the truth is that we all have a fear of some kind. There is always something that commands respect and awe from us.

"Welllll," he began in the long drawn-out analytical tone he always used before he launched into a deep, thoughtful explanation.

I held up my hand. "Never mind. You don't have to explain."

I thought about that encounter at the airport when he died in a horrible plane crash several years later. Did he have a premonition that ruffled him into discomfort about flying? Possibly. Sometimes that intuition just warns us.

But of all the times that the voice within has spoken to me, no experience has caught my attention more than the anticipated arrival of Darrell and Stevie Waltrip's second child. Stevie, who loves being a mom and had fervently hoped and prayed for a sibling for her daughter Jessica, called me excitedly in early January 1992 to share her good news—she was expecting again. She was only a few weeks' pregnant, with the baby due in late August.

A few days later, that voice within summoned me and went so far as to add a picture to the sound. I was driving home one night when suddenly a vision flashed in front of me. The highway, the scenery, everything disappeared and I saw a beautiful, blond baby girl in a diaper who was laughing and happy. I didn't hear a voice, but my mind processed words and sentences, like a ticker tape clicking. Whatever it was, I was suddenly filled with the knowledge that Stevie's baby would be a girl and that since she was a special God-sent blessing, I should tell the Waltrips that she should be named Sarah. I distinctly remember the phrase, "because in the Bible, Sarah was one of my chosen."

Then the vision was gone, but the knowledge and haunting chill remained. Tears of disbelief filled my eyes. Normally unflappable, I was completely shaken. For days I tried to forget about the unsettling experience, but the voice within urged me to call Stevie and tell her what had happened. Finally, with tremendous discomfort, I did. Stevie laughed—I can't blame her—and soothingly placated me by saying she would think about the name "Sarah" if it turned out that she was, indeed, carrying a girl.

I dropped the matter, but when prenatal tests revealed that the baby was a girl, I timidly reminded Stevie that I had told her so. Although she was being kind about it, I knew Stevie thought I was close to being loony. So I didn't pursue it. Besides, I didn't think for one second that it was any of my business what they named their baby. Her delivery was medically scheduled for August 25, and though we had talked many times during the preceding months, I had never again mentioned the name Sarah. However, on August 24, that dang voice started pestering me again. I was in my office, trying to work, when that voice within kept nudging me, "Call Stevie. Tell her again that she has to name that baby 'Sarah.'" I tried to brush it aside, but it kept talking and got louder and louder. Finally, annoyed beyond belief, I threw down my pencil and stormed, "Okay! I'll call her. Then, just leave me alone!"

I was trembling from slight nerves when I called Stevie again. After the perfunctory niceties, I launched bluntly into my mission. "Look, I know this is none of my business and I didn't want to mention it again but something keeps impressing me to call you and tell you that you should name the baby 'Sarah.' I am only doing what I feel led to do. So, there. I've told you again and now it's on your conscience. I'm passing the torch."

She started laughing. "Okay, okay. I tell you what I'll do—I'll pray about it. How's that?" I knew that she and Darrell were at something of a standoff about names and a decision had not been made. They hadn't found a name that appealed to both of them, and time was closing in.

So Stevie prayed. And without telling Darrell of my call or ever mentioning the name Sarah—a name that had never been discussed between them—she asked him to pray about it, too. I'm sure they already had been praying, because they are the kind of people who pray for guidance in every aspect of their lives. Nonetheless, they both began to pray with a renewed zest and purpose.

The next day, after Stevie delivered a healthy, lovely girl, Darrell sat down on the bed beside her to coo over their welcomed addition.

"Have you thought of a name yet?" Stevie asked.

He nodded. "I've been praying very hard about it since yesterday. Honey, it's the strangest thing but the only name I can think of, the only one that sticks in my mind, is one that we've never discussed."

"Okay. What?"

"I feel very strongly," Darrell replied, "that we should name this baby Sarah."

Stevie told me that chills swept through her body and tears sprang to her eyes. She threw her arms around Darrell and said, "Oh, yes, honey, I think that's what we should name her—Sarah." Then, for the first time, Stevie told Darrell about both my calls, the one seven months before and then the one on the previous day. He, too, was stricken with the emotion of the event and his eyes filled with tears. They were absolutely certain that they were giving their daughter the perfect name.

If the tale ended here, it would be remarkable. But it doesn't. What happened next was even more so. When Darrell went home to shower and change clothes, the phone rang. It was one of Stevie's closest friends.

"Darrell, I've been trying to reach you," she said urgently. "Have you named the baby yet? I wanted to tell you that I've been praying about this since yesterday as Stevie asked me to do and I keep getting one name as the answer."

"What is it?" Darrell asked.

"Sarah Kaitlyn."

Darrell again choked up. "Well, you're not going to believe this, but—"

The Waltrips had named their new baby girl Sarah Kaitlyn.

Boy, after that, I never questioned that voice again. Unfortunately, I sometimes stray into my own understanding and make mistakes. But if I listen to that voice and follow through with what it tells me to do, I'm rarely wrong. Sometimes it tells me things that I don't want to hear—like Earnhardt's being gone. Still, I realize that you have to take the good with the bad. I learned from that one vivid experience to try not to let analytical reasoning override instinct. The compass in our soul always leads us in the right direction.

About a year or so later, I had another remarkable experience. On New Year's Eve, when 1994 had melted into 1995, around four in the morning, I had a vivid, eerily realistic dream. I dreamed that Kenny Schrader was in a hospital bed, immobile, close to death. Suddenly, I was conscious, no longer asleep, and again words were filling my mind as if someone were talking to me: "Kenny is in serious peril, and he needs your friendship. He needs all his friends right now. Call him."

With a pounding heart, I sat straight up in bed. I felt there was someone close to me in the dark of my bedroom. That, combined with the fear I felt for Kenny, shook me fully awake. Again, I heard the words, "Call him."

And then, just as in the visionary glimpse I had of Sarah Kaitlyn, a ticker tape appeared before my eyes with the phone number of Kenny's race shop. For a second I was frozen, but I recovered enough to grab a pen and paper from my nightstand and scribble down the number. Now, here's the deal. I hadn't talked to Kenny in two or three years and, to be honest, I hadn't thought of him in quite a while. The number that ticked in front of me was a phone number I had dialed many times when we worked together as driver and publicist, so, granted, it was buried in my subconscious. But it was deeply buried. And the next day when I searched through my files and address books, I did not have that phone number written down anywhere. You might think that I would have learned my lesson with the Waltrip episode, but I had not. I tried to push the troublesome thought from my mind and ignore the voice within that kept telling me to call Kenny.

The following day, New Year's Day, I was in my office working—in the same office and at the same desk where I had been when the voice pushed me into calling Stevie. Well, wouldn't you know it? That voice kept prompting me to call Kenny. A couple of times, I picked up the phone and started to dial but hung it up again. Kenny is such a rascal that I knew if I called out of the blue for the first time in several years with such an absurd story, he would laugh me into the next century. For an hour or so, I argued with the voice, as I had in Stevie's case.

"It's New Year's Day. He's not going to be in the shop today. I'll call him later." I really didn't plan to do that, I was just saying that to get some peace. Still, the voice within kept saying, "Call him."

Finally, I grabbed the phone and dialed the number quickly before I could change my mind. I was confident that it was a waste of time and that Kenny would not be there, but at least I would have made the effort. The phone rang several times, and just as I started to hang up, I heard a familiar voice say, "Schrader Racin'."

Shocked and suddenly trembling all over, I asked, "Kenny?" I was torn between hanging up and crying. Instead, I plunged ahead, talking at lightning speed. I told him who I was and why I was calling.

"I know this is crazy and you're gonna think I'm nuts, but I had a terrible dream about you last night. You were in a hospital bed and couldn't move. Something told me that I should call you because you need all your friends right now. I know this is nuts, but are you all right?"

He was silent for a second, and I was dying on the other end of the phone, certain that his speechlessness was caused by his concern for my sanity. Quietly, he said, "Tell me more about this dream, and then I'll tell you something."

Encouraged, I told him more, including the phone number that had flashed before my eyes. When I finished, he said, "This is weird. It's spooky, but I just got outta the hospital. I was in there over Christmas because I have the Guillain-Barré virus. Do you know what that is?"

"No." I had begun to relax, but now I was tensing again over the eeriness of what I was hearing.

"It's a virus that attacks the central nervous system. I didn't have no feeling in my legs and arms. That's the most scared I've ever been in my life. I didn't know if I'd ever walk again. I had a friend back in St. Louis that got it, and he wound up on a respirator."

"Are you all right now?"

"Yeah. I'm getting there. But it's tough. I still don't have a lot of strength in my legs and arms. I'm not as scared as I was, but I'm still scared. I thought I wasn't ever gonna race again."

"Oh, my gosh." Chills covered my body and tears filled my eyes. "This is incredible."

"I know," he agreed. "I don't hear from you in years, then you have a dream just like what happened to me."

"Yeah, and what about your phone number flashing before my eyes? And you know what, I wasn't going to call you because I never dreamed that you'd be at the shop on New Year's Day." Then another thought suddenly popped into my head. "This is the first time I ever remember you answering the phone at your shop when I called."

"I *don't* answer it. And you wanna know something else? I just stopped by the shop for a minute to pick up something I needed. I was goin' out the door when the phone started ringin', and I had no intentions of answering it. I got outside the door and something told me to come back and answer it. This whole thing's just too weird."

I agreed. But there was a purpose, a very special purpose, in the dream and the voice that prompted me to call Kenny Schrader. I suspect it was to assure Kenny that he wasn't alone during one of the most frightening periods of his life.

"I'm going to pray for you," I promised as we concluded the conversation.

"Thank you," he said softly. "I need it." By the time he arrived in Daytona for the 1995 500, he had regained complete strength in his arms and 80 percent in his legs, and eventually he recovered entirely.

For me, it was another powerful lesson that the voice within speaks strongly only when it's important. It's not for me to try to figure out why I'm directed to do the things it tells me to do; it's only for me to listen and to do them. There's always a purpose and a reason. Of course, that doesn't make it any easier for me to intrude into the personal lives and decisions of others, so I still argue with that voice on occasion. But I have learned to listen because sometimes not listening is nothing short of selfishness and foolish pride, while at other times I'm only hurting myself.

That was the case when the voice told me to stop by and see an older friend of mine who had lost her husband several months earlier, and whom I tried to visit or call once a month. I slowed to turn into her driveway and then decided against it for some stupid, selfish reason like lack of time. Two days later, she suffered a massive stroke, and I never had the opportunity to give her the box of chocolates I had for her in my car. I was sick with grief and remorse at not listening to the voice within.

Fortunately, though, there have been other times—as in the cases of the Waltrips and Kenny—when I did listen. Thank God that I'm not always obstinate. But let me underscore something here. The voice I'm talking about here is one filled with good intentions, the kind that makes things better for others or for yourself. It is not the kind that would ever direct us to hurt someone in any way. In fact, I've never had that voice tell me to do anything mean-spirited or unkind, although it has pushed me to the point of discomfort when I had to intrude into someone's personal life—where good manners would tell me to keep out.

I don't know what, if any, difference that incident made in Kenny's life, but as for Stevie, she once asked me to write this down for her so that this remarkable story would never be forgotten. And now I have.

HEROES AND ZEROS

Richard Childress lifted a clutched fist in triumph and grinned broadly as the fans in the grandstands roared their approval. The sponsor reps who surrounded him atop the race hauler, from where they were watching qualifying for the spring race at Talladega, high-fived each other and slapped the veteran car owner on the back. His driver, Kevin Harvick, had just turned a lap fast enough, at least for the moment, to move him to the front row for the Sunday race. It was a moment of sweet, welcome bliss.

Still beaming happily, Childress glanced my way as he whipped out a tiny cell phone and punched in some numbers. "Don't go away," he instructed. "We'll find a quiet place and talk." That isn't easy when you're with the most famous, most recognizable car owner in the Winston Cup Series. Harder still is pulling him away from the legion of people who constantly want a moment of his time for business purposes, and from the well-wishers, con-dolers, and autograph seekers—and the media, which have always sought him out but now have become an ever-present stalking shadow.

Finally he was ready to escape and tugged my arm, urging me to move quickly. But neither of us was quick enough for the three tele-vision news teams that stopped him and asked for interviews. Ever gracious and mindful of the responsibility that comes with success, fortune, and fame, he smiled and nodded, and the cameras rolled. The questions from all three news teams were painfully identical. I grimaced the first time I heard them, frowned the second time, and scowled impatiently the third time. Childress, however, never flinched or appeared annoyed. He didn't even shorten his answers. He patiently gave each reporter solid sound bites, the kind that would be certain to make their producers smile.

"How hard is it to be in Talladega for the first time without Dale Earnhardt?"

"How are you and the rest of your team coping with his death?"

"What would Earnhardt think of the job that Harvick is doing for the team?"

"Dale Earnhardt won more races at Talladega than any other driver. Do you think that record can be broken?"

"What's the future of Richard Childress Racing without Dale Earnhardt?"

He finished the last torturous interview, stepped to my side quickly, and steered me toward a clear path where no one was wait-ing to ambush him. "That," he said softly, throwing a thumb over his shoulder, "is why it's so hard to start healing."

Richard Childress is my hero. Not because of his courageous conduct when his best friend and driver, Dale Earnhardt, died when he smacked the wall going into the fourth turn of Daytona International Speedway. The final lap of the 2001 Daytona 500 was the final lap of Earnhardt's life, the man who was loved like a brother by his car owner. Those two were uncommonly close, as if they shared the same heart and soul. Of course, they did share the same dream. The whole world knew that and marveled at how effortlessly they turned that dream into reality.

With six championships to their credit (Earnhardt won one championship before joining Childress) and more than $45 million in winnings since 1984, the pair ruled Winston Cup racing as no single team had ever done before. In the face of a tragedy played out live to millions, a racing accident that dominated the front pages of every major American newspaper and grabbed the covers of *Sports Illustrated, People*, and *Time*, Childress had no choice but to share his grief and agony with a world of strangers. Can you imagine how difficult that is?

More than fifty million watched on live television as the popular modern-day gladiator died before their eyes. Over the next few days, millions more saw endless replays of the tragedy. Stunned and in pain, fans of the sport, and particularly of the number 3 team, wanted to reach out via the media and unite their grief with that of Childress, his team, and Earnhardt's wife and family. Those fans with prying eyes who wanted to see deep into the personal pain were not motivated by a freakish impulse to stare at another's sorrow. Instead, they were compelled by hearts of compassion, hearts that were hurting badly, and the need to grieve with kindred spirits.

Still, that intrusion made grieving more difficult for those of Earnhardt's tight-knit circle, who were entitled to mourn the most. The majority of us would have run, retreated to a place of solitude where well-intentioned people from waitresses to hotel clerks to gas station attendants could not share their heartfelt sympathy for a fallen hero and serve as a constant reminder of what had happened. But Richard Childress is not a coward. When life gets tough, he gets tough. But he does so in such a beguiling, gentle fashion that the best way to describe him is as a tender-hearted, tough-minded man. He made it look easy and effortless, but I know it wasn't. Each time he was forced to do an interview or acknowledge an expression of sympathy, it felt like a pin-sharp claw pulling across the open wound of his heart, a woeful reminder of the friend who was gone forever.

But the admirable way that Childress has conducted himself in the face of adversity and public intrusion into his grief is not what has made him my hero. He has been my hero for many years, almost from the first moment I met him in 1985. One day in the garage, a friend of Childress's said to me, "Richard Childress asked me who you were." I was used to this. At that time, a woman in the NASCAR garage stood out like a hillbilly at a debutante ball.

"Who?" I asked.

"Richard Childress."

"Who's that?"

The guy rolled his eyes. "If you're gonna work here, you're going to have to learn who everybody is. RC owns Dale Earnhardt's team."

"Oh," I replied with a shrug.

The next time I passed the Childress-Earnhardt truck, I went over and introduced myself to the team owner. From that moment forward, I called him "Childress," not "RC" or "Richard" as most people do, but always by his surname. I have never called him anything else, except "my friend" and "one of my very favorite people in the world." Of course, I am not alone in my great admiration. He is enormously kind and compassionate, his word is his bond, and he speaks only positively of people and circumstances—and although he is a power broker, a star maker, he is a man of the highest ethical convictions.

He is also an exceptionally smart man, as he proved in 1981.

Childress is the personification of the American dream, in which the kid with nothing grows up to become the man with everything. When I first met Childress, life for him was better than it had ever been, but it was nowhere near as good as it was going to get. At that time, the number 3 truck was filled with cases of pork and beans and packages of bologna for sandwiches, which everyone ate for convenience. A few years earlier, though, they had eaten this food out of necessity, unable to afford fancier foods or the luxury of dining in restaurants. But in time, Childress no longer had to count each dollar carefully or worry constantly over making the race or finishing high enough to get to the next race. Dale Earnhardt and a sponsorship from Wrangler Jeans changed all that.

Oh, and a nudge from Junior Johnson that would mark the beginning of stock car history.

Earnhardt had captured the attention of the racing world by winning Rookie of the Year honors in 1979, then backing it up with the sport's championship in 1980, becoming the first driver to ever win those honors back to back. But by the 1981 season, he had grown disgruntled with his car owner and was looking for somewhere to land. With the explosive, hard-charging Earnhardt came an added bonus—the Wrangler Jeans sponsorship. Wrangler's slogan "One Tough Customer" matched perfectly with the aggressive Earnhardt, so the Wrangler folks had promised their driving sensation, "If you leave, we leave; and where you go, we go." In a time when sponsor dollars were incredibly hard to find, Earnhardt had a sponsorship but no team. Childress had a team but no lucrative sponsorship.

Junior Johnson, the moonshine runner turned stock car driver, had gone from driving to car owning. With the brash, brave Darrell Waltrip, he had found fame and fortune. After hearing of Earnhardt's dilemma, he conferred with his buddy Richard Childress, an independent driver who had struggled for years. "Get outta the car and put the kid in," Johnson advised. "You'll make a lot more money as a car owner. You'll be set for life."

Childress once told me that it was the hardest decision he ever made. "I loved driving. It was my life. But I knew that if I ever got out of the car, I had to make the commitment to stay out of it. I had to choose my course and stick to it."

When Childress sets his mind to something, he is as tenacious as a bulldog. He would never step on anyone to get ahead, but he would walk the roughest terrain barefoot to reach his goals. Once Earnhardt was in the 3 car, Childress was determined to be the best car owner possible. Which explains what he did next. As the 1981 season wound down, the new car owner and the champion racecar driver had a heart-to-heart talk.

"I told Dale that he was better than my team," Childress explained. "He was a champion and I was just starting out as a team owner, and I didn't want to hold him back. I told him that he needed to go to a good, well-established team; meanwhile, I would work on building my team—and when it was good enough for him, we'd get back together. I didn't want to hold him back."

A reluctant Earnhardt moved over to drive for veteran car owner Bud Moore, and the youngster Ricky Rudd moved into the Childress car. But two years later, the men destined to become the greatest team in NASCAR history rejoined each other in a professional marriage that would last for the next seventeen years. Only death could end the most brilliant, most compatible partnership in NASCAR history.

"I have never seen such brotherliness between two men in all my life," I commented to Childress after Earnhardt's death. "I don't think the world appreciates how close you two were or how devoted you were to each other. I can tell you this—Dale could have left you anytime he wanted and taken big sponsorship money to drive for his own team. But he didn't."

Childress nodded. "You're right—he could have left anytime he wanted. But he said, 'Man, we're in this together.' And we were."

Earnhardt, to his great credit, knew he had a good thing going. He was driving for a shrewd businessman whose mind never rests—who is always trying to figure out a way to make the car better and to go faster. Childress is a proven winner, but he never stops trying to improve. "It's much harder to stay on top than get on top," he declared to me after they'd already won four of their six championships.

Earnhardt, a bit of a skeptic from time to time, had found in Childress a man of his word, bound by his promise as much as by a hundred-page contract. He never forgets his friends and is always generous with help, money, and favors. I remember being in Pocono once when one of the media people had a family emergency. Childress, without hesitation, offered his plane and pilots for a quick trip home.

I have my own story of Childress's unparalleled generosity. When my first book was auctioned to publishers in New York and astounded me by earning a substantial advance, Childress was one of the first people on the phone to congratulate me, and he followed up with flowers and a thoughtful message that I cherish immensely. When the book was published, he offered to put its title on one of his cars in Talladega and then instructed his public relations people to push the deal with a press release and to set up interviews for me. Of course, we got a lot of media attention with a racecar carrying an advertisement for a book about Southern women. On the morning of the race, I was on the 3-truck, talking to Childress, Earnhardt, and David Smith, when Chocolate Myers stepped onto the truck and said, "Hey, there's some TV guys out there who want to interview Ronda about the name of her book being on the car yesterday."

"Okay!" I replied enthusiastically, and I started to leave.

"Hey, wait a minute!" Childress called. "Do you know where your car finished yesterday? They're going to ask."

My eyes widened. I was stumped. Sheepishly, I shook my head.

"Third." He held up three fingers, like an adult working with a child.

"Okay!" Again, I started to the door.

"Wait a minute!" Childress demanded again. "Do you know the name of your driver?"

I smiled. "Of course, I do. It's Kenny Harwick."

Childress rolled his eyes. "Kevin Harvick."

"Oh. Kevin Harwick."

"Har-*vick*." He shook his head in amused despair. "Look, Ronda. If you're gonna do television interviews about this deal, you gotta remember your driver's name!"

To illustrate Childress's business acumen, there's the story of a discarded slogan that Chevrolet had commissioned but never really used. Childress ran across the slogan, loved what it said, and thought it was so perfect for his race team that he had the words painted across the race hauler. That year in Daytona, Chevy executives spied the slogan and, captivated, asked Childress where he had gotten it. "It's yours," he replied. "I ran across it in some old advertising stuff and decided to use it."

The executives returned to Detroit with a mandate to their advertising department to build a campaign around it. "Chevrolet—the heartbeat of America" became one of the most popular and most memorable campaigns in American advertising.

Not all my memories of my life in Winston Cup racing are pleasant. I encountered a few of the kind of people who aren't good and loving but rather take, use, and abuse. But the sport has an amazing way of choking these people out—all the ones I knew are no longer involved in NASCAR. They've gone on to torture others elsewhere. Interestingly, the abusive people I knew, despite the wealth or influence they brought into the sport, were never successful. They usually ended up tucking their tails between their legs and limping away, often in disgrace and humiliation. Still, I am grateful for what they taught me, for from them I learned how *not* to treat others. I also learned to be strong and to fight for what's right. I'm grateful to those people because I learned as much from the zeros as from the heroes. I just happen to enjoy the heroes more.

There's Bobby Allison, who has battled back from more adversity than any other person I've known. There's Richard Petty, who always takes time to treat everyone with kindness and friendliness. And there's the entire Petty family, who showed such dignity and grace in dealing with the death of Kyle's son Adam, the scion who appeared destined for greatness before being killed in a crash at the age of twenty. Carolyn Rudd, who never fails to reach out a hand to a soul in need, will always be an inspiration. And I will always remember the Elliott family for taking a young girl and putting her on the path to a wonderful career as well as for defying the odds against them. There are many people in the sport who are heroes, people who have inspired me. But my greatest hero is, without question, the man behind the Man in Black.

Richard Childress is the same today as he was the day I walked over to him, stuck out my hand, and introduced myself. I am delighted but not surprised that fame and fortune have not changed him. A couple of years ago, I was trying to have a conversation with him in the garage, but it became impossible because of the constant stream of autograph seekers and reporters. He finished signing and turned back to me.

"Now, what were you saying?" he asked.

"Well, Mr. Big Shot, I was saying that—" He interrupted me before I could continue. At first, he recoiled in exaggerated horror, but then his look turned to genuine hurt. His voice, always soft and gentle, was a little stronger, more assertive than normal.

"Now, Ronda, you've known me for a long time. I'm the same person I've always been. Have I changed?"

I had to tell the truth. I didn't have the heart to tease him. I smiled. "No, Childress, you've haven't changed a lick. And I'm proud of you for that."

He nodded. "I'm just a lot busier than I used to be, but I'm still the same ol' RC."

Well, I'm not sure that he eats as many bologna sandwiches, Vienna sausages, and soda crackers as he once did. Now, he has a racing empire and shop facilities second to none, a fleet of planes, a home near Winston-Salem, and a hunting lodge in Montana. Richard Childress may not have changed, but life for him certainly has.

I've absorbed a lot of wisdom from Richard Childress about business, racing, money, people, and life, but the greatest lesson he has taught me is about dealing graciously with tremendous success. I wrote earlier that success can destroy you because it's insidious— it pulls you into thinking that it's a friend, not a foe. We let down our guard and welcome success without a moment's thought for the destruction it can bring. We can begin to believe, egotistically, that we alone are responsible for the success that comes our way; we forget the combination of a kind and gentle fate that rained opportunity upon us and the many people who helped us along the way.

When Earnhardt died, the media talked endlessly of his superiority as a driver, glossing over the importance of his partnership with Childress. Earnhardt would have been a great driver without Richard Childress, but he was a greater one because of him. Childress is a hands-on car owner who not only knows which gear, springs, and shocks are in the car on any given day but helps to choose them. On race day, he'll be able to rattle off the rear end ratio or the final drive ratio (how many times the engine will turn over in relation to how many times the tires turn). A racecar prepared by Richard Childress is a masterpiece of automotive excellence. Yet he will modestly tell you that his talents lie strictly in being able to choose the best people who can build the best racecar, and that he is a very small part of the team. This isn't an act. It's something he sincerely believes. If you doubt how good those racecars are, think of Harvick, the young man chosen to step into Earnhardt's ride. A rookie with no experience in the major league of racing, he won in only his third Winston Cup start, shattering any previous win records by a rookie.

Of course, his car owner, with a glance heavenward, quickly points out, "We had some help on that one." Still, fourteen races later, Harvick, the rookie forced into Winston Cup action earlier than planned, won again.

Thanks to Childress, I will never forget that the greater your success is, the greater is your responsibility to stay humble and to use your blessings to help others. It's something that is easy to remember when you have such an outstanding example, a man who teaches it and lives it. I am proud to know him, not for what he has achieved as a racer but for what he has achieved as a person and for the positive impact he has made on so many other lives. In the end, the real measure of a person is not how successful he is but how he deals with success. When you measure Richard Childress in those terms, he's a true giant.

THE CHECKERED FLAG

The first time I saw an Indy car race in 1986 at Michigan International Speedway, it took my breath away.

It wasn't the cars that impressed me—they looked like identical matchbox cars—and it wasn't the speeds, but rather the grandeur that surrounded that sport and its people. It was unlike anything I had ever seen in my life. The Winston Cup circuit raced twice a year at the beautiful track owned by Roger Penske. I knew it well and loved it; it is one of my favorite tracks because of the humidity-free weather, the gorgeous countryside, and the meticulous attention to detail that the Penske people give. But I was not prepared for what I saw when the CART folks infiltrated the place. The grounds, garage, and paddock became majestic, splendid beyond words. The difference between how the track looked with the CART teams in residence as opposed to the NASCAR folks was like the Metropolitan Opera versus the Grand Ole Opry, Broadway versus a small-town community play, a symphony orchestra versus a Saturday night hoedown. It was uptown versus down home.

Walking toward the garage with my friend Martie, I stopped to gawk in wonder at the paddock area where big buses, like the ones used by music stars for touring, were lined up beside each other. Those customized vehicles worth hundreds of thousands of dollars belonged to drivers and team owners who retreated to the mobile homes away from home for rest and a reprieve from the constant attention and activity. I shook my head in amazement. On the NASCAR circuit, the drivers retreated to the back of the transporters, where, if they were lucky, there was a chair. If not, they hoisted themselves up to sit on the counter, the same space they used to fiddle with spark plugs, gears, and carburetors. Dale Earnhardt, however, had figured out a better way; he slung a hammock across the back end of the Wrangler truck. There he positioned himself to sleep or keep a sluggish eye on the garage and, whenever the mood suited him, summon passersby over to shoot the breeze.

"You are the laziest person I've ever seen," I commented wryly when he called me over one day.

He snarled, "Why?"

"Because you're always in this hammock. Everytime I walk by, you're laid up in here."

"I'm thinkin'."

"Really?"

"Yeah. I'm tryin' to figure out what in the hell it is that you do around here." I spent a lot of useless time trying to one-up the master of one-ups.

The luxury buses were also used by the wives and families of the CART participants, who watched the races on satellite television. On the NASCAR circuit, wives and children crowded into rental cars and into borrowed vans to listen to the races on radio. All those buses were impressive, certainly, but it didn't stop there. I was astounded to see that each bus had its own little hospitality area where round tables covered with fine linen were set up. Each table was set with glistening, expensive crystal, china, silverware, elaborate silver candelabras, and towering center arrangements of fresh-cut flowers. It was absolutely awesome. When I was a reporter, I had covered a couple of steeplechases where I had seen similar indulgences, though without the motor homes, in big cow pastures. But I had never seen anything remotely as glamorous at a stock car racetrack. We were reduced to standing on the back of the trucks and eating peanut butter sandwiches wrapped in paper towels.

Perhaps most impressive were the chefs, dressed in traditional white and puffy white toques, who were preparing exquisite meals. For a moment or so, I was speechless. Then I sighed wistfully, spread my hands, and remarked to Martie, "Now, *these* are *my* people!"

When I recounted the experience to my best friend, Debbie, along with my personal assessment of the grandeur, she laughed gaily. "That's my buddy!" she chuckled. "Not to the manor born but determined, nonetheless, to get there!"

"I'm serious," I continued. "I was meant to dine in the lap of luxury as opposed to eating pork and beans out of a can in a gritty garage."

I was teasing. But only slightly. It is safe to say that in those days, I had definitely gotten above my raising despite my mama's constant admonishments against any such. I wasn't, however, fooling anyone. About that same time, Debbie and I decided to take a trip abroad, a plan which I shared with my good friend Doc Bundy, a famous racer on the hooty snooty sports car circuit—he races in places like Le Mans and Monte Carlo, while NASCAR races in Alabama and Tennessee.

"Debbie and I are going to Paris during the off-season," I commented casually to Doc one night during one of our normally lengthy phone conversations. My proclamation was met with deep guttural laughter, which lasted for a minute or two. I was puzzled. I couldn't imagine what was so funny.

"What are you laughing about?" I finally asked.

It took a while before he could stop his hysterics long enough to answer. "I'm laughing at the thought of you two country bumpkins in Paris!" To add further insult to deep injury, he started laughing again.

This, of course, started a bit of a bicker between us, but he refused to back down. It was obvious that I thought more of my worldliness than he did. This probably explains why, when I saw the decadent spoils of the Indy car folks, I thought I was ready to graduate from the beer masses to the champagne classes. And I can add a footnote: Doc hasn't changed his tune much. He still has basically the same opinion of me. He continues to race those rich-boy cars and is frequently gone, but when he's home he lives only a few miles from me. One night recently, he was having dinner at my house and while I made the salad, he sat on a stool at the kitchen counter and talked about how he, a native of Ohio, had found his way to the South more than twenty years ago and made his home there.

"I've always been a southerner at heart," he explained. "I would have moved here earlier, but I saw *Deliverance* and it scared me so bad, it took me longer to take the plunge."

I almost threw the head of lettuce at him. Instead, I narrowed my eyes, shook my head, and said, "Whenever I do speaking engagements outside the South, I have to carefully explain that *Deliverance* is *not* a documentary. It's a work of fiction." Then, remembering that argument years earlier, I added with a devilish smile, "But I guess you were just meant to be a country bumpkin, too! You fit right in with the rest of us."

He howled with laughter. "Which is why I shouldn't have been teasing you about it in the first place!"

Doc, however, was not alone in his perception of those of us in stock car racing. A lot of people outside the sport and outside the South sniggered at us and called us country bumpkins and rednecks behind our backs *and* to our faces. It was disheartening at times, but we believed in what we were doing and, most important, we were following the passion of our hearts and making a living—a very good living—at what we loved to do. As hard as it is to believe now, the NASCAR circuit, no longer second to anyone, was at that time the undisputed second fiddle in the band of racers. We longed to outplay the others and become the leader of the band.

While it wasn't impossible, it did seem improbable.

During the 1970s and 1980s, the media focused on racers with names like Foyt, Unser, and Andretti and therefore the nation knew more of these speedsters than they knew of the guys named Yarborough, Waltrip, and Allison. I will say that Richard Petty, however, was as well known as A. J. Foyt because his racing accomplishments were nothing short of astounding—200 wins, seven Daytona 500s, and seven national championships. No one in any other form of racing can claim a record even close to that.

Still, we suffered from a stigma. We were made to feel that we were second-class citizens, not as good as the Indy-car guys. Their purses paid more, they received more press, and their lifestyle, obviously, was much grander. In NASCAR, we were the redheaded, freckle-faced stepchildren of motorsports. Or, perhaps more appropriately, the redneck cousins. Interestingly enough, it was a redheaded, freckle-faced redneck named Bill Elliott whose phenomenal year in 1985 would signal the changing of the guard and open the door that brought in more media and more fans. He and his family are owed much for their role in the modern-day evolution of stock car racing.

It would be the 1990s before NASCAR reached the pinnacle of its popularity. Until then, though, we continued to dream of having the prestige, star power, and clout of our rivals. That was the essence of everything we worked for in those days. We wanted the respect, the glamour, the money, the fans, and the media attention just like they got. In fact, we wanted more. And we got it.

I believe the upturn started with two major events: the entrance of cable networks and Procter and Gamble. With the fledgling ESPN looking for events to broadcast, NASCAR races proved to be a natural, and the guys who called the races turned out to be interesting, smart, and good. The ratings were so impressive that soon every NASCAR race was carried on national television by CBS,

ABC, ESPN, WTBS, or TNN. Suddenly every American had access to a sport that was once coveted and owned solely by southerners.

When Procter and Gamble arrived as a sponsor, it was akin to a papal blessing because in the world of advertising, P&G was revered for its marketing savvy. Corporate America opened a floodgate of sponsor dollars, reversing the fortunes of the previously poor racing relations. Add to these fortuitous events the fact that stock car racing is a colorful sport filled with interesting people who speak clearly to middle America because they *are* middle America. While many sports car and open-wheel drivers are born into a kingdom of wealth and privilege, most stock car drivers and owners are born into blue-collar rural families who take a desire and turn it into the American dream.

There is something enormously appealing about a rags-to-riches story, because it instills hope into hapless hearts. Such stories are common in NASCAR, an organization befittingly founded by a visionary who spent years trying to raise enough funding to build Daytona International Speedway. The poverty-to-prosperity stories are the rule in the Winston Cup garage. (Tim Richmond, the silver-spoon-fed heir to an industrial fortune, was the exception.) Because of the human appeal of this very human sport, the fan base began to grow to mammoth proportions. As a result, existing tracks doubled their seating capacity and clever entrepreneurs built grand new tracks and *then* begged for a date on the racing schedule.

While Philip Morris was pouring money into the CART circuit, R. J. Reynolds, the cigarette maker based in Winston-Salem, North Carolina, blew money into stock car racing after tobacco companies were banned from television advertising. Say what you may, this was undoubtedly one of the cleverest maneuvers in the history of marketing. Winston was not allowed to buy television time, yet it emblazoned cars, tracks, and drivers with its logo, which was prominently, even brazenly, exhibited during televised races. During the 1985 championship banquet at the Waldorf, NASCAR and R. J. Reynolds made a joint announcement that what had long been called the Grand National Series would henceforth be known as the Winston Cup Series. To ensure that stubborn reporters, who resist using sponsors' names, would not continue to call it the Grand National, the Sportsman division, the one below the top echelon, was renamed Grand National. Later, it, too, would have a corporate name—the Busch Series.

This was one of the craftiest moves I've ever seen. Jerry Potter and I, both at *USA Today* at the time, had flown up from Washington for the banquet, and when we heard the announcement, we looked at each other and shook our heads. I said, "They've got us. No way around it." We knew that from that moment forward, every story we wrote would have to advertise that brand of cigarettes, regardless of editorial policy.

Brilliant move. The astute men who ran the sport continued to make clever decisions, applying textbook marketing strategies and perfect calculations. As new fans poured into the sport, so did corporate dollars, and soon large newspapers across the nation covered NASCAR and carried qualifying and race results in the agate section, next to baseball and golf. With the arrival of big sponsorship money came an obligation to polish the diamonds in the rough and project the image expected by CEOs in glistening, big-city high rises. Good ol' boys like Earnhardt and Elliott were soon being coached by top-notch New York media consultants, ordering custom-made suits and tuxes, and sharing their thoughts on the sport with *Business Week*, *Forbes*, and *Fortune*.

The role of publicists like me became crucial in the refinement of the sport's image as we schooled our drivers and teams on press etiquette and damage control and pleaded with them, time after time, to tone down their colorful remarks because "the sponsor won't like it. You're their representative, and if you're going to take their money, you have to act accordingly." Remember how I begged Darrell Waltrip to watch what he said after The Winston incident with Rusty Wallace? Over a relatively short period of time, comments like the one Davey Allison made after crashing in Daytona— "That little brown-eyed weasel wrecked me. He's an idiot!"—soon disappeared and were replaced with perfectly appropriate corporate remarks such as "That's racin' " and "Those things happen." All this drained color from a sport that had won legions of fans because of its colorful drivers and their unpredictable remarks. But those image-conscious public relations people had to go and mess up a good thing. Damn them.

Soon the rednecks had plenty of greenbacks, with most teams owning several planes, and the fabulously luxurious buses that I had first seen on the CART circuit crowded the parking areas around the garages. Team owners, drivers, crew chiefs, team managers, and probably an engine builder or two were each installed in a motor coach worth more than half a million dollars. What I had first seen at the Michigan Indy car race was duplicated tenfold by my friends in the Winston Cup, and the joke was on me—my good ol' friends had unwittingly become what I had referred to as "my people." Things changed, and the close-knit camaraderie began to unravel as the drivers and teams became more physically segregated. Gone now are the days when everyone congregated in the garage and clowned around and friendships were made strong through old-fashioned bull-shooting sessions. Now, the drivers dodge from their buses to the garage, just in time to hop into the cars for practice, then out of the cars and straight back to the buses. It's awfully hard to find a driver hanging around his transporter anymore.

For a while, it was possible to catch the drivers on Sunday morning as they headed from the garage to the platform for introductions. No more. Now, they're loaded onto a bus in the garage and driven to the ceremony. The men made by the people are now sequestered from them, for the most part. While I think it's terribly sad, I can't blame them, because the life they lead is hectic and these luxuries make a hard-paced life easier. It is a grueling existence, and I completely understand their need for a refuge.

But I, and many of my friends in the sport, still have a hankering for the good ol' days when a downpour of rain forced us to crowd into the race trucks, where we told stories or played cards. I miss the days when Earnhardt hung out in a hammock; for that matter, I miss Earnhardt and the other precious friends I have lost. Sometimes, in fact, the pain over losing all of them is even greater than all the happiness they brought to me. I'm still sentimental for the days when the silliest things were the most important.

Once, in Pocono, I was on the 3 truck with some of Earnhardt's guys and their sponsor rep, and we got into a discussion over which was our favorite cartoon. The Jetsons won by a large margin, and we started singing the theme song, but no one could remember the dog's name. It was absolutely critical that we figure it out.

"Kyle will know," someone said. Kyle Petty is really cool. He always knows kid stuff. So someone went over to the garage office and had Kyle paged.

"Kyle Petty, report to the 3 truck. Kyle Petty to the 3 truck," the authoritative voice boomed. Immediately, Kyle came scurrying over, and we said in unison, "What was the name of the dog on the Jetsons?"

"Astro, man! Astro!" Kyle shot back with a big grin.

"Of course!" we all said, as we moved on to another subject of equal importance.

I miss the days of horseplay and foolishness, like the scorching day in Talladega when I was being interviewed by a Birmingham teleevision station. I had painstakingly primped before I stepped in front of the camera. My hair was combed, and my lipstick was perfectly applied. I was in the midst of the on-camera interview when Kenny Schrader sneaked around behind the camera and hit me full in the face with a blast of water from a garden hose. He drenched me for several seconds, and when the water stopped, I wiped the streaming black mascara from my face, pushed the dripping hair from my eyes, and without a second thought took off after him, screaming, "Kenny Schrader! I'm gonna kill you!"

I was in high heels, but I could run as fast as he could because I'd had more practice in running in high heels than he had in running at all. A crew guy who saw what had happened ran up to me and handed me a bucket of water. When I caught Kenny, my aim was right on target and I soaked him with it. Of course, that little caper, which had been filmed in its entirety, led the sportscast that night and began with a voiceover that asked, "Just how hot was it in the Talladega garage today?"

Those days are gone. In their place are days of greater notoriety, more money, increased propriety, greater influence, and increased media attention. It's the greatest lesson in this entire book: Be careful what you wish for. You might get it. And when you get it, you might not want it.

Still, my friends are the same people at heart as when they were poor and struggling, ridiculed as backwoods racers with a legacy owed to the business of moonshine. Now, we no longer bristle when we're called rednecks. We wear the title with honor because that was a nickname given to good, common people, with a strong work ethic and solid integrity, who labored in the hot sun until their necks were burned red. We also realize that this sport born in the mountains of the South now reigns supreme over haughtier forms of athletics and has become the number one spectator sport in the nation. That's not too shabby, is it?

Even Doc Bundy, world-renowned hooty snooty sports car racer, has to admit that it's no longer a joking matter. "Okay, okay," he agrees, laughing. "I know I used to poke fun at you guys over in NASCAR, but let me assure you—ain't nobody laughing anymore. NASCAR is the hottest ticket around, and it's the merry-go-round that everybody wants to play on now."

Turns out that the majority of Americans are common people, middle-class dwellers who prefer stock cars over cars they don't recognize or can't afford. It's this simple: there are more beer drinkers than champagne sippers, more Chevy owners than Porsche owners, more pickup truck drivers than sports car drivers, more working-class folks than trust-fund babies, more people looking for heroes who rise up from a similar hard-luck dollar-poor existence than for heroes who inherit their prestige. This keeps the American dream alive. Dale Earnhardt grew up in a small mill village where the majority of the town earned a living by working in a textile factory like the one depicted in the movie *Norma Rae*. Yet he pulled himself up by his blue-collar roots to become a hero to the common man, and where he came from was never a point of shame for him—it was a point of pride. It signified, as with the Elliotts, that where you come from doesn't matter. All that matters is where you go.

I'm a simple country girl at heart, and while there was a time when I tried to disguise that fact, I don't any longer. When someone calls me a country girl now, even if it's in a derogatory tone, I grin and say, "You bet I am."

I love the days when I can leave my watch in the jewelry box, put on my jeans and T-shirt, and walk barefoot through the grass as my dachshund, Dixie Dew, scampers along by my side. I love living in a home surrounded by woods, with no close neighbors, where the breeze gently rustles the leaves and the river ripples peacefully by on its way to the sea. I could sit for hours on my terrace and watch the deer as they prance and play in my backyard. I even buy food for them. I suppose the greatest gift that NASCAR gave me was the peace I now have with who I am and where I come from. Like most stock car people, my roots run deep in the mountains of the South, and I'm happiest when I'm there. But, also like my racing friends, I'm perfectly at ease with dressing up in expensive couture and dining in ritzy restaurants with some of the nation's most distinguished politicians and celebrities. I adore spending an evening on Broadway as much as I love winter evenings in front of my fireplace. What a wonderful gift to have—that of being able to step back and forth between such dissimilar worlds and yet appreciating the value of both worlds and their people. That's why NASCAR-bred people are unique—we're as comfortable at a black tie dinner at the Waldorf as we are at a backyard barbecue.

Of course, we all had to learn that. I remember that one year, one of the sport's top car owners was very perplexed when he got his invitation for the championship banquet at the Waldorf. The invitation, of course, said "Black Tie Only." A bit worried and agitated, he called his sponsor and said, "Look, I just got my invitation to the banquet and it specifically says, 'Black Tie Only.'"

"That's right," the sponsor rep replied. "Is there a problem?"

"Yeah!" the car owner replied. "You said you wanted us to wear red ties and cummerbunds with our tuxes to match our car colors."

"Yes," the rep said, puzzled. "So?"

"Well, according to this, we can only wear black ties! We can't wear red like you want us to!"

Over the years, as we all toiled to take the sport to the level of prestige it resides at now, we learned to turn a deaf ear to aspersions cast our way or the monikers we were given. Eventually, when you make enough money, become famous enough, and appear on the covers of enough national magazines, the tide turns and no one calls you anything but "successful" and "a star."

One day, my niece and nephew were verbally sparring with each other over something unimportant. My niece said rather haughtily to her brother, "Oh, that is such a redneck thing to do."

Before he could throw back his retort, I interjected, "Hey! Hey! I take offense to that," I said in a playfully defensive tone. "Some of my best friends are rednecks." I paused for a second and smiled slyly. "Of course, they're *rich* rednecks with their own private jets. But they're still rednecks."

Everyone started laughing as we all realized that it doesn't matter what the world calls you as long as *you're* comfortable with who you are. Here's the final thought to remember: follow your heart and do what you yearn to do, even if it isn't popular. It's a law of the universe. Everything eventually comes into vogue and becomes a cultural phenomenon. Even rednecks and country bumpkins.

ACKNOWLEDGMENTS

First and foremost, my heartfelt appreciation to three people who enthusiastically believed in this book: my agent, Richard Curtis; my editor, Tom Dupree; and my publisher, Michael Morrison. Thank you for your support and encouragement.

More than words can adequately express, I am grateful for the love, prayers, and support of my family and friends. The outpouring of kindness and affection of those close to me is always enormous. In addition to my beloved family, I am indebted for various reasons to Guy and Pinky Cabe, Debbie Lunsford Love, Brenda McClain, Jennifer Finley, Doc Bundy, Rich Luker, Janet Spurr, Linda Kish, Larry Tannahill, Dr. Bill Coates (my pastor, who really ought to pray for me more than he does), Judy Baker, Chantel Dunham, Dr. Sam Richwine, Jill Rice, Karen Peck Gooch, Ruth Sklar, Amy Longhouse Powers, Bill and Virgie Miller, Tina Andreadis, Yung Kim, Jo Obarowski, Arthur Cohen, Diane DeBartlo, Debbie Steir, Travis Massey, Charles and Beverly Connor, Jerry Potter, Dr. Johnny Burns, Richard Higgins, and, most especially C. B. Fair, who has been one of the greatest warriors of encouragement in my life. Thank you to Ed and Randy Parks, who among other things, gave me a quiet retreat in which to write at a time when I needed it most.

This book would never have been possible without the wonderful people in Winston Cup racing, the teachers who taught me the greatest lessons. I hope I have adequately demonstrated my appreciation for those people in the previous pages, but I also wish to express my appreciation for the friendship of Martie Rompf, John Singler, Martie Schneider, Clyde Bolton, Godwin Kelly, David Smith, Chip Williams, Darrell Andrews, Dave Rodman, Judy Parrott and her entire family of racers, Buddy, Todd, and Brad, Mike Smith, Max and Jean Helton, and Ed Clark.

The idea for this book belongs solely to Jack Friedman. Thank you, my friend, for a wonderful idea.

Additionally, I am deeply grateful to those friends who helped me double-check facts: Deb Williams, Dan Elliott, Richard Childress, Richard Petty, Carolyn Rudd, Bobby Allison, Johnny Thomas, Debbie Lunsford Love, Ed Parks, Randy Parks, Troi Hayes, Gordon Pirkle, and Doc Bundy. Thank you for your time, patience, and guidance.

And to all who read my words: thank you for giving me the kind and generous gift of your time.

God bless all of you.